# Tourism and Local Economic Development in China

English-language Series of the Institute of Asian Affairs, Hamburg No. 4

VERBUND STIFTUNG
DEUTSCHES ÜBERSEE-INSTITUT

The Institute of Asian Affairs forms, together with the Institute of Comparative Overseas Studies, the Institute of African Affairs, the Institute for Ibero-American Studies and the German Orient Institute, the Foundation German Overseas Institute in Hamburg.

The object of the Institute of Asian Affairs is to promote research on contemporary political, economic and social developments in the various Asian countries.

In doing so, the Institute endeavours to encourage the expression of various opinions. The reader should note, however, that the views expressed are those of the authors and not necessarily those of the Institute of Asian Affairs.

First Published in 1999
by Curzon Press
15 The Quadrant, Richmond
Surrey, TW9 1BP

© 1999 Gang Xu

Printed and bound in Great Britain by
TJ International, Padstow, Cornwall

*British Library Cataloguing in Publication Data*
A catalogue record of this book is available from the British Library

ISBN 0–7007–1152–X

# Tourism and Local Economic Development in China

## Case Studies of Guilin, Suzhou and Beidaihe

*Gang Xu*

CURZON

# CONTENTS

# Contents

# Acknowledgments

The present study is completed as part of a project entitled 'The Impact of Tourism on Socio-Economic Change and Regional Development in the P. R. of China', which was led by Prof. Dr. E. Gormsen and supported by the Volkswagen Foundation, at the Johannes Gutenberg-University of Mainz, Germany.

Prof. Dr. E. Gormsen deserves my special thanks for his consistent and many-sided supports to this study. He has not only introduced me to the subject of study, but helped me in conducting research at all stages. He has helped me in so many ways in and outside my academic life in Germany that a complete list of his supports would be too long.

Especially, it is under his guidance that I have begun to *lernen kritisch zu sein*. 'To be critical' in addressing some development issues related to a country in which the author has grown up is indeed neither easy nor painless. Nevertheless, it is such a cross-cultural academic environment that has made the study more stimulating to me, and helped me to strengthen and sharpen the arguments made in the text.

I would like to thank Prof. Yu Xiaogan, Director of Nanjing Institute of Geography, the Chinese Academy of Sciences, for his support to this study. Especially, much of the 11-month fieldwork in China would not have been possible had not Prof. Yu provided me with strong organizational supports. I would also like to thank Mr. Ge Mingyi and Mr. Chen Lesheng, Bureau of International Cooperation of the Chinese Academy of Sciences, for their support.

I am greatly indebted to Prof. Dr. J. Nipper (University of Köln), Prof. Dr. W. Taubmann (University of Bremen), Prof. Dr. T. Heberer (University of Trier) and Prof. Dr. M. Domrös (University of Mainz) for their invaluable suggestions to this study and many-sided supports to my academic endeavors in Germany.

## Acknowledgments

For financial supports, I would like to express my indebtedness to the Volkswagen Foundation, the Friedrich Ebert Foundation and the Max-Plank-Gesellschaft.

I would like to express my thanks to all those *danwei* in China, especially in the study areas, which have provided valuable information and source materials for this study.

I also greatly appreciate the provision of a range of research infrastructure at the Johannes Gutenberg University of Mainz, especially the Institute of Geography.

Last but not least, I feel especially indebted to my wife Wanxiao and our son Jiajia. This study could not have been completed without their understanding and tolerance. To my parents, I would like to say many *xiexie* for their long-year support.

# List of Tables

## List of Tables

# List of Figures

# List of Figures

# Abbreviations

| | |
|---|---|
| CAAC | Civil Aviation Administration of China |
| CITS | China International Travel Service |
| CTS | China Travel Service |
| CYTS | China Youth Travel Service |
| FDI | Foreign Direct Investment |
| FEC | Foreign Exchange Certificate (An equivalent of RMB which was issued specifically for international tourists to China. Officially, FEC expired in 1994.) |
| FYP | Five-Year Plan |
| NTA | National Tourism Administration |
| RMB | Renminbi (People's Money, i.e. the Chinese currency) (The basic unit of Chinese currency is a yuan. 1 yuan = approximately 0.17 DM, or 0.12 US$, as of Dec. 1995.) |
| SOE | State-Owned Enterprise |

# Part I

# Theoretical and Empirical Background

# 1

# Introduction

## 1.1 Tourism Impact Assessment: a Neglected Issue in China

The central theme of the present study is the impact of tourism on local economic development in China.

The booming of tourism to and in China is a quite recent phenomenon. Yet, with 42 million border arrivals and 4.6 billion US$ receipts in 1993, China has become one of the leading destinations of international tourism within a short period of time. Still more spectacular is the rapidly rising travel demand of the Chinese people themselves. It is estimated that in recent years some 300–400 million Chinese have, in one form or another, taken part in domestic tourism per annum, yielding a total revenue of 86 billion RMB yuan.[1] Possible statistical inaccuracies notwithstanding, a mere look of the rough orders of these figures suggests that the recent growth of the travel and tourism industry in China is enormous by any standard.

What has been the impact of tourism boom in China? What role can tourism play in the socio-economic change and regional development in China?

These are broad questions related to a research field that has given rise to much controversy in the past few decades. As an expanding economic sector and a socio-cultural phenomenon, interna-

---

[1] *Yearbook of China Tourism Statistics* (henceforth: NTA) 1994, and various reports of the NTA.

tional tourism to the 'pleasure periphery' has since the 1960s caught considerable attentions from both academics and policymakers.

The size of the literature on tourism is formidable. Geographically, tourism studies cover most parts of the 'pleasure periphery' which have been involved or 'integrated' in international tourism businesses.[2] Thematically, besides studies on tourism's industrial structure (its operation, management and marketing) and geographical structure (models of spatial development and interactions), research into the effects of tourism expansions in the developing countries, including economic, socio-cultural, political and environmental repercussions, has been the major focus of the literature.[3]

The key issues raised in the study of tourism and its effects in the developing countries cut across the heart of the major concerns in the field of development studies of the 'periphery' in the post-war period.[4] However, much dispute exists not only about the nature and extent of the effects of tourism development but over the ways in which they might be assessed.

## (1) Economic effects:

The alleged economic benefits brought about by tourism to the developing countries were the major arguments of early tourism advocates. However, due largely to the cross-sectoral nature of the tourism industry as well as paucity of empirical data, controversial statements have arisen about the following issues:[5]

- the contribution of tourism to the 'balance-of-payments';
- the quantity and quality of tourism employment;
- the extent of 'multiplier effects' of tourism growth; and
- the role of tourism in balancing sub-national development.

## (2) Socio-cultural consequences:

Perhaps as a reaction to the accelerating globalization and as a result of a renewed desire to capture some of the 'authentic' life, there has been a growing recognition of the value of cultural diversity worldwide. Consequently, tourism impacts on the host societies, such as

---

[2]Gormsen 1983a, pp. 149–65, 1983b, pp. 608–17; Vorlaufer 1990, pp. 4–13; Harrison 1992b, pp. 1–18.

[3]Bryden 1973, pp. 71–96; Kadt 1979, pp. 1–68; Gormsen 1983a, pp. 149–65, 1983b, pp. 608–17; Vorlaufer 1990, pp. 4–13; Sinclair and Stabler 1991, pp. 1–14; Harrison 1992b, pp. 1–18, 1992c, pp. 19–34; Shaw and Williams 1994, pp. 1–17.

[4]Cf. Kadt 1979, pp. 1–68; Bryant and White 1982, pp. 3–20; Hemmer 1990, pp. 506–50; Bardhan 1993, pp. 129–42; Krueger 1994, pp. 3–9.

[5]See footnote 3.

erosions of local cultures and traditions, cheapening effects on arts and crafts, and rising consciousness of 'relative deprivation', have been assessed increasingly in an undesirable light. At the same time, more weights are being given to critical studies of the issue 'who benefits from tourism?'[6]

## (3) Environmental repercussions:

Less controversial is the discussion about the environmental 'costs' imposed by hitherto tourism expansions, though unfortunately only very recently. In this regard, the consensus-building seems rapid. Although detailed studies remain scant, it is generally held that on net balance the hitherto tourism expansions have been negative for the quality of natural environment. Therefore, genuine concerns for an environmentally friendly tourism development have fostered a worldwide constituency rapidly gaining political potency, reflecting the growing awareness of global environmental problems at large. Physical environment begins to take 'center stage' in tourism development and management.[7]

Most recently, as 'sustainable development' has become a catchword at the international level, calls for a paradigm shift in future tourism development are receiving increasing attentions from both academic and industry communities. New concepts, such as 'sustainable tourism', 'appropriate tourism', 'soft tourism', 'low impact tourism' and 'eco-tourism', are emerging in effect as the 'impact statements' of future tourism initiatives. However, while some pragmatic issues related to such a paradigm shift are being addressed, most discussions to date remain philosophical and heuristic in nature.[8]

Tourism started in China when the first boom of international tourism to the developing world had run its course, and concerns over the socio-cultural and environmental 'costs' associated with tourism expansions began to come to the forefront of international debates. Despite the enormous growth, disputes over the 'benefits and costs' of tourism development and recent movements toward a new paradigm have found hardly any echoes in China.

---

[6]Cf. Kadt 1979, pp. 34–68; Gormsen 1985, pp. 7–10, 1983b, pp. 42–47; Bentley 1991, pp. 55–58; Harrison 1992c, pp. 19–34; Crick 1992, pp. 135–47.

[7]Ritchie 1991, pp. 149–58; Edgell 1991, pp. 194–96; Coates 1991, pp. 66–71; Kurent 1991, pp. 78–82; Briassoulis et al 1992, pp. 8–20.

[8]Ibid. See also Freyer 1988, pp. 354–59; Kleiner and Patzak 1991, pp. 173–77; D'Amore 1991, pp. 170–72, Lillywhite 1991, pp. 162–69; Lee and Malek 1991, pp. 210–12; Romeiss–Stracke 1993, pp. 363–69.

Policymakers at both national and local levels are interested primarily in projecting tourism growth and devising tourism policies and long-term strategies which supposedly should be conducive to 'healthy' development of tourism and, more recently, 'market-confirming' in nature. Most researchers have been preoccupied with tourist resource surveys and 'tourism planning' at various levels.[9] On the whole, neither policymakers nor indeed tourism researchers have taken an adequate account of the impact issues.

Obviously, in a transitional society in which economic growth is regarded as an overarching objective of all development efforts, the prime interest of the Chinese government in tourism promotion is economic. However, even in the economic respect, the need for critical assessment of the outcomes of hitherto tourism development has not been given sufficient attention. Lessons from other parts of the world in tourism development have been largely ignored. Still rarer are considerations about possible socio-cultural and environmental consequences of tourism expansions. Issues of degradation of cultural and physical environments are more often than not just papered over. Obviously, a myopic stance toward tourism can be costly, both economically and socio-culturally.

## 1.2 Tourism and Its Effects: Comparative Perspectives

China is a big developing country which, though still labeled as a socialist one, finds itself in a dramatic transitional process. As a developing country, China shares some features and, especially, problems which are characteristic of the developing world in tourism development, such as capital shortage, infrastructure constraints, lack of marketing know-how, and so on.

Nevertheless, the tourism boom and the socio-economic contexts within which it has taken place in China are apparently different to the situations previously formulated in the tourism literature.

### (1) International vs. Domestic Tourism
Up till now, studies of tourism and its effects in the developing countries have centered almost exclusively on the international tourism. Issues related to domestic tourism in the developing countries are at most a footnote of the existing literature. Underpinning such a

---

[9]Cf. Guo and Bao 1989, pp. 2–8; He 1990, pp. 115–21.

mainstream bias seems the assumption (albeit implicit) that domestic tourism in the developing countries is neither quantitatively nor economically significant. According to most tourism advocates, the major justification for international tourism promotion in the developing world is its alleged contributions to the 'balance-of-payments' of the host countries on the one hand, and the search for new tropical and exotic destinations of the tourists from the developed countries on the other.

A parallel development of international and domestic tourism is one of the most salient features of the tourism boom in China.[10] Though the primary interest of the Chinese government in tourism promotion is to earn desperately needed hard currency, domestic tourism has become an integral part of China's tourism industry. The surge of mass domestic tourism has not only documented many aspects of social, political as well as economic changes taking place in contemporary China, but has shown its significant economic effects at both national and local levels.

## (2) Institutional Context

Compared to those of other countries, the institutional system governing tourism development in China is unique. China is a big socialist country which is in a rapid move toward a 'socialist market economy'. Such an institutional context has important implications not only in tourism development itself but for a study of tourism impacts.

First, the governing system of tourism development in China is transitional in nature. Among others, it is characterized by:

- a changing government-business relationship, but pervasive state interventions in and often political influences on tourism development;
- an increasing role of the market mechanism in tourism supply, but frequent and multifold institutional conflicts characteristic of a transitional society at the threshold of a market economy;
- a rapidly growing non-state tourism sector in co-existence with a dominant public sector in key tourism supply areas;
- a growing recognition of the priority of efficiency in tourism investment, but a propensity to 'quantitative maximization' thinking;

---

[10]For discussions of China's tourism development at the national level, see Gormsen 1989, pp. 65–72; 1990b, pp. 127–35; 1993, pp. 137–79; 1995b, pp. 131–40; Sun 1990, chapter 1, 3, 6; Lew and Yu 1995.

- an increasing weight being given to local well-being, but a lack of the mechanism which favors people-centered, community-responsive and socially responsible approaches in tourism planning and policy formulations;
- rapidly rising local and individual initiatives in tourism development, but an apparent absence of broad-based participation in decision-making of local population upon whom tourism developments affect. Local participation is thus partial and inconsistent.

Second, special cautions are warranted in addressing tourism impact issues in China, in particular at the national level. In many respects, it seems very difficult to distinguish clearly between what are 'tourism impacts' and what are general outcomes of the rapid changes taking place in a socialist transitional society.

## (3) The significance of sub-national dimensions

The issue of sub-national dimensions in tourism development and the need for comparative studies of the effects of tourism in different type of destinations have been often overlooked in the previously formulated analytical framework.[11] Besides data limitations, this seems due largely to the fact that a large number of 'classic' destination countries, which have been most often studied, are small in size and, in many cases, unique in cultural and/or physical environment.

China represents a different case. The country's huge population and area size and, especially, the apparent regional diversities in social and economic development as well as in cultural and physical environments give particular weight to the sub-national dimensions in studying tourism and its effects in China. At the national level, while the impact of tourism seems less apparent in a big country than in smaller ones, overall statements about tourism impacts in China, be they desirable or undesirable, economic, socio-cultural or environmental, are easily to be partial, if not misleading.

China has a wide variety of tourism destinations in terms of primary attraction, type of tourism, stage of development, position in national development schemes as well as their regional contexts. Obviously, different types of tourism development bring with them specific structures and, consequently, different economic, socio-cultural and environmental impacts to the destination areas in question.

---

[11] Müller 1983, p. 4; Pearce 1991, pp. 178–79.

While tourism may appear to be a significant 'change agent' in some small and remote areas, its role in the structural changes in the metropolitan areas where though tourist flows are highly concentrated, may be comparatively smaller or of another nature. This seems especially so with respect to the socio-cultural impacts of tourism. Tourism expansions may exert perceivable impacts on the local social and cultural changes in areas dominated by minority cultures in the western part of the country, while such effects tend to be much less discernible in the urbanized areas, especially in the east coastal region where internationalization of 'mass culture' is rapid. In many respects, much social and cultural change in such areas would have taken place without or with a smaller size of tourism.

Up till now, China has played a minor role in the 'tourism vs. development' debate. Knowledge about the nature and consequences of the recent tourism boom in China remains scant. The largest part of Chinese literature on tourism, though sizable, deals exclusively with description of tourist resources, issues of tourism planning, and interpretation of national tourism policies.[12] Except few global discussions on the growth of tourist arrivals and receipts, solid structural analysis of China's tourism industry is scant. Still rarer are detailed empirical studies focusing on the nature of tourism growth, both international and domestic, and its effects on regional and local structural changes.

Literature in foreign languages about China's tourism development remains few and far between. Only recently, publications of Western scholars on this subject tend to be in growing. And, some of them began to break new grounds and shed lights on the contours of tourism phenomenon in China.[13] More or less systematic case studies in such areas as Huangshan and Dali have produced knowledgeable insights into the nature of tourism development at the local level.[14] However, comparative studies of tourism and its effects in different types of destination areas are still non-existent.

---

[12] *Lüyou jinji* (tourism economy), 1984–93. This publication is informative for reviewing Chinese literature on tourism. It collects papers and documents on this subject, and provides an index of papers not included. For a review of Chinese literature on tourism, see also Guo and Bao 1989, pp. 2–8; He 1990, pp. 115–21.

[13] Gormsen 1989, 1990 a and b, 1993, 1995 a and b; Gormsen et al 1991; Gerstlacher et al 1991; Krieg 1993; Lew and Yu 1995.

[14] Gormsen et al. 1991; Hemberger 1990 and 1991; Wagner 1990a and b.

# 1.3   Scope and Research Questions of This Study

## (1) The main research questions

The purpose of this study is to examine the role of tourism in local economic development in different type of areas in China, and try to identify those factors which are decisive in determining the success or failure of a tourism-oriented development strategy at the local level.

Guilin, Suzhou and Beidaihe have been selected as the case study areas. They represent three important types of destinations in the eastern part of China:

- Guilin (Guangxi province) is a worldwide famous destination in South China. Its primary attraction is rooted in the unique karst landscape. Guilin is one of the 'key tourist cities' of China, enjoying top priorities in national tourism development.[15] It is a most favored destination of both international and domestic tourism in China. Tourism is expected to play a key role in local development. However, the regional economic basis for tourism development in Guilin is very weak.

- Suzhou (Jiangsu province) is an internationally well-known tourist city whose attraction is rooted in numerous historical and cultural sights, especially the classical Chinese gardens. Suzhou is among the 'key tourist cities'. It is an attractive place for international and domestic tourism in East China. Tourism in this area is growing on the basis of an industrialized and diversified regional economy.

- Beidaihe (Hebei province) is the largest seaside resort of China. Since the early 1980s, it has changed rapidly from a recreational center of the elite of the Chinese society into a leading destination of mass domestic tourism in North China. Though sizable state investments have flown into the recreational sector, the growth of domestic tourism in the strict sense has been characterized by a development 'from below'. On the whole, international tourism plays hardly any role in this place.

As tourist destinations, the differences between Guilin, Suzhou and Beidaihe are substantial. However, it is such differences that constitute the very basis for the central concern of this study, that is, the impact of tourism on local economic development in different

---

[15]The remaining 'key tourist cities' are Beijing, Shanghai, Guangzhou, Xi'an, Hangzhou and Hainan. Cf. section 3.1.

regional contexts. On the whole, Guilin provides a case for the study of the role of tourism (both international and domestic) in a less developed local economy. Suzhou is selected to examine the impact of tourism (both international and domestic) on a more-mature local economy. Beidaihe is a place for a study of the effects of domestic tourism on local structural changes.

The present study centers on six key research questions:

(1) *The incentives for local participation in tourism development*
In the post-reform period, regional and local initiatives in tourism development in China are enormous. Without a critical look of the disputes and lessons reported from other parts of the world, many regions and cities in China seem to see a much rosier prospect in this new industry than in traditional ones. Tourism has been widely viewed as a good candidate to development. In this connection, it is to ask what are the factors that have stimulated nationwide local initiatives in tourism development? what are the motives underlying a tourism-oriented local development strategy? what types of areas will be dealt with in this study? and what are their goals in tourism promotion? Obviously, such issues need to be examined in the broader development contexts at both national and local levels. These are the central concerns of Chapter 2 and 3.

(2) *Growth and structural changes of international tourism*
After a period of steady and rapid growth, China's international tourism has been undergoing remarkable structural changes since the late 1980s.[16] What are the similarities and differences in demand structure and growth pattern of international tourism at national and sub-national levels? What are the regional implications of the changes in international markets in general and in specific market segments in particular? Furthermore, as overseas marketing authorities have been decentralized since 1982, competitions among Chinese tour operators in the international market have become increasingly intensified. What are the regional implications of such a decentralization policy? These issues will be addressed in Chapter 4.

(3) *The nature and structure of domestic tourism*
Until very recently, mass domestic tourism in China has not received adequate attention from the central government, nor from most research institutions. In view of the still low average income and living standard of the largest part of the Chinese population, the rise of

---

[16]Gormsen 1993 pp. 137–79; 1995b, pp. 63–88.

mass domestic tourism seems rather puzzling in many respects.[17] What are the rough orders of domestic tourism, in relation to international tourism, in such key tourist cities as Guilin and Suzhou, and in Beidaihe where international tourist activities are negligible? In different types of destinations, who tend to make up the major part of domestic travelers? What are their travel motives? And how do they organize their trips? Can any descriptive models be developed to highlight the basic features of domestic tourism in contemporary China? And what are the social, political and economic underpinnings of such demand patterns? These are some of the major issues addressed in Chapter 5, which is one of the centerpieces of this study.

*(4) The role of the non-state sector in tourism infrastructure development*

In a public-sector dominated economy, direct state involvement (via SOEs as well as tourism boards and ministries) in the tourism sector is extensive, especially in international tourism businesses. Nevertheless, from the point of view of ownership structure, China's tourism industry has been undergoing a pluralistic development, stimulating the growth of a non-state sector in the tourism supply system. What are the major business areas of different investors in the tourism marketplace? What part has the non-state sector played in recent tourism development at the local level? These issues will be addressed with particular reference to the involvement of FDI in the international hotel sector (Chapter 6), and the participation of small investors in the domestic accommodation sector (Chapter 7).

*(5) Distribution of tourism revenues*

In response to the change of mainstream theories in critical social sciences, the issue of distribution of 'tourism benefits' has attracted much interest in tourism studies since the late 1960s.[18] Most discussions to date have focused on the patterns of distribution of tourism revenues between multinational corporations and the host economies.

---

[17]In recent time, there has been a dispute over the 'real' size of the Chinese economy or the 'real' standards of living of the Chinese people. According to the 'conventional' criteria employed by the World Bank (i.e. foreign exchange parity), China is classified as a 'low-income' country with a per capita GNP of about 470 US$ in 1992. But, according to the calculation of IMF at 'purchasing power parity', this figure allegedly amounted to 1,800 US$ by 1993 (BMZ 1994, p. 9). For discussions on this issue, see also Segal 1994, pp. 44–45; Cable and Ferdinand 1994, pp. 243–44.

[18]Kadt 1979, pp. x–xiii; Richter 1991, pp. 189–93; Harrison 1992a, pp. 8–17.

Ownership and contractual relationships, development strategies and the stage of general economic development of the host countries are often pointed as the key factors in determining the net effects and, thus, the contributions to the 'balance-of-payments' of tourism as an earner of foreign exchange.[19] However, issues of revenue distribution within host societies have received comparatively little attention.

Under a centrally planning regime, regional and local objectives used to be regarded as identical with and subsequent to the national goals in China. In the course of decentralization and economic liberalization, there has been a growing awareness of local and individual interests. Obviously, the national and local goals of tourism development are not necessarily mutually compatible. As pursuit of local and individual interests, however vaguely-defined, has been legitimated in China, it is of importance to ask what are the distributional patterns of tourism revenues? What factors are decisive in determining the local shares of tourism revenues? And what factors appear to favor or impede the 'spillovers' of tourism growth? With respect to domestic tourism, there is a need to examine its role in inter-regional re-distribution of national income. The growth and distributional patterns of tourism revenues will be examined in Chapter 8.

(6) *The role of tourism employment in local labor markets*
The employment effects generated by tourism are often assessed in a favorable light. However, research findings on the significance of tourism employment vary from rather optimistic statements in some cases (albeit small countries) to explicit reservations in others. Furthermore, in view of the dualistic structure of tourism employment, the role of tourism in human capital accumulation has been sharply questioned.[20] Nevertheless, as in many other countries, the alleged role of tourism in job creation is very appealing to the policymakers in China. Tourism is widely regarded as a labor-intensive sector which can generate not only direct job opportunities but also secondary employment effects, though solid inter-sectoral comparative studies are non-existent. By 1992, China's tourism industry had created about 2.1 million direct jobs, contributing about 1.3% of total employment in the urban sector, or 3.0% of urban tertiary sector employment.[21] Obviously, such rough numbers tell nothing about the

---

[19]Bryden 1973, 71–83; Kadt 1979, pp. 28–32; Harrison 1992b, pp. 13–14; Sinclair and Stabler 1992, pp. 1–10.

[20]Kadt 1979, pp. 34–49; Vorlaufer 1990, p. 12; Harrison 1992b, pp. 14–17.

[21]If both urban and rural sectors are included, these figures go down to 0.4% and 1.8% respectively. NTA 1993, pp. 112–13; ZTN 1993, pp. 97–112.

type and structure of tourism employment, its role in the local labor markets of those areas with a stronger presence of tourism. Issues related to the size and structure of tourism employment, and its effects on rural-urban migration will be dealt with in Chapter 9.

## (2) Scope and research approaches

Basically, the present study has followed an empirical research approach. Its main findings are based primarily on author's 11-month fieldwork in China. The major part of empirical research was conducted during: (1) September–October 1991 in Suzhou; (2) May–October 1992 in Guilin, Beidaihe and Suzhou; and (3) September–October 1993, together with Prof. E. Gormsen, including visits to Beijing, Xi'an, Guilin, Shanghai, Suzhou and Nanjing.

In this study, Guilin, Suzhou, and Beidaihe refers to Guilin *shi*, Suzhou *shi*, and Beidaihe *(cheng)qu* respectively, unless noted otherwise. The term *shi* is used in this study to refer to *jianzhi shi*, or 'designated city'. A 'designated city' (*shi*) has an officially approved city status, and consists basically of two parts: urban districts (*chengqu*) and suburban districts (*jiaoqu*).[22] Table 1–1 gives an overview of the geographical scope of the areas which are covered in author's empirical studies.

Large-scale mapping, interviews, accounting, personal observations, and collections and compilation of local documents and data made up the major part of empirical studies. Besides direct interviews with tourists, and employees in the private sector, the main contact partners in China include: (1) tourism bureaus, park management bureaus, statistical bureaus, economic planning committees and economic research centers at the municipal level; (2) the National Tourism Administration (NTA) in Beijing and (3) various research institutions.

Last but not least, it is noteworthy that statistics in China are poor at detecting causality. Especially, information about China's domestic tourism remains scant and inconsistent. A considerable part of the data presented in this study are based on author's field surveys. Though dozens of notes have been made, cautions are still called in interpreting data in the text.

---

[22] In the literature on China's urban development as well as in Chinese statistics, the term *shi* may have other connotations. Due to lack of standardized terms, the use of such a term as *shi* has caused much confusion in studying China's urban development (e.g. size of urban population). For a detailed discussion of the definitions (and confusions) of the frequently used terms in Chinese urban studies, see Taubmann 1986, pp. 114–23; Ma and Cui 1987, pp. 373–95.

**Table 1–1: Geographical Scope of the Empirical Studies**

| Study area | Scope of Empirical Research | Population (1991) Total | Non-Agricultural |
|---|---|---|---|
| Guilin | Guilin city (*shi*) | 516,800 | 372,400 |
| | Yangshuo town (*zhen*) | 20,000 | 15,000 |
| | Chuanyan village (*cun*) | 420 | – |
| Suzhou | Suzhou city (*shi*) | 850,000 | 714,300 |
| Beidaihe | Beidaihe district (*qu*)[1] | 54,500 | 24,000 |
| | Nandaihe resort[2] | n.a. | n.a. |
| | Changli resort[3] | n.a. | n.a. |

[1] The resort place Beidaihe is an urban district of Qinhuangdao *shi* (city). In 1991, Qinhuangdao *shi* had a total population of 514,100, of which 376,300 non-agricultural;
[2] in Funing county (*xian*);
[3] in Changli county (*xian*).
Sources: *Statistical Yearbook of Chinese Cities* 1992; Statistical Bureau Yangshuo and Beidaihe.

# 2

# Incentives for Local Participation in Tourism Development

## 2.1 Decentralization and Local Development Initiatives

One of the leitmotivs of the Chinese reform policy is a far-reaching philosophy of decentralization.[1] Decentralization turns out to be not only a 'cleaver strategic move' of reformers to advance the transition process, but a decisive explanatory factor to the macro performance of the Chinese economy in the post-reform era.[2]

Besides substantial downward delegation of powers in routine decision-making, the most appealing element of the decentralization policy, from the local standpoint, is the fiscal reform schemes. The kernel of China's fiscal reforms involves inter alia the so-called *caizheng fenzao chifan*, or 'revenue-sharing' in the 1980s and, more recently, fenshuizhi, or a federalism-like tax-sharing system, among various administration levels.[3]

Such decentralization as has taken place in China unambiguously leaves lower level governments a bigger steak in the prosperity of local economies, though such benefits differ widely from one region to another, depending on local capacity and 'tactics' in political bargain-

---

[1] In the light of organization theory, 'decentralization' in the Chinese case tends to fall into the category of 'deconcentration', instead of 'devolution'. Cf. Bryant and White 1982, pp. 160–61; Davey 1985, pp. 9–10.

[2] Roland 1994, pp. 32–38; Sachs and Woo 1994, pp. 102–105; Yusuf 1994, pp. 75–97.

[3] Cf. Guo 1988, pp. 10–14; Yusuf 1994, pp. 75–79.

ing and policy lobbying, among others. The net outcome of such a decentralization approach is a rapidly rising consciousness of regional and local interests, which in turn has spurred enormous 'bottom-up' initiatives in local development in the post-reform period.

Yet, decentralization is in its very nature a double edged sword. A sheer downward shift of the locus of decision-making, in and of itself, will not generate adequate capacity for local development. Obviously, what used to serve local authorities well in a centrally planning regime is not necessary their assets in pursuit of local prosperity under the new policy of economic liberalization. As development issues have been progressively delegated to lower levels, local success rests squarely with the initiative of local authorities and community actions.

One of the biggest challenges in a transitional economy is that there is neither a uniform concept of development to strive for nor a self-evident development path to follow. Though the substantial improvements in local economic well-being associated with such success stories as Sunan Model and Wenzhou Model are visible to all, few can deny that such models of development are unlikely to fit in with the local conditions in most parts of the country.[4]

In pursuit of local development, many regions and cities in China have embarked on a tourism-oriented development course. Tourism industry is widely viewed as a new 'window of opportunity' for local development. The theoretical reasoning for such a policy choice is 'classic':

- First, endowment of local resources. In sharp contrast to the red lines of the Maoist development policies which underlined regional 'self-reliance' by establishing 'complete sets' of industries, China's new development policy places increasing weight on regional specialization and inter-regional trade. The latter-day local authorities are told to take into account the 'comparative advantage' of their regions in devising local industrial policies. Since many areas, both developed and less developed, claim to have 'comparative' or 'absolute advantage' in tourist resources, tourism promotion is thus a logical choice.

- Second, investment and industrial strategy. From very beginning on, tourism has been monolithically advocated as a

---

[4] *Sunan Moshi* (Sunan Model) is characterized by a rapid rural industrialization and urbanization; Suzhou is a core part of the Sunan Model. *Wenzhou Moshi* (Wenzhou Model) (in Zhejiang province) is featured by a rapid growth of the private sector. Cf. Heberer 1989, pp. 419–23; Ma 1990, pp. 223–38.

'sunrise' industry which allegedly 'requires little investments to achieve quick results'.[5] Plagued by dozens of problems in promoting local development, especially capital shortage, many local authorities suddenly see a much rosier prospect in this new industry than traditional ones.

Thus, the tourism industry is consigned an important role to play in local development in China. The idea that tourism industry could serve as a catalyst for local prosperity began to gain good currency in the early 1980s. It was widely held that once a region gets tourism moving, the tourism industry would do the rest.

Besides theoretical reasoning, there are several incentive factors at the national level which seem to support a tourism-oriented local development strategy. The rapidly growing travel demand, preferential treatment of the international tourism sector, the inflow of large-scale FDI, and deregulation and decentralization in tourism development are especially noteworthy. These factors will be spelt out in some details in the following two sections.

## 2.2    Tourism as a New Development Factor

Till the mid-1970s, China remained a blank space on a world map of international tourism businesses. As China began to open its 'door' in the late 1970s, the country's plentiful tourist resources were soon mobilized to serve its new development goals. At the beginning of tourism expansions, international tourism was still promoted under a flag of enhancing 'mutual understandings' between peoples, and perhaps as a window showcasing China's new image to the outside world. Subject to economic needs, however, these rumblings soon got marginalized.

By the early 1980s, provision of tourist services had become commercialized nearly in a wholesale manner (Tab. 2–1). Since then, China's tourism industry has been growing at an unanticipated rate (Tab. 2–2).[6] In the 7th 'FYP' (1985–1990), tourism industry was for the first time integrated into the 'National Social and Economic Development Plan', indicating that China's tourism sector had graduated from an infant industry.

---

[5] Cf. Cai 1986, pp. 146–155; Wang 1986, pp. 201–206; Qiu et al. 1990, pp. 11–44; Zheng 1990, pp. 78–90.

[6] For a detailed discussion of tourism development at the national level, see Gormsen 1990, 1993 and 1995; Sun 1990; Lew and Yu 1995.

## Table 2–1: The Changing Model of Tourism Development in China

|  | 1950s to mid–1970s | Since the early 1980s |
|---|---|---|
| Motivation and Goals | .political considerations<br>.government reception<br>.without cost-benefit analysis | .an economic sector<br>.foreign exchange<br>.profit-making drive<br>..job creation |
| Mechanism | .centralized planning<br>.state monopoly<br>.state as the sole investor | .market mechanism<br>.diversification of owner-ship<br>.local participation |
| International Tourism | .guests and visitors from other socialist countries | .foreigners from all over the world<br>.*compatriots* and overseas Chinese |
| Domestic Tourism | .politically-motivated population movement<br>.limited business travel<br>.controlled travel demand | .emerging mass domestic tourism<br>.diversified travel motives |

## Table 2–2: China's Tourism Industry, 1978–1996

|  | 1978 | 1980 | 1985 | 1990 | 1996 |
|---|---|---|---|---|---|
| International tourism |  |  |  |  |  |
| Arrivals (million) | 1.8 | 5.7 | 17.8 | 27.5 | 51.1 |
| Receipts (billion US$) | 0.26 | 0.62 | 1.25 | 2.22 | 10.2 |
| Balance (billion US$) | ... | ... | 0.94 | 1.75 | 5.77 |
| International hotels (number) | 431 | 508 | 995 | 2,039 | 4,418 |
| Rooms (1,000) | 74.6 | 84.5 | 150.8 | 305.4 | 594.5 |
| Domestic tourism |  |  |  |  |  |
| Domestic visitors (million) |  |  | 240 | 280 | 640 |
| Revenues (billion yuan) |  |  | 8 | 17 | 164 |
| Tourism firms (1,000) |  |  |  | 98.3 |  |
| Tourism employment total (million) |  |  | ... | 1.70 | ... |
| International tourism |  |  | 0.17 | 0.62 | 1.19 |
| Domestic tourism |  |  | ... | 1.08 | ... |

Source: NTA 1986–1997.

The rapid rise of a commercial tourism sector is a significant economic event in the post reform era. Due to its enormous size and rapid growth, tourism has opened a new dynamic marketplace in the Chinese economy.

From the local standpoint, the following features of China's tourism industry are particularly noteworthy:

### (1) Preferential treatment of international tourism sector in the national industrial policy

One of the strongest momentums of the Chinese economy in the post-reform era is export orientation. Since the early 1980s, all regions have been greatly encouraged to participate in export markets as far as possible, and to seek to become a focus of FDI. In China, international tourism industry is treated as an export sector which enjoys national incentive legislation. Regions or enterprises engaged in international tourism businesses receive favorable treatments in terms of investment, taxation, revenue-sharing, and so on.[7]

Obviously, in a partial reform course, the orientation of national industrial policy has crucial effects on local development thinking. As a reaction to the explicit sectoral and geographical unevenness in policy environment, all regions are eagerly seeking those economic sectors which enjoy priorities in national development policies and incentive legislation. Thus, international tourism industry seems to be a good candidate to development.

### (2) International tourism sector as a focus of FDI

In its course of development, international tourism, especially the hotel sector, has become one of the leading sectors in use of FDI in the entire Chinese economy. During the first 10 years of the 'open-door' policy, some 550 tourism projects had attracted 7.3 billion US$ FDI, accounting for about 20% of all FDI which had flown into the country in the same period.[8]

By April 1994, China's tourism sector had used around 10 billion US$ FDI. The realized FDI made up 53.3% of all tourism investment in the country. If taking into account all planned or contracted FDI, then the share of FDI reached nearly 73%.[9] Furthermore, in 1994 there were still 1.88 billion US$ FDI projects under construction.[10]

That international tourism industry has become a focus of FDI is apparently very appealing to many local authorities, especially at a time when the absolute size of FDI a region can attract has become almost a synonym of success. Thus, promotion of international tourism in areas where it seems 'appropriate' is at least worthy of try.

---

[7] Cf. Li 1991, pp. 182–200.
[8] Zhao 1990, p. 230.
[9] *Renmin Ribao* (People's Daily), 2 June 1994.
[10] *Ibid.*

## (3) The dominance of *compatriots* in international tourism

Despite the importance of Western tourists, especially in monetary terms and at early stages, the recent growth of China's international tourism has been in larger measure favored by:

- the political restructuring in the Asia-Pacific region, especially the emerging 'Greater China';[11]

- the travel boom stimulated by the dynamic Asian economy;[12] and

- the historical and cultural relationships, and contemporary economic interactions between China and other Asian countries and regions.

Obviously, all these factors are to the advantage of tourism boom in China. At the same time, such an international background has led to a salient feature in the demand structure of international tourism in China. That is, an overwhelming dominance of the *compatriots* from Hong Kong, Taiwan and Macao (over 90% of all border arrivals), and an increasing share of Asian travelers, among whom the number of overseas Chinese from Southeast Asia, especially the ASEAN, is on the rapid increase.[13]

On the whole, the travel demand of *compatriots* has shown a strong spatial preference to the southeast coastal provinces. Nevertheless, the 'home-town' areas of *compatriots* and overseas Chinese, to visit them is an important motive of their travels to the mainland, involve a larger part of the country.[14] This fact has significant regional implications with respect to local tourism initiatives:

- first, the visits of *compatriots* and overseas Chinese to their home-town areas have in effect transmitted a message of tourism business opportunities to many parts of the country, especially to those areas outside the 'key tourist cities', though the number of visitors to these areas remains not very large;[15]

---

[11] Hornik 1994, pp. 28–42; Vincent and Ferdinand 1994, pp. 243–61.

[12] According to Nozawa (1991, p. 103), the number of outbound tourists from the Asia-Pacific region as well as travel within the region have shown remarkable growth since 1985. As this market is still 'untapped', the prospect of tourism businesses in the Asia-Pacific region is promising.

[13] NTA 1986–94.

[14] For a discussion of the 'existential tie' of *compatriots* and overseas Chinese to mainland China, see Law 1995, pp. 155–75.

[15] In this respect, the arrivals of Western backpackers as 'pioneers' tend to have similar effects in the remote areas of the country. Cf. Gormsen 1990; Hemberger 1989.

- second, to accommodate the travel needs of *compatriots* and overseas Chinese, no matter in which part of the country, is regarded of not only economic but also political importance in the Chinese tourism policy;

- last but not least, local speculations on possible follow-up investment of some *compatriots* or overseas Chinese may, in many cases, have also played a certain part.

### (4) Low barriers to entering into domestic tourism supply market

At the macro level, mass domestic tourism has a certain role to play in China's domestic economy. As a new area of consumption, domestic tourism can withdraw a certain amount of over-supplied domestic currency, and thus contribute to stabilizing an inflated economy. This appears to be one of the most important considerations underlying the central government's liberal attitude toward domestic tourism since the mid-1980s.[16] In addition, domestic tourism has inter-regional re-distributional effects, which are on the whole to the advantage of economically less developed areas. However, such re-distributional effects have not received sufficient attention in policy discussions in China.

Besides its macro-economic effects, the rise of mass domestic tourism is of importance for local economic development in several respects:

- first, because of its enormous size, domestic tourism has opened up a huge demand market;

- second, China's domestic tourism is expanding continuously to a larger part of the country, providing a broader basis for local participation;

- third, and most importantly, subject to the low standard of living, the travel demand of most individual tourists remains low-budgetary in nature. Thus, the barriers to entering into the supply market are low, providing plentiful market chances for local small private investors.

---

[16]In the period from 1985 to 1992 Chinese households spent 2.4% to 3.2% of their total spendings on domestic travel. During this period China's domestic tourism helped withdraw equivalent of 22% to 60% of the amount of domestic currency that had been issued each year. ZTN 1992, pp. 611–620; 1993, p. 666, and various documents.

## 2.3 Regional Implications of National Tourism Policies

As spelled out elsewhere, the Chinese reform course is characterized by a pragmatic approach. Policy liberalization is desirable to the extent that it is in the interest of economic development, at least potentially.[17] In this regard, the policy of pluralistic development of tourism is a case in point.[18]

### 2.3.1 Institution vs. Deregulating

To meet the need of 'institutionalized' development of international tourism, tourism promotion in China began with a 'top-down' instituting in early 1978. At the national level, the former 'Travel Service Administration Bureau' was upgraded to a ministry status.[19] In the same year, a complex tourism administration system was established at the provincial level, which has extended to lower levels in the following years.

However, 'instituting' was only a marginal aspect of the events taking place in China's tourism industry system. In responding to the overall policy of economic liberalization, tourism development has followed a deregulation and decentralization approach, especially since the mid-1980s. It is such a policy that has made nationwide local participation possible.

Already in late 1978, as the first signal of decentralization, a large number of then existing state-owned hotels with relatively higher standards were consigned to either province-level tourism bureaus or the regional bureaus of CITS. A big step in decentralization was taken in 1982 when the authority of overseas marketing began to be delegated from the NTA to regional enterprises, especially to the 'Overseas Tourism Corp.' at the provincial level and in some 'key tourist cities'.

Clearly, the decentralization of management and marketing authorities has given regional enterprises a bigger room to maneuver in capturing tourism businesses. Unfortunately, problems associated with this decentralization policy have become serious since the mid-1980s. One of the main problems, according to Chinese tourism plan-

---

[17]Heberer 1989, pp. 432–41; Ellmann 1994, pp. 1–21.

[18]For an overview of tourism policies at the national level, see Bai and Li 1990, pp. 91–119; Zhang 1995, pp. 3–17.

[19]This national 'Bureau' was renamed as National Tourism Administration (NTA) in 1982.

ners, is the excessive competition via price-cutting among Chinese tour operators themselves in the international market.[20]

### 2.3.2 Tourism Enterprise Reforms

The core issue in tourism enterprise reforms concerns the so-called 'separation of ownership from management' without substantive change in property rights. By such a separation, it is alleged, the financial performance of many deficit-ridden enterprises could be improved, and a uniform market-led tourism supply system be established.

According to this reform scheme, since 1980 all 'agencies' engaged in tourism businesses have been ordered to transform themselves into enterprises, and to be self-responsible for their 'profits or losses' by establishing independent book-accountings. At the national level, CITS became independent from the NTA in 1982. A 'responsibility system' was introduced in 1983. In order to mobilize the initiatives of individual enterprises, 50 international hotels were selected in 1984 'to learn from *Jianguo* Hotel'.[21] Since the late 1980s, enterprise reforms have focused on the organizational innovation of the SOE systems, such as building large-scale 'enterprise groups' based on CITS, CTS and CYTS systems, and reorganizing CAAC in air transport.[22]

Despite these developments, the 'principal-agent' issue of SOEs in the tourism sector, as in other sectors, remains extremely complicated. Tourism enterprises can be the 'agencies' of government departments or *danwei* from any administration spectra and at any levels.[23] Individual firms or *danwei* are subject only, if any, to 'regulations' in their own administration spectra.[24] This complicated ownership structure has led to the persistence of 'soft budgetary constraints' at the enterprise level on the one hand, and the absence of

---

[20]Cf. Bai and Li 1990, pp. 95–100.

[21]*Jianguo* Hotel was the first joint-venture hotel in China. Since its opening in 1982, this hotel has not only achieved excellent financial performance, but also gained good reputations for its service quality. The number of hotels that should 'learn from *Jianguo* Hotel' grew to 114 by 1991. Cf. Gao and Wang 1984, and NTA 1993.

[22]In 1985, the former CAAC was reorganized into Air China (CA - the national flag carrier) and seven regional airlines. Cf. Zhang 1995, p. 11.

[23]*Danwei* (working unit) is a basic organizational unit of Chinese institutions. In the pre-reform period, *danwei* had not only economic functions but social and political functions as well. The importance of *danwei* has been decreasing in the post-reform period, though.

[24]Even in a single city like Guilin, 68 international tourism enterprises belonged to 31 government departments or *danwei* (fieldwork 1992)!

'rule of game' binding actors in the supply market on the other. The latter is especially acute at a time when 'smashing' tends to outpace the necessary re-instituting of a market-confirming regulatory framework. The consequences of this unsolved 'principal-agent' problem have been well documented in the problematic expansions of the hotel sector, among others, in many parts of the country.

### 2.3.3  The 1984/85 Tourism Policy

In many important respects, the tourism policy issued in 1984/85 was a milestone in tourism development in China. The highlights of this policy package involved the so-called *sige zhuanbian*, or 'four transformations' in overall tourism development, and *wuge yiqishang*, or approximately 'five investors going into action simultaneously' in tourism infrastructure development (Tab. 2–3).

#### Table 2–3: The 1984/85 Tourism Policy

| Four Transformations | From | To |
|---|---|---|
| Investment Orientation | Reception facilities | Both resource development and reception facilities |
| Tourism Promotion | International tourism | Both international and domestic tourism |
| Investors in Infrastructure Development | The state as the major investor | *Wuge yiqishang*, i.e. the state, local governments, departments (*bumen*), collectives, and private individuals; *Liyong waizi*, i.e. 'self-reliance' and use of foreign capitals |
| Enterprise Management | Government agencies | 'Independent' firms (*qiyehua jinying*). |

Source: Various Chinese documents.

The regional effects of the 1984/85 policy turned out to be enormous. While its effects on the anticipated 'transformations' in investment orientation and enterprise management remain unclear, what is clear is that this policy has stimulated enormous local initiatives in tourism development in many parts of the country, and given a big boost to the surge of domestic tourism.[25]

---

[25]The effects of the 1984/85 policy on domestic tourism will be dealt with in section 5.1.

As later developments have shown, the signals of deregulation and decentralization embedded in the 1984/85 policy package were quickly and well understood by many private investors as well as local authorities. Policy liberalization has evoked a widespread and long-standing wave of 'investment fever' in tourism development at sub-national levels beyond the control of the central authorities.[26]

During the 7th 'FYP' (1985–1990), a total amount of 13.2 billion RMB yuan were planned to invest in China's tourism industry, of which 2.5 billion yuan (19%) were direct state investment of the central government via the NTA.[27] Local tourism investment has three major sources, namely,

- the financial resources of local governments. Beside the investment in public facilities, the participation of local governments takes place principally via the investment of locally-run SOEs;[28]

- FDI, which makes up a large part of all tourism investment;

- the investment of individual households and small collective *danwei*.

Clearly, in a public ownership dominated economy, state interventions in tourism development remain pervasive, even at the regional level. Besides its regulatory role, the state has been directly involved in the key business areas of international tourism, including exclusive controls in air transportation, a large state-owned sector in travel services, considerable involvement in hotel businesses, and so on.[29]

Nevertheless, from the point of view of ownership structure, the tourism expansions over the past decade have been characterized by a pluralistic development. On the whole, the non-central and non-state investors have an ever-bigger part to play in the tourism marketplace, pushing the tourism sector further marketwards. In general, non-state tourism investment consists of two major parts, namely,

---

[26]Local and private participation was planned to take place primarily in infrastructure constructions. In fact, it turned out that pluralistic development has expanded to almost all sectors of the tourism industry. Cf. Qiu, Wei and Shi 1990, pp. 34–37.

[27]Zhao and Wei 1990, p. 237.

[28]Such developments have been supported by the unfolding financial reform schemes such as changes in industrial investment from budgetary allocations to loans and credits.

[29]A 'strong state' can be plausible as far as the national interests are concerned, such as taking cautions in appropriate use of FDI, negotiating contract terms and building strategic domestic tourism supply industries, and so on. Unfortunately, however, such issues have failed to receive sufficient attentions in China either.

FDI in joint-ventures established principally in the international hotel sector; and the investment made by individual households and 'small collectives' in such service sectors as accommodation, restaurant, and souvenir businesses (Fig. 2–1).

**Figure 2–1: The Role of Various Investors in China's Tourism Industry**

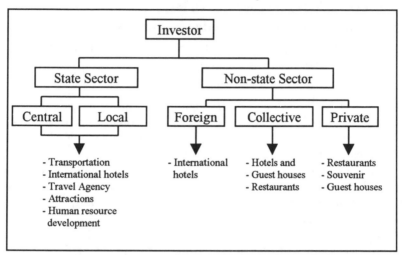

Indeed, deregulation and decentralization has stimulated enormous regional and local initiatives in tourism development. However, one caveat is warranted. That is, such local participation as has taken place in China remains partial and inconsistent. Obviously, due to political constraints, broad-based participation in decision-making of the local population upon whom tourism developments affect is still absent. At the same time, people-centered, community-responsive and socially responsible approaches in tourism planning and policy formulations remain unknown in China.

## 2.4 National and Local Goals of Tourism Development

The primary goal of tourism promotion at both national and subnational levels is economic. To many tourism planners and decision-makers, the economic 'benefits' of tourism development, especially international tourism, seem self-evident, though the means to achieve them is less clear.

At the national level, a commercial tourism industry has been envisaged as a new development factor and one of the most dynamic sectors of the Chinese economy. According to the National Tourism Development Plan of the 8th 'FYP' (1990–95), the goals of tourism promotion at the national level were:[30]

- to earn foreign exchange receipts;

- to generate 'spillovers' to other economic sectors;

- to withdraw a certain amount of over-supplied domestic currency via domestic tourism, and

- to create job opportunities.

Obviously, the Chinese tourism planners have in large measure accepted the early arguments regarding the potential economic benefits of tourism in the national economy, with a creation of the role of domestic tourism in an inflated economy.

In the course of economic reforms, pursuit of regional, local and individual interests has been legitimated in China. However, the goals of tourism development at the local level, especially on the part of local authorities, appear to be only vaguely-defined, though the desire for local prosperity looms large. In general, local objectives in tourism promotion can be examined under following three major headings:

1. Tourism revenues. The expected revenue effects include foreign exchange receipts, domestic tourism revenues, and the revenues to be generated by other economic sectors whose existence or expansions are supposedly associated with a growing tourism industry.[31]

2. Tourism 'externalities'. The envisaged 'externalities' involve first and foremost the expected improvement in regional infrastructure and urban facilities, which constitute a decisive component of local investment climate. Substantial improvements in local investment climate via tourism development are often regarded as vital to attracting FDI and justifying preferential policy treatments such as financial subsidiaries, tax relief, grants-in-aids, and the like.

---

[30]NTA 1991; Sun 1991, pp. 102–104.

[31]The motive to earn hard currency for local economies arises from a central-local contract in sharing international tourism receipts. Compare section 8.2.1.

3. Employment and personal income.  Not very surprisingly, employment and personal income objective has not been a major policy concern on the part of local authorities in many tourism areas.  However, such concrete objectives are obviously at the heart of individual participants in the tourism businesses.

Apparently, due to different regional social and economic conditions, the underlying motives of tourism promotion vary significantly from one area to another. This will be exemplified by the cases of Guilin, Suzhou and Beidaihe.

# 3

# Regional Settings of Tourism Development

## 3.1  Guilin, Suzhou and Beidaihe in National Perspectives

As a country with a vast territory and long history, China possesses a rich diversity of tourism potentials. Historical and cultural sights, native cultures of minority communities, picturesque landscape and unique natural scenery as well as modern urban centers are but some examples on a long list.

At the national level, besides numerous tourist sights in the economically prosperous and fast growing coastal region, an even larger part of the country's plentiful tourism resources find themselves in the inner territory where regional economic development is far behind the coastal region, and most minority population is concentrated. Recent studies show that the potential for tourism development in the western part of the country is huge.[1]

However, achieving regional goals by setting up tourism industry in the economically lagged areas has not been actively pursued in China. On the contrary, selective allocation of incentives and state participation, and the provision of tourism infrastructure have in fact favored tourism development in the coastal provinces, leading to an explicit spatial concentration of tourist activities. Underpinning such a spatial preference are, among others, the infrastructure

---

[1]Cf. Xing et al. 1990, pp. 251–75; Gormsen 1995, pp. 63–88; Zhang 1995, pp. 41–58.

constraints and the 'unbalanced' regional development strategy in the post-reform period.[2]

The uneven tourism development strategy has manifested itself most apparently in the selection of the so-called 'key tourist cities' which enjoy top priorities in national tourism development. In the 7th 'FYP' (1985–90), seven places were selected as 'key tourist cities':

- Beijing, Shanghai and Guangzhou. They are promoted both as travel destinations in their own right and the gateways to and showcases of the whole country;

- Guilin and Xi'an. They are the destinations which possess 'monopolistic' attractions, and are a 'must' for tourists on packaged tours; and

- Suzhou and Hangzhou. Together with Shanghai, they build an attractive group destination.

Except Xi'an (in province Shuanxi), all other 'key tourist cities' are located in the coastal provinces.[3] Since the 8th 'FYP' (1990–95), 'key tourist cities' have been expanded to eight cities (areas). Besides redefinitions of Guangzhou (city) to Guangdong (province) and Suzhou (city) to Jiangsu (province), Hainan province has been added to this list.

In 1992, China started a new round of tourism infrastructure construction, which should give another big boost to China's tourism development in the next century. According to this scheme, 11 'national tourism and recreational centers' will be established. Except Kunming (in province Yunan), ten of the 11 planned 'Centers' are located in nine coastal provinces.[4] Obviously, such tourism projects are most likely to further the concentration processes on the supply side.

---

[2]Scholars are divided regarding whether or to what extent the Maoist development model had differed from the classic 'inverted-U'. Little disputable seems that respectable, though not necessarily rational, top-down attempts in coping with regional inequalities were seriously undertaken in the pre-reform period. In the post-reform era, however, the mainstream paradigm of regional development is an explicit 'unbalanced' strategy. Cf. Taubmann 1987, pp. 26–29; Cannon 1990, pp. 28–59; Lyons 1991, pp. 471–506; Putterman 1992, pp. 467–93; Tsui 1993, pp. 600–27.

[3]Xi'an is most famous for its archeological sites of the ceramic army.

[4]*Renmin Ribao* (People's Daily), 23 October 1992.

The study areas of Guilin, Suzhou and Beidaihe are located in the eastern part of China (Fig. 3–1). They represent three important types of tourist areas (Tab. 3–1). Guilin and Suzhou are among the 'key tourist cities' of China. They play an important role in tourism development in the whole country. Guilin and Suzhou are the favored destinations of both international and domestic tourism in China. Yet, differences between them are fundamental. While tourism in Guilin is dominated by landscape sightseeing, tourism in Suzhou is cultural sightseeing in character. While Guilin's tourism is growing on a weak regional economic basis, Suzhou's tourism is supported by a strong, diversified and dynamic regional economy. Beidaihe represents yet another type of destination. It is the largest seaside resort of China, which is exclusively for domestic tourists.

**Figure 3–1: Location of Guilin, Suzhou and Beidaihe**

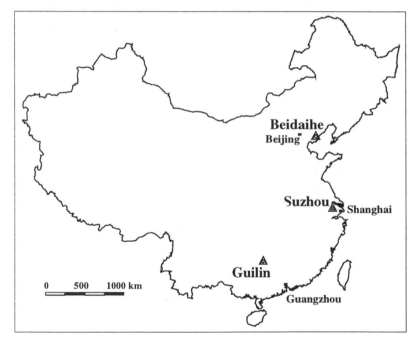

**Table 3–1: Types of Tourist Areas of Guilin, Suzhou and Beidaihe**

|  | Guilin | Suzhou | Beidaihe |
|---|---|---|---|
| Location | Guangxi | Jiangsu | Hebei |
|  | 400 km from Guangzhou; 600 km from HK | Shanghai metropolitan area | Beijing-Tianjin metropolitan area |
| Primary Attraction | karst landscape | a 'historical-cultural city' | sun and sand |
| Position | a 'key tourist city' | a 'key tourist city' | seaside resort |
| Type of Tourism | international; domestic; natural sightseeing; | international; domestic; cultural sightseeing; | domestic seaside recreation |
| Goal | a leading sector | 'externalities' of tourism | spontaneous |
| Major investors | state; foreign investors; individuals | state; collectives; individuals | state; individuals |
| GDP per capital[1] 1991 | 1,991 | 4,178 | 2,277 |
| 1978 | 454 | 634 | 376 |

[1] City-region averages in RMB yuan. National averages: 375 yuan in 1978, and 1,758 yuan in 1991.

Sources: Statistical Bureau Guilin, Suzhou and Beidaihe; *Statistical Yearbook of Chinese Cities 1992; Forty Years of Urban Development in China.*

## 3.2 Guilin

### 3.2.1 Tourism in an Economically Less Developed Area

Guilin is worldwide famous for its unique karst landscape. It is located in the northeastern part of Guangxi Zhuang Autonomous Region (province). The karst landscape in Guilin area is famous at home and abroad since historical times.

Historically, Guilin area is associated with the ancient construction – *Lingqu* Canal, which was dug in the 33rd year (214 B.C.) of the First Emperor of the *Qin* Dynasty (*Qinshihuang*). In Chinese history, the construction of *Lingqu* Canal was of great political, military as well as economic importance, because it connects China's two large river systems: the Changjiang and Zhujiang river systems.[5] Due to its strategic geographical location, Guilin gained importance in the development of Southwest China, and became a hub linking Central and South China during that time.[6]

The original city walls of Guilin were built in the 6th year (111 B.C.) of the *Han* Dynasty. The name 'Guilin' derived from the fact that many sweet-scented osmanthus trees were planted in this place. By the early of the *Tang* Dynasty (618–960), Guilin had become the political center of the whole region of Guangxi (today's Guangxi province). During the *Song* Dynasty (960–1279), Guilin witnessed significant economic and cultural development and became a 'Capital of the Southwest'. During the *Ming* (1368–1644) and *Qing* (1644–1911) Dynasties, Guilin was the provincial capital of Guangxi, and the city of Guilin saw a considerable expansion.[7]

Travel activity has a long history in Guilin. During historical times, Guilin was a favored destination of the political prominent of the Chinese society as well as scholars. Already in the *Tang* Dynasty (618–960), the picturesque landscape of Guilin had become famous at home and abroad, and attracted a large number of Chinese scholars. By the *Song* Dynasty (960–1279), travel activities in Guilin had allegedly developed to a considerable extent.[8]

Modern tourist activities began in Guilin in the early 1970s when the city was officially opened to international tourists in 1973.[9] In 1982, Guilin was named as one of the 24 'historical and cultural cities' of China. Of particular importance for Guilin's tourism development was the designation of Guilin as one of the seven 'key tourist cities' of China in 1985. Since then, Guilin's tourism has been growing at a rapid pace. Today, as a most important 'key tourist city' in the whole country, Guilin has become not only a 'must' for most international

---

[5]The major part of Lingqu Canal is located at Xing'an (county), which is about 60 km from the city of Guilin. *Lingqu* Canal links Xiangjiang river (the Changjiang river system) with Lijiang river (the Zhujiang river system). Today, however, this historic construction plays no roles in tourism promotion in Guilin.

[6]Li 1990, pp. 5–20; Zhao 1985, pp. 57–58.

[7]*Ibid.*

[8]*Ibid.*

[9]GLERC 1989, p. 20.

tourists on packaged tourism in China, but a most favored destination of domestic tourists.

In geographical terms, Guilin is a 'key tourist city' which is far away from China's major gateway cities. To its nearest gateways, Guilin is about 400 km northwest from Guangzhou, or 600 km from Hong Kong. From this perspective, the recent growth of international tourism in Guilin must be ascribed to the considerable expansions of its international airport.

Guilin airport is among the top 10 international airports in China. From 1978 to 1992, air passenger traffics had grown from 60,000 to 790,000 persons.[10] By 1992, there were 28 routes connecting Guilin with other leading tourist cities/big urban centers in China. Measured in flight frequency per week, passenger traffics are concentrated on the routes between Guilin and Guangzhou, Shanghai, Beijing and Xi'an, depicting the most favored travel routes of international tourists in China (Fig. 3–2). Since the early 1990s, daily charter flights between Guilin and Hong Kong have been in operation.

## Figure 3–2: Airway Connection and Flight Frequency (1992), Guilin

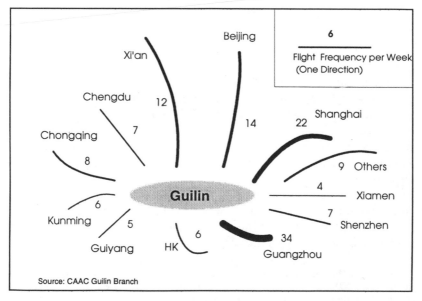

Source: CAAC Guilin Branch

---

[10]GLTN 1992, p. 420; 1993, p. 233.

In view of the decisive role of air transport in tourism development, a large international airport has been under construction in Guilin. This airport project is the only one in the whole country which has been invested by the CAAC during the 8th 'FYP' period (1990–95).[11] It is located in *Liangjiang*, about 6 km from the city Guilin (Fig. 3–3). The planned international airport has an area of 400 hectares, and a capacity of five million passenger turnover per annum. The new airport is planned to be completed by early 1997. Obviously, the major justification for such large-scale state investment in Guilin is its unreplaceable position in China's entire international tourism.

### Figure 3–3: Lijiang River Scenic Spots

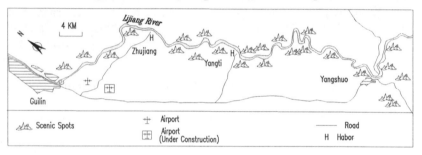

With respect to domestic tourism, Guilin is a remote destination. It is far away from China's major metropolitan areas. Compared to its air connections, Guilin has a much less advantageous location on the national railroad network. In 1991, there were nine pairs of passenger trains passing by Guilin per day, and four trains starting from Guilin to Guangzhou, Nanning, Liuzhou and Hengyang. Inadequate provision of inter-regional transportation remains one of the most apparent bottlenecks in domestic tourism development. In December 1995, a big railroad project was started in Guilin, which aims at building Guilin into one of the major inter-regional railroad transport nodes in Central-south China.[12]

---

[11] In 1992, the central government approved a tourism-specific grant-in-aid of RMB yuan 900 million for this airport project. Foreign investors invested RMB yuan 150 million in the airport road project. GLTN 1993, pp. 399–400; *Renmin Ribao* (People's Daily), 20 January 1996.

[12] *Renmin Ribao* (People's Daily), 11 January 1996.

In Guilin, local expectations on the alleged 'growth effects' of tourism are extremely high. Over the past one and half decades, local government has set out almost entirely on the tourism industry. Tourism has been viewed as a growth sector in which Guilin enjoys 'absolute advantage'. A growing tourism sector is expected to play the role of a 'leading' industry, through whose expansions the 'take-off' of Guilin's local economy could take place. For this reason, an extensive economic restructuring program was carried out in the mid-1980s. 27 manufacturing factories, which had been classified as incompatible with tourism, were shut down. Other 46 pollution-generating industrial units were either relocated or properly treated.[13]

However, compared to other 'key tourist cities' in the coastal region, Guilin is very weak in regional economy. According to a popular (albeit rigid) definition, Guilin (Guangxi province) belongs to the coastal region. However, in terms of economic development, Guilin area tends to share more features with the central and western parts of China than with the coastal region.

Local financial resources for tourism promotion are extremely limited. As a result, tourism development in Guilin has to rely heavily on foreign investment as well as state investment from higher-level governments, exemplifying an outside-induced development on an underdeveloped regional economic basis. On the whole, tourism in Guilin has followed a path of 'institutionalized' development.

### 3.2.2  Tourism Potentials: Karst Landscape

The primary tourist attraction of Guilin is the natural beauty of subtropical karst landscape in and around Guilin. Due to the unique geological structure and sub-tropical climate, Guilin area is most typical of the so-called *Fenglin* (tower) karst landscape in Southwest China.[14]

Famed as 'scenery unparalleled under the heaven', Guilin's karst landscape is characterized by four peculiar features:

- green hills in various shapes towering out of the ground;
- crystal-clear water flowing like green silk ribbons winding its ways through numerous weirdly shaped hills;
- fantastic caves displaying various magnificent constitutions and colors; and
- charming rocks being beautifully wrought.

---

[13]GLERC 1989, pp. 19–44.
[14]Zhu 1991 (1–3), pp. 51–62, 137–50 and 171–82.

## Figure 3–4: Tourism Infrastructure in Guilin

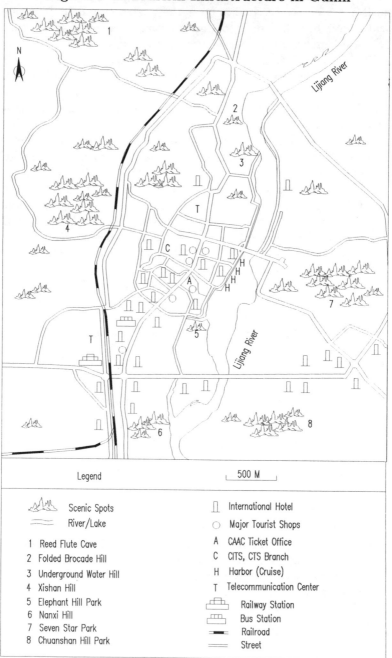

Legend

500 M

| | | |
|---|---|---|
| Scenic Spots | | International Hotel |
| River/Lake | | Major Tourist Shops |
| 1 Reed Flute Cave | A | CAAC Ticket Office |
| 2 Folded Brocade Hill | C | CITS, CTS Branch |
| 3 Underground Water Hill | H | Harbor (Cruise) |
| 4 Xishan Hill | T | Telecommunication Center |
| 5 Elephant Hill Park | | Railway Station |
| 6 Nanxi Hill | | Bus Station |
| 7 Seven Star Park | | Railroad |
| 8 Chuanshan Hill Park | | Street |

Numerous vivid fairytales of scenic sights often stimulate visitors' imagination of the natural beauty of Guilin's landscape. The highlights of Guilin's landscape include 'one river', 'two caves' and 'three hills' (Fig. 3–3, 3–4).[15]

## (1) The Lijiang River

The Lijiang river, with a total length of 437 km, meanders through hills in the northeastern part of Guangxi province. The most splendid part of Guilin's landscape finds itself along the 83-kilometer-long river valley between Guilin and Yangshuo, which is often praised as a 'fairyland on earth'.[16]

With zigzag streams, and peaks of fantastic shapes and greenery-covered cliffs, this river stretch (especially between *Yangdi* and *Xingping*) presents the highlight of the most favored one-day cruise on the Lijiang river (Fig. 3–3, 3–4). A boat ride along this stretch features limpid waters mirroring oddly-shaped peaks and picturesque fields on both sides, resembling a cruise in a landscape painting. Natural beauty is at its best under clear sky, and becomes almost poetic for the curling mist after rain.

At the beginning of tourism development, the Lijiang river was partly polluted.[17] Though further river pollution has been largely controlled thereafter, tourist activities on the Lijiang river began to be threatened by falling water-level in the mid-1980s, especially during the dry seasons (October–March).[18] Since the late 1980s, the start-point of river cruise during dry seasons (for international tourists) has to be relocated to *Zhujiang* or *Yangti*, about 20 km or 40 km from the city respectively.

## (2) Scenic spots within the city proper

Though Guilin is listed as a 'historical-cultural' city, the major tourist attraction within the city is also rooted in the natural beauty of karst developments. Among famous scenic spots are the magnificent karst caves at *Ludi* (Reed Flute) and *Qixin* (Seven-Star) park, and the karst-tower sights at *Diecai* (Folded Brocade), *Fubo* (Underground Water) park, and *Nanxi* and *Xiang* (Elephant) hill (Fig. 3–4). Vis-

---

[15]Zhao 1985, pp. 57–58; Liu 1987; GTB 1988; *Guilin shijing* (Ten Scenes of Guilin); *Lijiang shijing* (Ten Scenes of Lijiang); *Yangshuo shijing* (Ten Scenes of Yangshuo); Zhou 1988.

[16]The rest parts of the Lijiang river has not yet been developed as tourist attractions. Cf. GLERC 1989, pp. 83–128.

[17]GLERC 1989, pp. 83–128.

[18]GLURC 1990, pp. 33–35.

its to such scenic spots are not only an important part of the tour arrangements for international tourists, but the major activities of domestic visitors in Guilin.

### (3) Scenic sights in Yangshuo county

Yangshuo county is a place where 'hundred miles of river are paintings and green lotus peak has families'.[19] The county-seat town Yang-shuo*zhen* is about 65 km on the road and 83 km on the waterway from the city Guilin. It is the end-point of the one-day river cruise. About 43 km of the most intensively used river section is located in the Yangshuo county (Fig. 3–3).

The western part of Yangshuo county is not only rich in karst developments such as karst towers and caves, but especially famous for its 'untouched' natural rural landscape. Subject to the dominance of Guilin as well as the currently prevailing tour arrangements, however, tourist potentials in Yangshuo have hardly been developed. Except at such scenic spots as the 'Big Banyan Tree' and the 'Moon Hill', tourist activities are concentrated in Yangshuo town, a short stop-over of most one-day excursionists.

### (4) Minority Cultures

The province Guangxi is an autonomous region of China. *Zhuang, Miao, Yao* and *Dong* are the major groups among the 11 minority nationalities in this province. In Yangshuo and Lingui counties, which are under the administration of Guilin, there are eight minority groups living in compact communities.[20] However, native minority cultures have not been given sufficient attention in tourism promotion in Guilin.

Instead, a 'Folk Village' was established in the city of Guilin in 1991. Interestingly, this 'Folk Village' is a joint-venture of Guilin Tourism Development Co. and Taiwan Huawan Ltd.[21] It is located at *Liangjiang kuo*, about 4 km from the city center. The 'Folk Village' has an area of 3.5 hectares, consisting of a 21-meter high drum-tower (*Dong* minority) and a number of constructions representative of the native settlements of *Zhuang, Dong, Miao* and *Yao* nationalities. During tourism seasons, folk dance and songs are performed regularly.

---

[19] GLERC 1989, pp. 337–64.
[20] GLCPB 1988, pp. 10–12.
[21] About US$ 2.6 million were invested in this project, of which US$ 2 million from Taiwan-based Hauwan Ltd. GLTN 1992, p. 654.

# 3.3 Suzhou

## 3.3.1 Tourism in an Industrialized Area

Suzhou is a famous city which is not only of historical and cultural importance, but full of modern industrial and commercial dynamics in Southeast China. It is located in southern Jiangsu province, and only about 80 km west of China's largest metropolis Shanghai. As a tourist city, Suzhou's primary attraction is rooted in the numerous historical and cultural sights in and around the city.

Both historically and culturally, the Suzhou area is often referred to as the *Wu* region. At the beginning of the 6th century B.C., the capital of the *Wu* State was moved to the present-day site of the city Suzhou.[22] In 514 B.C., the 'Great City of *Helü* ' (virtually the entire old town of Suzhou) was built as a political and economic center of the Changjiang delta area. The years after the *Qin* (221–206 B.C.) and *Han* (206 B.C.–A.D. 220) Dynasties saw the rise of the 'great metropolis of the *Wu* '.[23]

During the *Sui* (589–618) and *Tang* (618–907) Dynasties, *Su* (Suzhou)-*Hang* (Hangzhou) area (also called *Taihu* area) had became the economic core region of the whole country.[24] The particular importance of this area was reflected most evidently in the construction of the Grand Canal, which was completed mainly during the *Sui* Dynasty (589–907), and aimed originally at linking up the economic core region in Southeast China with the political centers in North China. Suzhou was one of the most prosperous urban centers along the Grand Canal.[25]

In the *Song* Dynasty (960–1279), the *Su* (Suzhou)-*Hang* (Hangzhou) area was described as a 'paradise on earth', and became famous throughout the country. During the *Yuan* Dynasty (1279–1368), Suzhou was, in Marco Polo's words, a 'very great and noble city'.[26] The *Ming* (1368–1644) and *Qing* (1644–1911) Dynasties carried the advance of Suzhou's culture and economy still further.

Associated with its economic prosperity, Suzhou was an important cultural city and birthplace of scholars in Southeast China throughout historical times. Especially, since the early 12th century, when

---

[22]Before that, the capital of the *Wu* State was located about 16 km west of the present-day city of Suzhou. Cf. Shen and Jiang 1988, pp. 2–12.

[23]*Ibid.*

[24]Ma and Yu 1990, pp. 56–66.

[25]Compare section 3.3.2.

[26]Shen and Jiang 1988, pp. 2–12.

nomadic tribes swept down from the North and the imperial court moved to the south of the Changjiang river, a large number of aristocrats and cultural elite migrated to Southeast China. As a result of such cultural shifts, Suzhou became a favorite home of the scholar-gentry class and a hub of literary and artistic pursuits. In many fields, distinct styles appeared and were recognized as the '*Wu* Schools'.[27] In the meantime, Suzhou developed gradually into a recreational place for the wealthy and elite at the regional level.

Suzhou is among the cities which lead the country in opening to the outside world. Similar to Guilin, Suzhou was named as a 'historical and cultural cities' in 1982, and selected as a 'key tourist city' in 1985. The major justification for Suzhou to be selected as a 'key tourist city' seems the idea that Shanghai, Hangzhou and Suzhou together can build up an attractive group destination in the Changjiang delta area.

The Shanghai metropolitan area, including Shanghai, southern Jiangsu and northern Zhejiang, leads the country in overall economic development. Large cities in this agglomeration area have recently become one of the fastest growing tourist regions in the whole country.[28] Indeed, the recent growth of international tourism in Suzhou is attributable largely to its spatial proximity to the gateway city Shanghai, since Suzhou has no international airport.[29]

Parallel with international tourism, domestic tourism has also grown to an enormous size in Suzhou. Shanghai–Jiangsu–Zhejiang is a densely populated and highly urbanized region in China. In 1991, this metropolitan area had an urban (non-agricultural) population of 16 million.[30] Stimulated by the dynamic regional economy, recreational demand of the inhabitants of the delta area has been on rapid rise. Geographical proximity, and numerous cultural and scenic sights make Suzhou an ideal place for one-day excursions.

Standing on the Beijing–Shanghai railroad, Suzhou is well connected with big cities in many parts of the country. Besides daily passenger trains starting from Suzhou to Shanghai, Nanjing and Bei-

---

[27] *Ibid.*

[28] In 1993, this area (including Shanghai, Hangzhou, Suzhou, Nanjing and Wuxi) received 2.4 million international tourists, accounting for 15% of the national total (hotel arrivals). NTA 1994, p. 72–75.

[29] Suzhou has a small airport called *Shuofang* Airport, which is about 40 km from the city. Due to limited capacity (two fights per week to Beijing and Shengzhen), however, this airport plays a marginal role in tourist transportation.

[30] ZCTN 1992, pp. 52–53; Yao 1992, chapter 4.

jing, there are 33 trains via Suzhou per day. Suzhou has a developed road transport network connecting urban centers within the Changjiang delta area. The Hangzhou–Shanghai–Nanjing highway, which is under construction and planned to be completed by early 1997, will further improve the accessibility of Suzhou.[31]

Modern tourism development started in Suzhou when this area had already entered into a rapid industrialization stage. Today, the southern Jiangsu province (*Sunan*), of which Suzhou is a core part, is among the most prosperous and dynamic regions in China. The so-called *Sunan Model* is almost a synonym for rapid and successful rural industrialization and urbanization and, therefore, widely described as a 'success story' of regional development in China.

In the mid-1980s, a proposal of 'building Suzhou into one of the leading tourist cities in China' was drawn up as a guide line of the city's development strategy.[32] However, unlike in Guilin, tourism industry in Suzhou has been regarded mainly as a new developmental factor for the urban tertiary sector in an industrialized local economy.

In Suzhou, the underlying motive of tourism promotion tends to go far beyond tourism itself. Although foreign exchange receipts are also expected, the local government has placed even greater values on the envisaged 'externalities' of tourism development, including 'spillovers' of tourism growth on such a local economic sector as souvenir industry, improvements in local investment climate as well as the city's image-making. In addition, calculations of a more favorable policy environment for the entire local economy may have also played a certain part in tourism promotion.

### 3.3.2 Tourism Potentials: A Historical-Cultural City

As mentioned in the preceding section, Suzhou has 2,500 years of history. History has left Suzhou a handsome legacy of architecture, arts and crafts, literature, painting, etc. It is this legacy that builds up the prime attraction for modern tourism activities in Suzhou. Especially famous are the classical Suzhou gardens, the historical and cultural sights in and around the city, colorful local handicrafts, and part of its old townscape (Fig. 3–5).[33]

---

[31] *Renmin Ribao* (People's Daily), 30 May 1995.
[32] SZCPB 1985.
[33] For detailed descriptions of tourist attractions in Suzhou, see e.g. Zhong 1983; Zhao 1985, pp. 37–38; Shen and Jiang 1988; Qian and Zhu 1989.

## Figure 3–5: Tourism Infrastructure in Suzhou

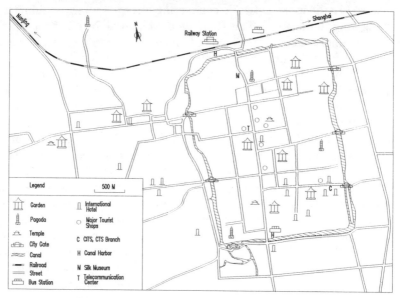

### (1) A 'City of Gardens'

Suzhou's reputed classical gardens are most representative of the private residential gardens in Southeast China. They were originally the private residential constructions of local landowners, rich merchants, aristocrats, officials and the like. Suzhou gardens were built mainly in the *Song* (960–1279), *Yuan* (1279–1368), *Ming* (1368–1644) and *Qing* (1644–1911) Dynasties. During the *Ming* and *Qing* Dynasties alone, more than 400 gardens were constructed in Suzhou.[34]

By the late 1950s, within Suzhou's old town there were still 114 gardens of various sizes, of which 38 were in full existence.[35] Due to political movements such as the Cultural Revolution as well as modern industrial expansions, however, most of Suzhou gardens had been destroyed by the late 1970s.

In the course of tourism development, considerable efforts have been made in restoring Suzhou gardens. The major gardens have been restored and renewed in their original styles. Today, there are 11 big gardens open to tourists, three of them are under the state protec-

---

[34] SZCPB 1988, pp. 20–22; SZGMB 1991, pp. 1–4.
[35] *Ibid.*

tion. The Humble Administrator Garden and the Linger-here Garden are famed as two of the four 'most famous Chinese Gardens'.[36] To enrich Suzhou's garden cultures, traditional cultural activities such as performance of classic music and folk dance have been recently added to the Garden of Master of Nets.

Suzhou's garden architecture holds a leading position in the Chinese architectural art and landscape gardening. In contrast to the magnitude imperial gardens in North China, such as the Summer Palace in Beijing and the Summer Resort Villa in Chengde (Hebei), Suzhou gardens are characterized by their small but fine garden techniques. Drawing upon nature, conceived in traditional Chinese painting and inspired by the spirit of *Tang* and *Song* poetry, Suzhou gardens have demonstrated a variety of artistic and imaginative techniques. They are so constructed as to achieve an impression of spaciousness, a poetic atmosphere, and a seemingly endless variety of spontaneous scenes by stimulating visitors' imagination.[37]

### (2) The Ancient Townscape

The old town of Suzhou was founded in 514 B.C. When *Wu Zixi*, a senior minister of the King *Helü* of the *Wu* State, built the 'Great City of Helü', he 'investigated the water and soil conditions, surveyed the terrains, and made astrological tellings'.[38] The 'Great City' had eight land gates and eight water gates, and its outer walls aggregated 24 km in length. Since its founding, the location, extent and overall layout of Suzhou's old town have remained virtually the same.

The prosperity and urban dimensions of the ancient city Suzhou is especially well recorded on the *Pingjiang* Map. *Pingjiang* is an old name for Suzhou. The *Pingjiang* Map is a scale map of the ancient city Suzhou, which was engraved on a stele in 1229 (the *Song* Dynasty). The *Pingjiang* Map is 2.8 meters in length and 1.4 meters in width. It is carved with hills, lakes, city walls, rivers, streets, gardens, temples, pagodas, commercial establishments, etc. The *Pingjiang* Map is now kept in Suzhou Confucian Temple.

The well-preserved structure of Suzhou's old town is representative of ancient Chinese cities, reflecting then prevailing sociopolitical structure as well as Chinese philosophy. The basic element of Suzhou's townscape is a so-called 'double-line chessboard', i.e. streets

---

[36]The other two are the Summer Palace in Beijing and the Summer Resort Villa in Chengde (Hebei).

[37]Peng 1988, pp. 1–51.

[38]Shen and Jiang 1988, pp. 2–12.

and alleys on close parallel with canals, with houses hanging at the water's edge. Famed as 'Venice of the Orient', Suzhou used to be described as a city with 'little bridges, flowing waters and residential houses'.

Unfortunately, Suzhou's tranquillity and elegance is definitely gone. Due to industrial expansions in the past decades, a large part of the city walls, typical small alleys and the inner-city canal systems have disappeared. According to Suzhou's city renewal programs, efforts are being made in restoring some of the historical constructions in the old town area. However, today the white walls, dark-gray roof tiles and small bridges over flowing waters, which used to be a symbol of Suzhou, can only partly be seen in the inner city.

### (3) A 'Metropolis of Arts and Crafts'

Arts and crafts is another area in which Suzhou takes great pride. Among most distinguished local handicrafts are silk products, embroidery, fan-making, and jade and padauk carving.

Suzhou has a 3000-year history of sericulture, enjoying a reputation of 'home of silks'. Skills of the past centuries have been well preserved, which find wide applications and rich motives in local handicraft productions. Suzhou is one of the leading silk production bases of China, contributing about one-sixth of the country's silk exports in the 1980s.[39] In the course of industrialization, however, sericulture as an economic sector has been losing its importance in Suzhou area. A large part of the cultivation of mulberry trees and the rearing of silkworms has shifted to the northern part of Jiangsu province. In order to restore the history of local silk productions, a Silk Museum was opened in 1991.

Delicate designs and exquisite workmanship of Suzhou's silk products are famed both at home and abroad. Suzhou embroidery is distinguished by its elegant, neat characteristics and excellent craftsmanship. Finely made sandalwood fans and jade carving articles, which draw on the essence of garden arts and traditional paintings, are works of art.

Local souvenir industry plays an important part in tourism development in Suzhou. Not only are many fine and colorful souvenir products frequently sought by tourists, but visiting some of the leading souvenir manufacturing plants makes up an attractive part of tour arrangements for many tourists. The local government is very aware of the role of tourism in promoting local souvenir industry. In an ef-

---

[39] *Ibid.*

fort to expand local exports and raise Suzhou's reputation, the local government began to sponsor the 'Suzhou International Silk Festival' in 1992.

## (4) Cultural and Scenic Sights in the Surrounding Areas

Suzhou's another attraction is the historical, cultural and scenic spots in its surrounding areas. Most of the tourist spots around Suzhou combine historical and cultural sights with the landscape typical of Southeast China. Besides such places as the Tiger Hill and the Cold Mountain Temple, which are among the most attractive for both international and domestic tourists, an ever larger number of suburban cultural and scenic spots are more often visited by domestic tourists. Among many others, the *Tianping* (Sky-Level) and *Linyan* (Miraculous) Hills are typical of the tourist spots in the surrounding areas.

The Suzhou area is often described as a typical 'water country' dotted with a large number of lakes, and crossed by rivers and canals. Since historical times, much attention has been paid to building water conservancy works. Of historical importance was the construction of the Grand Canal in the 7th century. The part of the Grand Canal south of the Changjiang river is often called *Jiangnan* Canal. By the *Song* Dynasty (960-1279), many rivers, canals and lakes in this area had been connected with the Grand Canal, and an elaborate network of waterways had emerged. For several centuries, this waterway network had provided the most important base of transportation in the whole region. Even today, the *Jiangnan* Canal still plays a role in regional transportation.

For many international tourists, the name of Suzhou is also closely associated with the Grand Canal. Running 1,790 kilometers from Tongxia county (near Beijing) in the North to Hangzhou in the South, the Grand Canal is often described as an engineering wonder which is as magnificent as the Great Wall. The Grand Canal flows across the western part of Suzhou, and links Suzhou with other tourist cities such as Wuxi and Hangzhou in the Changjiang delta area. The Grand Canal cruise from Suzhou to Wuxi and Hangzhou often appears in tour programs offered by travel agencies.

Along the Grand Canal in Suzhou area, there are many historical constructions such as bridges, gates, temples and pavilions worth visiting. Particular famous are the Coiling Gate (*Panmen*), the Cold Mountain Temple (*Hanshan Si*) and Maple Bridge (*Fengqiao*), and the Precious-Belt Bridge (*Baodai Qiao*).

The wide moat around Suzhou's old town is also linked with the Grand Canal. Within the old town, there once existed a dense inner-city canal system. However, in the course of city development, the largest part of this canal system has become defunct. Today, canal cruise within the city is possible only on part of the outer moat and some existing inner-city canals. In addition, incredible water pollution has also impeded the use of inner-city canals in tourism promotion.

A big tourism infrastructure project outside Suzhou is the planned 'Jiangsu-*Taihu* Tourism and Recreational Center', which is one of the 11 'Centers' in the national development scheme.[40] This planned Center consists of two parts, i.e. *Wuxi-Mashan* (in the neighboring city Wuxi) and *Suzhou-Xukou*. The Suzhou sub-center is located near *Xukou*, 25 km from the city Suzhou. This project is just under construction. Though the establishment of this center aims at promoting international tourism, its role in the future tourism development in Suzhou remains unclear.

## 3.4  Beidaihe

### 3.4.1  A Traditional Seaside Resort

Beidaihe is the largest seaside resort of China. It is an urban district of Qinhuangdao *shi* (city), which is located in the eastern part of Hebei province.[41] In addition to the resort Beidaihe, Qinhuangdao *shi* is famous for its modern harbor functions. It is the largest transshipment node of coal transportation from North to Southeast China.

The resort area Beidaihe is about 15 km southwest of the central part (*Haigang qu*) of Qinhuangdao *shi* (Fig. 3–6). Beidaihe is about 380 km east of the capital city Beijing, and 240 km east of the city Tianjin. The resort area is well connected via railroad (about 20 trains per day) with big urban centers in Beijing–Tianjin–Tangshan (*Jingjintang*) area. Beijing–Tianjin–Tangshan is the largest metropolitan area in North China, and had around 12 million urban (non-agricultural) population in 1991.[42]

---

[40]Compare section 3.1.

[41]For definitions, compare section 1.3.

[42]ZCTN 1992, p. 49. For a discussion on urban development in this area, see Yao 1992, chapter 4.

## Figure 3–6: Beaches in Beidaihe Area

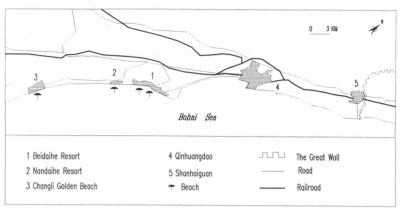

Traditionally, Beidaihe is the most important seaside resort of the elite of the Chinese society. The recreational value of the charming sea and long beaches around Beidaihe was discovered in the late 19th century when the *Jinshan* (Beijing–Shanhaiguan) railroad was built in 1893. The construction of *Jinshan* railroad provided the necessary transport connections between Beidaihe and the political center Beijing as well as other urban centers in North China. The first recreational villa in Beidaihe was built by an English engineer in 1893.[43] In the following years, numerous recreational facilities were established by both Chinese elite and foreigners.

In 1898, Beidaihe was officially declared by the *Guangxi* Emperor (the *Qing* Dynasty) as a summer resort of the imperial family.[44] In the same year, Qinhuangdao Harbor was opened as a foreign trade harbor in North China. This event gave the birth to more than 700 recreational facilities, which were established and continuously expanded as a summer resort not only for the ruling and wealthy classes of the Chinese society, but for many foreign diplomats, businessmen, and missionaries.[45]

Since the founding of the PRC, Beidaihe has become a recreational center for the late-day elite of the society. It was and is the place where the entire central government apparatus operates in the

---

[43]Li 1990, p.3; QTB 1990, pp. 14–16.
[44]QTB 1990, pp. 14–16.
[45]*Ibid.*

summer time. For this reason, Beidaihe is often called as China's 'capital in summer'. In the meantime, Beidaihe was also a recreational place for the late-day 'model workers and laborers'. Since the early 1950s, a large number of holiday quarters had been built by numerous *danwei* at various administration levels as well as the ministries of the central government. By 1966, there had already been 31 large-size danwei holiday quarters with more than 7,000 beds.[46] Till the late 1970s, Beidaihe remained indeed a place of 'mystery' for the mass of Chinese people. Having access to Beidaihe was regarded as a social prestige.

The curtain of the 'capital in summer' began to be drawn back when Qinhuangdao was opened to the outside world in 1979 and, especially, when it was designated as one of the 14 'coastal open cities' in 1984. Obviously, as a seaside resort, though Beidaihe is occasionally visited by foreign diplomats and experts who work for some time in Beijing, it has hardly any attractions to international tourists who need to travel long distances from their home countries, where they can reach better equipped seaside resort within a much shorter time.

Nevertheless, Beidaihe's attraction to domestic tourists is enormous. Within only a few years after its opening to mass tourists, Beidaihe's recreation amenities and then developed beaches became fully choked with holiday-makers and visitors from North China.[47] In order to divert the ever-growing tourist flows, Beidaihe resort has been supplemented by two newly developed beach areas since the mid-1980s (Fig. 3–6).

One of the newly-developed beach areas is Nandaihe resort, which is about 10 km south of Beidaihe. Nandaihe beach began to be developed in 1984 by the Tourism Development Company of Funing county (Hebei province). The first construction project, including 3 km long beaches and a 2.5 sq.km recreational area, had been fully completed by the late 1980s. More than 65 investors, including various *danwei* from 10 provinces as well as investors from Hong Kong, had invested 300 million RMB yuan.[48] Because of its spacious amenities and favorite conditions for recreational activities including parking possibilities, Nandaihe has diverted a considerable part of tourist flows from Beidaihe. In recent years, Nandaihe receives two to three million visitors per annum.

---

[46] *Ibid.*
[47] Compare section 5.4.
[48] FTB 1992, pp. 5–11.

Another resort area, the Changli Golden Beach has been established in Changli county (Hebei province) since 1985. Changli beach is about 17 km southwest of Beidaihe. Local tourism bureau reported that more than 70 investors have participated in this project. Since the late 1980s, this area receives ome to two million visitors per annum. One of the most attractive activities at this place is sand slide, which attracts a large number of visitors from Beidaihe and Nandaihe.

Since the early 1990s, the beach areas of Beidaihe, Nandaihe and Changli have been integrated by a high-standard road. Today, this resort area has become a destination of mass domestic tourism in North China, receiving about six to seven million holiday-makers per annum in recent years.

It should be emphasized that, till the late 1970s, though the central government and numerous *danwei* had invested heavily in expanding recreational facilities in Beidaihe, such 'developments' had hardly any links with the local economy. On the contrary, the political needs of higher-level bureaucracies appeared to the disadvantage of local development of Beidaihe, at least in economic terms. By the early 1980s, the area directly surrounding this resort was still dominated by an agrarian and fishery economy.

On the whole, the recent expansions in tourism supply outside the state-owned sector are spontaneous in nature. Under the shadows of powerful political influences, the role of local authorities in devising local development path remains marginal. Therefore, the rise of domestic tourism in the strict sense has been characterized by a development 'from below'. The initiatives of private households as well as small collective units are crucial to tourism development in this place.[49]

### 3.4.2 Tourism Potentials: Sun and sand

Sun and sand are the prime tourist attraction of Beidaihe. In geomorphological terms, Beidaihe is located on the northern coast of the *Bohai* Bay. Long and zigzag coastline, calm sea and soft sand make this area an ideal place for recuperation. Tucked away in a quiet corner, Beidaihe resort area leans against the green hills to the north, and faces the sea to the south. The sandy beach spreads over 10 km between the mouth of the Daihe river in the west and the Eagle Rocks in the east.

---

[49]Compare section 7.4.

However, most parts of the beach resources have not been developed for recreation purposes. Up to now, recreational activities are concentrated mainly in the Central Beach area around the Tiger Rocks. In this area, about 40 bathing facilities are in operation in tourism seasons. Most of them are temporary and simple in nature. In climatic terms, Beidaihe is located in the warm temperate zone. While the warm temperate zone covers a wide range of areas in China, Beidaihe is located on North China Plain.[50] Beidaihe is favored by a warm, maritime climate, with an annual temperature of 10.5°C and annual precipitation of about 700 mm.[51]

In Beidaihe, temperature rises quickly in Spring, with a small amount of precipitation. In summer, local temperature averages 2–3°C lower in Beidaihe than in neighboring cities in the metropolitan area (Tab. 3–2). About 60% of the annual precipitation is concentrated in July and August. Beidaihe has a short Summer and Autumn. By late October, average temperature declines to below 10°C.[52] Therefore, tourism activities are highly concentrated in the period from mid-July to mid-August.

### Table 3–2: Comparisons of Average Temperature in Beidaihe, Beijing and Tianjin

|                | Beidaihe | Beijing | Tianjin |
|----------------|----------|---------|---------|
| Annual         | 10.5     | 11.7    | 12.2    |
| June           | 20.4     | 24.4    | 24.0    |
| July           | 24.1     | 24.4    | 26.5    |
| August         | 24.1     | 26.0    | 25.8    |
| September      | 20.4     | 24.8    | 20.8    |
| Maximum        | 34.5     | 40.6    | 39.6    |
| ≥ 30°C days    | 7.6      | 62.1    | 57.4    |
| ≥ 35°C days    | none     | 8.1     | 5.2     |

Source: Li 1990, p. 5.

Scenic spots around Beidaihe, such as the *Lianpeng* (Lotus Seedpot) Hill and the Eagle Rocks, play only a secondary role. In recent years, some man-made tourist attractions, such as the Palace of the

---

[50]Domrös and Peng 988, pp. 263–65.

[51]Cf. Li 1990, p. 4.

[52]*Ibid.*

Emperor *Qinshihuang* (*Qinhuanggong*), have been established. *Qin-huanggong* Palace is built according to the historical records of the visit of the First Emperor of the *Qin* Dynasty (221–206 B.C.) to this area.

The major sightseeing attractions are located in Shanhaiguan area, which is about 35 km East of Beidaihe (Fig. 3–6). Shanhaiguan is especially famous because it is the place where the Great Wall starts. The partly renovated Great Wall in this area approaches the *Bohai* Sea at *Laolongtou* (the Old Dragon Head), which is the most attractive sightseeing spot in the whole region. Historical buildings and cultural sites in and around Shanhaiguan have been also restored. In recent years, this area has become an attractive destination of mass domestic tourism.

# Part II

# The Growth and Structure of Tourist Demand

# 4

# International Tourism

## 4.1 The Rise of Commercial International Tourism

### 4.1.1 Early 'Political Reception'

China's international tourism as a whole came into being in the late 1970s when the country began to open its 'door'. International tourist activities in Guilin and Suzhou took place much earlier. Even in the 1950s and 1960s, Guilin and Suzhou were among the few destinations in China which received international 'guests' from other socialist countries. Around the mid-1970s, international tourism began to take its shape in these two places. In Guilin, the number of international 'guests' and tourists rose from 1,000 in 1973 to 48,200 in 1978, and in Suzhou from 12,300 in 1975 to 27,700 in 1978.[1]

However, a large part of the provision of travel services to international tourists in the early years was non-commercial in nature. Apart from a small number of 'pioneer' international tourists, a large part of early visitors were not tourists in the strict sense. In fact, they were 'guests' of higher-level governments including the central government. By the late 1970s, more than 50 large-size foreign delegations consisting of government leaders, numerous diplomats, prominent figures and the like had already visited Guilin. At the local level, such travel services were usually arranged by the so-called *waiban*, or 'Offices of Foreign Affairs'. Receiving such international 'guests' was a top-down political task in the pre-reform period.

---

[1] GLERC 1989, pp. 146–51; SZTN 1949–1885, p. 400.

Nevertheless, the early efforts of Guilin and Suzhou in receiving numerous foreign guests turned out to be a great payoff for the later-on development of international tourism in one important respect. That is, such frequent visits of foreign delegations from many parts of the world had in effect made Guilin and Suzhou worldwide famous within a short period of time. Obviously, this is a favorable factor for the rise of modern international tourism in Guilin and Suzhou since the late 1970.

### 4.1.2 The Growth Since the Early 1980s

Thanks to their unique attractions, Guilin and Suzhou are among the leading destinations of international tourism in China. Especially, the selection of Guilin and Suzhou as 'key tourist cities' has given a big boost to international tourism in these two cities. From 1978 to 1993, international tourist arrivals had grown at an average rate of about 17% per annum in both places. In 1993, Guilin received around one half million international tourists, and Suzhou about 300,000 visitors (Fig. 4–1).

### Figure 4–1: International Tourist Arrivals in Guilin and Suzhou, 1978–1993

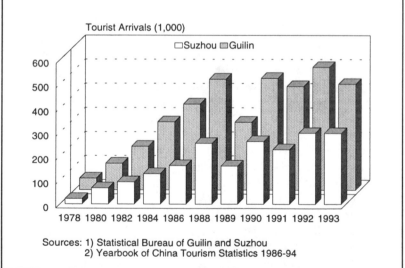

Sources: 1) Statistical Bureau of Guilin and Suzhou
2) Yearbook of China Tourism Statistics 1986-94

The largest part of the growth of international tourism in Guilin and Suzhou took place before 1989. During this period, tourist arrivals (taking 1978 as base-year) increased by nearly 10 times in

Guilin and nine times in Suzhou, accounting for 90% (Guilin) and 85% (Suzhou) of the total increase during 1978–92. In 1989, both places had to suffer a substantial decline in tourist arrivals, or 153,000 in Guilin and 95,000 in Suzhou. The development of international tourism after 1989 has been characterized by ups and downs. The general tendency is that tourist arrivals in both places stagnated.

## 4.2   Structural Changes in Tourist Demand

### 4.2.1   Foreigners, Compatriots and Overseas Chinese

According to the classification employed by the NTA, international tourists are roughly divided into three groups, namely, foreigners, *compatriots* and overseas Chinese. Recent studies have shown that these three demand groups have played widely different roles in international tourism development at different stages and in different parts of the country.[2]

Alongside substantial growth, the recent development of international tourism in Guilin and Suzhou has been accompanied by remarkable structural changes which are characterized by (Fig. 4–2, 4–3):

- first, the major source of growth in tourist arrivals pre and post 1987 was apparently different;
- second, individual market segments have played very different roles in the ups and downs since 1989; and
- third, the changes in tourist demand structure in Guilin and Suzhou tend to be substantially different to those observed at the national level.

#### (1) Foreign tourists as the major source of demand prior to 1987

Till the mid-1980, foreign tourists had played a leading part in international tourism in Guilin and Suzhou. From 1982 to 1986, foreign visitors contributed about 80% of the total increase in tourist arrivals in Guilin, and even 90% in Suzhou. In 1986, this demand group made up 75% of all hotel arrivals in Guilin and 83% in Suzhou. The dominance of foreign tourists suggests that both Guilin and Suzhou are among China's most attractive destinations of international tourism in the strict sense.[3]

---

[2]For discussions on demand structure and its changes at the national level, see Gormsen 1989, pp. 65–72; 1990a, pp. 143–56; 1990b, pp. 127–35, 1993, pp. 137–79; 1995a, pp. 63–88; Lew and Yu 1995.

[3]The share of foreign tourists at the national level was 9.6% in 1982, 6.5% in 1986, and 11.2% in 1993. NTA 1994, p. 30.

**Figure 4–2: Source of Growth/Decline in International Tourist Arrivals in Guilin and Suzhou, 1983–1993**

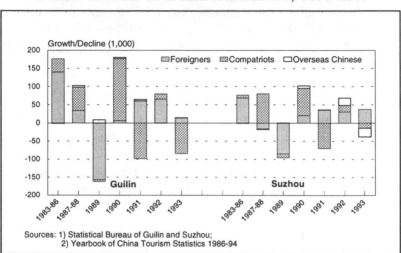

Sources: 1) Statistical Bureau of Guilin and Suzhou;
2) Yearbook of China Tourism Statistics 1986-94

**Figure 4–3: Structure of International Tourist Demand in Guilin and Suzhou, 1982–1993**

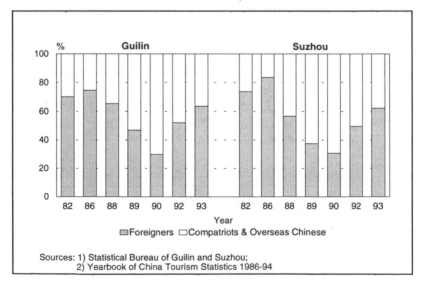

Sources: 1) Statistical Bureau of Guilin and Suzhou;
2) Yearbook of China Tourism Statistics 1986-94

## (2) The surge of the *compatriots* segment during 1987–88

In 1987, significant changes began to set in the composition of tourist demand in Guilin and Suzhou. During 1987–1988, over 62% of the increase in hotel arrivals in Guilin was contributed by the *compatriots* segment, though the number of foreign tourists was also on the increase. In Suzhou, the demand of foreign tourists and overseas Chinese travelers even declined in these two years. However, the arrivals of a large number of *compatriots* had not only fully offset such declines, but made a substantial growth possible. As a result, by the end of 1988 the share of *compatriots* had climbed to 33% in Guilin and 43% in Suzhou. Furthermore, author's field surveys suggest that 70–80% of such increases had resulted from the *compatriots* from Taiwan, who have been allowed to visit the mainland since 1987.[4]

## (3) The Development of Individual Market Segments after 1989

The decline of international tourism in Guilin and Suzhou in 1989 was remarkable. As the case at the national level, the travel demand of *compatriots* in Guilin and Suzhou was much less sensitive to the political incidents of 1989, compared to that of foreign tourists. In 1989, 97% of all decrease in tourist arrivals in Guilin resulted from the part of foreign tourists. This share was 88% in Suzhou.

While the source of the 1989 decline was more or less similar at the national and regional levels, the role of the three demand groups in the after-1989 recovery and development of international tourism in Guilin and Suzhou has been apparently different to the aggregate pictures at the national level.

The international tourism industry in Guilin and Suzhou had recovered from the deep recession at a much faster rate than the national aggregate. By the end of 1990, tourist arrivals in Guilin and Suzhou had already climbed over the 1988-level, whereas total border arrivals of international tourists recovered 87% of the 1988-level.[5] The role of the *compatriots* segment in this immediate recovery was decisive. In Suzhou, over 73% of the recovery in 1990 was contributed by the *compatriots*. In Guilin, this share reached 94%.[6] As a result, by 1990 the share of *compatriots* in all hotel arrivals had risen to about 66% in both places.

---

[4]Cf. Gormsen 1993, pp. 141–42, 1995a, pp. 71–72; Qui 1990, pp. 41–42; Zhong 1991, pp. 127–32.

[5]NTA 1994, p. 30.

[6]At the national level, *compatriots* contributed about 90% of the immediate recovery. *Ibid.*

The re-surge of travel demand of the *compatriots* in 1990 tended to be stimulated partly by the special situations in the supply market after the 1989 political incidents. As most tourism enterprises suffered from apparently inadequate demand, international tour operators were in fact in a typical buyer's market, putting substantial downward pressures on the supply-side. Tourism Bureaus of Guilin and Suzhou reported that at that time nearly all service suppliers had to compete savagely to offer tour operators with ever lower prices, leading to a widespread price-cutting practice in the whole supply market.

High price-elasticity of the travel demand of *compatriots* also explains a large part of the seemingly puzzling drop in hotel arrivals in the following year. As the 'lowest-price maintenance' campaign was launched nationwide in late 1990, tourism enterprises began to be forced to raise their service price to a certain extent.[7] Local travel agencies reported that, due to the consolidation and strengthening of market disciplines, in 1991 many Hong Kong-based tour operators withdrew a considerable part of business contracts which had been made in the previous year. Thus, while hotel arrivals of foreign tourists increased in 1991, the remarkable decrease in *compatriots* segment resulted in a drop in all hotel arrivals in both places.

In contrast to the immediate recovery stage around 1990, the major source of growth in 1992 was the demand of foreign tourists. In Guilin, over 82% of the total increase was attributable to the part of foreign tourists. Though this share was lower in Suzhou (about 45%), still it was much higher than that of *compatriots* (26%). In 1993, foreign tourist arrivals remained on increase in both places. However, a remarkable drop appeared in hotel arrivals of *compatriots* in Guilin, and a slight decrease in Suzhou.

In summary, it can be argued that the course of tourism development in Guilin and Suzhou after 1988 has been full of fluctuations. Such fluctuations resulted principally from the *compatriots* segment. Though foreign tourist arrivals were especially sensitive to the political incidents of 1989, they have been on stable increase from 1990 on in both places. Taking the period of 1990–1993 as a whole, all international tourist arrivals had a recovery of 157,000 in Guilin and 136,500 in Suzhou, to which foreign visitors had contributed 94% and 91% respectively. This makes a sharp contrast to the pattern

---

[7] Compare section 6.3.

of recovery at the national level, whereby the *compatriots* segment contributed over 80% (border arrivals) during the same period.[8]

### 4.2.2 Nationalities of Foreign Tourists

In recent years, one of the remarkable changes in foreign tourist demand taking place at the national level is the declining role of the traditional leading market segments, especially the Japanese and American tourists. The rapid rise of cross-border travels of the citizens of former USSR to China has made a significant contribution to the after-1989 recovery, though the largest part of such travel demand tends to serve trading purposes, instead of tourism in the strict sense.[9]

The after-1989 recovery in foreign tourist arrivals in Guilin and Suzhou is totally different to the pattern at the national level. While the border arrivals of Russian travelers have surpassed those of Japanese and American tourists in recent years, the role of Russian tourists in Guilin and Suzhou remains negligible (Tab. 4–1).

### Table 4–1: Nationalities of Foreign Tourists in Guilin and Suzhou, 1990 and 1993 (%)[1]

| Nationality | Guilin | | Suzhou | | China[2] | |
|---|---|---|---|---|---|---|
| | 1990 | 1993 | 1990 | 1993 | 1990 | 1993 |
| Japan | 33.4 | 21.5 | 38.8 | 40.4 | 26.5 | 19.6 |
| USA | 12.6 | 11.8 | 7.3 | 9.1 | 13.3 | 8.6 |
| France | 5.3 | 7.3 | 4.5 | 10.2 | 2.9 | 2.5 |
| Germany | 5.6 | 5.5 | 2.9 | 4.4 | 3.2 | 3.0 |
| UK | 6.4 | 11.0 | 2.8 | 5.8 | 4.5 | 3.3 |
| Canada | 2.0 | 1.7 | 1.7 | 1.8 | 2.7 | 2.3 |
| Australia | 2.3 | 2.2 | 0.9 | 1.0 | 2.8 | 2.1 |
| Singapore | 1.8 | 4.5 | 3.1 | 5.5 | 4.1 | 4.3 |
| Thailand | 2.3 | 1.5 | 1.7 | 0.8 | 3.9 | 3.3 |
| USSR | - | - | 0.2 | 0.3 | 6.3 | 19.9 |
| Philippines | 0.5 | 0.4 | 0.7 | 0.4 | 4.5 | 3.2 |
| Others | 27.8 | 32.6 | 35.4 | 20.3 | 25.3 | 27.9 |
| | | | | | | |
| Top-three[3] | 52.4 | 44.3 | 50.6 | 59.7 | 46.1 | 48.1 |

[1] % of all foreign tourist arrivals; [2] for comparative purposes; [3] the share of top three sending countries.

Source: *Yearbook of China Tourism Statistics* 1990–94.

---

[8]NTA 1994, p. 30.
[9]Cf. Gormsen 1993, pp. 139–144, and 1995a, pp. 66–73.

From 1990 to 1993, foreign tourist arrivals in Suzhou had a recovery of 104,000, to which the top-three sending countries (Japan, USA and France) alone contributed 67%. In this place, the top-three concentration ratio is still on the increase. The considerable reliance of Suzhou's international tourism on the single Japanese market segment can be explained by two major factors.

- First, due to historical and cultural relationships, Suzhou's cultural sights seem especially attractive to the Japanese tourists. In visiting Suzhou's gardens, for instance, many Japanese tourists appear to have high interests in appreciating gardens' historical backgrounds, legends, classical Chinese calligraphy and paintings, stone tablets, architectural styles, etc.

- The second explanatory factor is the spatial proximity of Suzhou to the metropolitan Shanghai. Among China's leading tourist destinations, Shanghai is the city which has the highest share of Japanese tourists in all hotel arrivals, or about 48% in 1993.[10] Obviously, most Japanese tourists who visit Shanghai usually also make a short visit to Suzhou.

Compared to Suzhou, the recovery of international tourism in Guilin tends to have more diversified sources. From 1990 to 1993, about 35% of the recovery (131,000) in this city was contributed by the top-three sending countries (Japan, USA and UK). The declining top-three concentration ratio suggests that in recent years a restructuring process has been taking place within the foreign tourist segment. Especially apparent is the declining share of the Japanese tourists.

## 4.3 Organization and Form

### 4.3.1 Overseas Marketing

The way of international tourism promotion in Guilin and Suzhou has changed significantly over the past decade. The centerpiece of such changes is a rising role of local initiatives in generating tourism businesses. Take the CITS system for example.

During the early years, the CITS branches in Guilin and Suzhou had little room to maneuver in expanding their business size. What kinds of and how many international tourists they could receive used to be determined by the CITS headquarters in Beijing. The allocation

---

[10]NTA 1994, pp. 78–79.

of tourism businesses among CITS regional branches was allegedly done according to the importance or attractiveness as well as other unknown criteria of the tourist cities concerned.

The monopoly of the national travel agencies in doing overseas travel businesses was broken down in late 1982, when a big step was taken in decentralizing the authority of overseas marketing to the provincial level.[11] In the light of this new regulation, the leading travel agencies at both national and regional levels are encouraged to enter into international tourism market as far as possible. Because of their leading position in national tourism development, Guilin and Suzhou have been granted to set up 'Overseas Travel Corp.' which are authorized in doing overseas marketing directly in the international tourism market.

Thus, the local capacity in overseas marketing has become increasingly critical to the success in international tourism businesses. As a result, in Guilin and Suzhou the share of international tourists assigned from the CITS headquarters has decreased significantly since the mid-1980. In both places, this share had dropped to about one-half of their all travel businesses by the late 1980s, and tends to decrease further. However, author's field surveys suggest that a considerable part of the non-centrally assigned travel businesses in Guilin and Suzhou tend to result from 'horizontal' or inter-regional business contracts, instead of direct overseas marketing.

Obviously, decentralization in overseas marketing authorities has stimulated enormous regional and local initiatives in tourism promotion, and exerted increasing pressures on tourism enterprises. They are increasingly compelled to improve their service qualities in order to maintain their market shares. On the other hand, however, such a decentralization has also led to dozens of problems. This involves, among others, excess competitions among Chinese tour operators themselves in the international tourism market.

The 'Overseas Travel Corp.' in Guilin and Suzhou reported that, due to continuous 'price-combats' from other regional enterprises, they have to suffer from increasing downward pressures on service prices in overseas marketing. Over-competitions have resulted in continuing price-cutting and, in many cases, unfavorable terms of contracts such as delays in payment. Another apparent problem is the lack of human resources and technical know-how in overseas marketing, which is characteristic of many tourist cities in China.

---

[11]Bai and Li 1990, pp. 91–119.

## 4.3.2 Tour Arrangements

With respect to tour arrangements, the overwhelmingly dominant form of international tourism in Guilin and Suzhou is package tourism. In recent years, about 90% of all hotel arrivals are generated by tourists who are on inclusive package tours. Though the number of individual tourists tends to be on slight increase, they play a marginal role in Guilin and Suzhou. It seems that up to now the need for more tailor-made products has not been a concern in tourism promotion in these two places.

As 'key tourist cities', Guilin and Suzhou are among the most attractive destinations in China. Since most international tourists usually visit several places in a single trip, their average length of stay in Guilin and especially in Suzhou is very short (Tab. 4–2).

**Table 4–2: Average Length of Stay of International Tourists in Guilin and Suzhou, 1986 and 1993 (days)**

|  | Foreigners | Overseas Chinese | *Compatriots* |
|---|---|---|---|
| Guilin |  |  |  |
| 1986 | 2.5 | 2.6 | 2.7 |
| 1993 | 2.0 | 2.2 | 2.3 |
| Suzhou |  |  |  |
| 1986 | 1.2 | 1.3 | 1.2 |
| 1993 | 1.4 | 1.4 | 1.7 |

Source: *Yearbook of China Tourism Statistics* 1986 and 1994.

In Guilin, packaged tours are organized in two directions:

- First, from south to north. International tourists on packaged tour in this direction usually start from Hong Kong or Guangzhou. The majority of them are *compatriots*. Some Japanese tourists and overseas Chinese from southeast Asian countries also take this route. Apart from a small fraction of tourists traveling to destinations such as Kunming in Southwest China, most of them travel further north, typically to Beijing, Xi'an or Shanghai.

- Second, from north to south. Most of the international tourists in this direction are travelers from North America, Western Europe and Japan. Typically, they travel from Xi'an, Shanghai or Beijing, and fly further to Guangzhou or Hong Kong.

Suzhou is basically a part of the group destinations centered on the gateway city Shanghai. The recent development of international tourism in Suzhou is attributable largely to its spatial proximity to the metropolitan Shanghai. On the other hand, Suzhou's international tourism has developed certain dependencies on Shanghai. Nearly all international tourists on packaged tours as well as most individual travelers arrive in Suzhou via the gateway city Shanghai, leading to an apparent similarity in the composition of tourist demand between these two places. Typically, tourists arrive in Suzhou by train, stay there for about one and half days, and then return to Shanghai.

## 4.4 Tour Activities

### 4.4.1 Guilin

Lijiang River Cruise
International tourism in Guilin is natural sightseeing in nature. A large part of tourist activities are concentrated on the Lijiang river. The most favored one-day cruise starts from *Jiefang* Bridge or *Yangti* (in dry seasons), and ends in the county town of Yangshuo.

Along the Lijiang river between Guilin and Yangshuo, there are two major types of tourist attractions. First, the picturesque landscape of karst developments. Among many others, most famous scenic sights are the Elephant Hill, Tunnel and Pagoda Hills, Cock-Fighting Hills, Drum-Stick Hill, Fresco Hill, Yellow Cloth Shallow, Pretty Girl Peak, etc.

The second type of attraction is the scenes of native local life and settlements. Along both sides of the Lijiang river, there are several fishing villages and small rural towns dotted in the natural landscape, which are famous for their history, colorful local life, and commercial activities (e.g. periodic rural markets). Most famous villages and rural towns include the *Weijia* Ferry Village, *Qifeng zhen* (Peculiar Peak Town), *Daxu* Town, *Caoping zhe* (Meadow Town), *Banbian* Ferry Village, *Taoyuan* (Peach Blossom) Village, *Yangti* (Poplar Dyke) Village and *Xingpin zhe* (Town).

These fishing villages and rural towns are connected by numbers of ferries. Waterway transportation still plays a key role in local economic activities. Moreover, fishing seems to remain an important part of local rural life. Indeed, bamboo rafts, cormorants (a kind of bird which is a dab at fishing), fishing nets and old fishermen are traditionally part of Guilin's landscape.

Till 1988, Lijiang river cruise was organized by both public and private transport firms. Individual tourists could make excursions by renting private boats. Today, all private firms are subject to the 'unified' management of the Waterway Transportation Center of Guilin. This Center is responsible for not only selling tickets (or via its agents) at uniform prices, but the allocation of cruise businesses. Such assignments are allegedly made on a fair basis. Though such local regulations have been made in the name of establishing market rules and serving local economic interests, the real ground for this 'unified' management seems to protect those state-run firms which once suffered from increasing competitions from the private sector.

Due to the improvements in air transport between Guilin, Guangzhou and Hong Kong, a small but increasing number of travelers begin to make one-day trips to Guilin only for the purpose of river cruise, leading to an outpace of growth in river arrivals than in hotel arrivals since the mid-1980s (Fig. 4–4). Such one-day visitors are exclusively *compatriots* and businessmen.

**Figure 4–4: The Number of International Tourists on Lijiang River Cruise, 1979–1991**

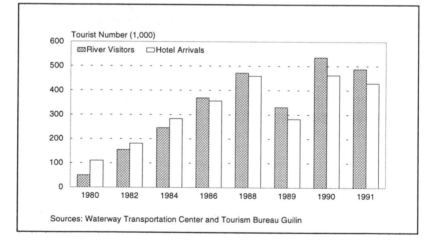

Sources: Waterway Transportation Center and Tourism Bureau Guilin

Tour activities in Yangshuo county

As described in section 3.2, the Yangshuo county is a place of great potential in tourism development. However, due to the complicated administration relationships between Guilin and Yangshuo, the development of local tourist infrastructure in Yangshuo has been hindered. By 1991, Yangshuo had 4 low-standard hotels (about 280 rooms). Two of them are former guest houses of the county government. Up till now, Yangshuo county remains merely a supplier of tourist attractions for the city Guilin.

Tourist activities in Yangshuo take place in two forms. First, as the end station of Lijiang river cruise, the small town *Yangshuo zhe* receives a large number of tourists each day during tourism seasons. *Yangshuo zhe* is not only famous for the scenic spots around the town, but for active souvenir trading in the town.

The main street of *Yangshuo zhe* is about one kilometer long, with 2–4 storied buildings (partly old) on both sides. Surrounded by hills and towering green peaks, this street links main tourist harbors with the old part of *Yangshuo zhe*. Since the mid-1980s, this street has developed into the busiest business area of the whole town. The major manifestation of tourism in this town is a large number of private souvenir shops and restaurants along both sides of the street. Tourist shops provide a wide variety of souvenirs such as paintings, antique articles, embroidery, stone- and bamboo-carvings, etc. According to author's field survey, 95% of the souvenir goods which appeared in Yangshuo came from other parts of the country. Besides souvenirs, some local products are also provided.

Tourist activities in *Yangshuo zhe* are very short. After one hour sightseeing and souvenir shopping in and around the town, most of the visitors return to Guilin by tourist buses. It was estimated by the local tourism bureau that in recent years more than one million such tourists visit this small town per annum.

The second part of tourist activities in Yangshuo are generated by individual tourists. According to the information from Tourism Bureau of Yangshuo, in recent years 15,000 to 25,000 individual tourists visited this place per annum. Most individual tourists are foreigners, especially young people. In 1991, foreign tourists made up 94% of all hotel arrivals in Yangshuo, and their average stay was 3 days. Most favored sightseeing places are the rural areas with nearly 'untouched' karst landscape in the western part of the county.

Sightseeing in the city of Guilin
Besides river cruise, international tourists usually spend one day visiting 2–3 scenic spots within the city proper. Such sightseeing activities are concentrated in only a few places. In 1992, about 80% of all park

visits took place in the *Ludi* and *Fobu* Park.[12]   Visiting the 'Folk Village' has become a new item on tourism arrangements. Souvenir shopping plays a marginal role in Guilin.

Temporal distribution of tourist arrivals
There are two major tourism seasons in Guilin (Fig. 4–5). Foreign tourist arrivals are concentrated in the second half of a year, especially in September and October. Visits of *compatriots* take place mainly in the months from February to May. The considerable travel demand of *compatriots* in February tends to be stimulated by such Chinese traditions as family-visits during the 'Spring Festival'.

**Figure 4–5: Distribution of International Tourist Arrivals in Guilin and Suzhou by Month, 1991**

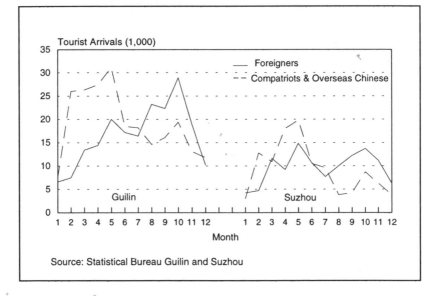

### 4.4.2   Suzhou

Tour activities of international tourists in Suzhou are arranged mainly within the city proper. Typical tour programs consist of two parts:

[12]Information from Guilin Park Management Bureau.

- First, sightseeing. Most favored sightseeing spots are the classical Chinese gardens and historical sites. As most tourists stay only a very short time in Suzhou, their tour activities are especially concentrated. In 1991, about 85% of all visits took place in three most famous gardens and parks, i.e. the Tiger Hill, the Humble Administrator Garden and the North Temple Pagoda.[13]

- Second, souvenir shopping. Souvenir shopping and visiting souvenir manufacturing plants are another important activity in Suzhou. Most frequently sought local handicrafts include silk products, embroidery, famous paintings and calligraphy, pottery and sandalwood fans. Souvenir shopping takes place either at big state-owned shops in the downtown area or at small private shops nearby hotel plots or tourist spots.

Visiting souvenir manufacturing factories is also very attractive to many international tourists. Though not all souvenir plants are open to tourists, several big factories have been selected as visiting spots for tourists. Most frequently visited souvenir plants include the No.1 Silk Factory, Silk Printing Factory, Fan Manufacturing Plant, and the Embroidery Research Institute. Typically, at such places there are well-decorated display rooms and big retail sales shops selling their own products. Money exchange service is usually available at retail sales shops. Some well trained English-speaking guides are good at showing tourists, especially group tourists, various parts of the manufacturing processes.

Tour activities of individual tourists in Suzhou are more flexible. Many individual travelers prefer hiring bicycles as local transport means, with which they can go into narrow and winding streets in order to enjoy a sense of discovery and delight in new experience. They often participate in individual tour programs such as 'night cruise of classical gardens', 'canal cruise', and so on.

As in Guilin, hotel arrivals of *compatriots* in Suzhou are concentrated in the first half of a year, especially in April and May. The concentration of foreign tourist arrivals in Suzhou appears to be less apparent than in Guilin. According to the information from local travel agencies, Japanese travelers are the main demand group in the Spring.

---

[13]Information from Suzhou Garden Management Bureau.

# 5

# Domestic Travel and Tourism

## 5.1 Mass Domestic Tourism: a National Perspective

### 5.1.1 Policy Trade-offs

Mass domestic tourism in China is a phenomenon of the post-reform era. The surge of domestic travel demand gave rise to much debate in the early 1980s. The debates over the desirability or undesirability of domestic tourism involved a learning process for the central authorities and many tourism planners. The central element of such debates concerns the role of domestic tourism in social and economic development of the country.[1]

(1) Traditional elements of domestic travel
Historically speaking, travel for pleasure-seeking purposes belongs to the privilege of a few social groups in China, such as ruling classes, the wealthy and the educated. With regard to the mass Chinese people, traditional travels appeared primarily in two forms, namely, 1) travel to cities and, 2) travel to religious sites. On the whole, such travels were characterized by:

- first, the dominant motive of rural Chinese to visit cities was economic in nature;

---

[1] For discussions on domestic tourism at the national level, see Gormsen 1989a, pp. 65–72, 1990b, pp. 127–35, 1993, pp. 151–57, 1995b, pp. 131–40; Tang 1990, pp. 143–81; Krieg 1993, pp. 10–14; Gerstlacher et al. 1993, pp. 53–55; Qiao 1995, pp. 121–30.

- second, pilgrimage travels used to take place at the local level; and

- thirdly, such travels most often took place on an individual or family basis, and were primitive in forms, short in duration, and lowest in spending.

Unfortunately, even such moderate travel demand had been fully prohibited for nearly three decades after the Chinese people 'stood up', though the travel traditions of the elite of the society were largely maintained.[2] Till the mid-1970s, religious practices and pilgrimage were forbidden on ideological grounds. Subject to rigid controls through such measures as the so-called *hukou*, or household registration systems, individual private travels were hardly possible.[3] As a result, the mobility of the Chinese society in the pre-reform period was minimal. Pleasure-seeking travels remained unknown to most urban Chinese, let alone the earth-bound Chinese peasantry. One exception was the travel activities of family-visits during Chinese Spring Festival.

(2) Restrictive policy in the early 1980s
Mass domestic travel demand of the Chinese people began to break out in the late 1970s when the country embarked on a reform course. Early policy reactions toward this new phenomenon of population movement seemed not sensible. In the early 1980s, policymakers still squarely insisted on that 'it is temporarily not suitable to promote domestic tourism'.[4] Obviously, the primary interest of the Chinese government in tourism promotion was to earn hard currency. Plagued by dozens of problems in the tourist supply system, especially the over-loaded transportation infrastructure, most tourism planners held that, for the sake of international tourism, domestic tourism should be controlled. In addition, concerns over social stability may have also played a certain part in taking such a restrictive policy stance.

(3) Significant changes in tourism policy since the mid–1980s
In the mid–1980s, the central government was pushed to change its early policies. The first push came from the demand side. By the mid–1980s, grassroots travel demand had become brisk in some parts of the country. Though the rising travel demand maintained some of

---

[2]Cf. Gormsen 1993, pp. 151–53, 1995b, pp. 131–32; Krieg 1993, pp. 10–14.

[3]For a discussion of the Chinese population policy, see Taubmann 1991, pp. 161–78, 1993a, pp. 163–85; Scharping 1993, pp. 77–93.

[4]Cf. Tang 1990, p. 144.

its traditional elements, it was new in several respects. First, its size and pace of growth was unknown before. Second, the participating groups had far out-ranged its traditional dimensions. Third, the new travel demand arose at a time when the incidence of political and administrative disciplines began falling significantly.

The second push was economic. Despite of the hesitates in policy-making of the central government, local authorities in some parts of the country had become aware of the potential effects of domestic tourism on local economic development. In some areas, local resources began to be mobilized to promote this growth sector, and tended to achieve sizable payoffs. Ironically, it was those 'non-strategic' tourist areas that had showcased the potential economic effects of domestic tourism.

In view of the already buoyant demand and the showcasing of the economic effects brought about by domestic tourism, the argument that ignorance of domestic tourism was 'inappropriate and misleading' began to gain good currency in the mid–1980s. Consequently, official attitudes toward domestic tourism had changed first from 'temporarily not suitable' to 'correctly to direct', and then 'actively to promote'.[5] In this regard, two policy packages are especially noteworthy.

The 1984/85 tourism policy

- The first big boost to domestic tourism resulted from the tourism policy issued in 1984/85. It was in this document that domestic tourism had for the very first time been advocated by the central government. In this document, the rising travel demand was viewed as a logic outcome of China's economic liberalization policy, and a concomitant of the rising standard of living. Therefore, 'domestic tourism should be actively directed and steadily promoted in line with local conditions'.[6]

- The policy effects of this document on the supply side were also substantial. The pluralistic approach advocated by this policy package had stimulated enormous local initiatives including the private sector in building domestic tourism infrastructure.[7] Considerable expansions of local infrastructure made it possible for many tourist areas to accommodate more domestic travel demand.

---

[5] *Ibid.*

[6] *Ibid.*

[7] Compare sections 2.3.3 and 7.4.

The 'First National Conference on Domestic Tourism'

- Another big boost to domestic tourism was the 'First National Conference on Domestic Tourism', which was held in Tianjin in 1987. This conference was important because it contributed significantly to the consensus-building regarding several key issues of domestic tourism.
- The main themes of this conference included definitions of domestic tourism; the relationships between international and domestic tourism; the need for relevant research and planning; necessary financial and administration resources and policy instruments for domestic tourism promotion; the role of domestic tourism in national and regional development, and so on.[8]
- It is especially noteworthy that during this conference domestic tourism began to be regarded as a development factor. Besides its macro-economic effects, the potential role of domestic tourism in regional development was seriously discussed.

In summary, it can be argued that, like policy-making in many other fields, domestic tourism policy was discussed and formulated at a time when much development had already taken place in many parts of the country. Nevertheless, it was the growing knowledge about the potential economic effects of domestic tourism that has created a favorable policy environment for its rapid growth. In this regard, the payoff of this learning process is enormous.

## 5.1.2  General Patterns

(1)  Data Problems

Due to negligences, nationwide statistics on domestic tourism are not existent. Rough Information about the size of domestic tourism originated from irregular reports of the NTA.[9] However, the approaches in arriving the aggregate figures are unknown.

In Chinese language, there are three terms that are relevant to domestic tourism, namely, *liudong renkou* (floating population), *lüke* (travelers or passengers), and *youke* (tourists). A definitive differentiation between them is hardly possible, though each of them has not only statistically but socio-economically different meanings. It remains unclear which parts of 'travelers' and/or 'floating population' have been included in the data delivered by the NTA.

---

[8] Cf. *Lüyou jingji* (Tourism Economy) 1987, 1: 13–15.
[9] Compare Tab. 2–2.

First in 1994, the *Yearbook* provided some information about the structure of domestic tourism at the national level (Tab. 5–1). Such information was allegedly produced on the basis of 'sampling and surveys'.[10] Author's fieldwork in Guilin, Suzhou and Beidaihe suggests that data basis for such aggregates does not exist at regional and local levels. The most commonly employed data source is the number of visitors accounted by tickets sold at major tourist spots. It was reported that in recent years efforts are being made to establish a nationwide system of domestic tourism statistics.[11]

### Table 5–1: Domestic Tourism in China, 1993[1]

| | Arrivals | | | Revenues | | |
|---|---|---|---|---|---|---|
| | Million | % of Total | % of Population | Billion Yuan | % of Total | Yuan per Tourist |
| Total | 410 | 100.0 | 35.0 | 86.4 | 100.0 | 211 |
| Urban Travelers | 160 | 39.0 | 49.4 | 71.4 | 82.6 | 446 |
| Rural Travelers | 250 | 61.0 | 29.5 | 150 | 17.4 | 60 |

[1] Compare Tab. 2–2.

Source: *Yearbook of China Tourism Statistics*, 1994, p. 9.

## (2) Size and Structure

Despite vague definitions and statistical inaccuracies, only if the orders of these aggregate figures are roughly correct, then China's domestic tourism can be outlined as follows:

- The quantitative size of domestic tourism is enormous by any standard. By the early 1990s, the number of domestic visitors had grown to 300–400 million per annum. This means that 25–35% of the Chinese population have taken part in domestic tourism;

- domestic travel demand is generated by both urban and rural Chinese. In 1993, about one-half of urban Chinese participated in domestic tourism, making up 39% of all tourist demand. Yet, the travel demand from rural China seems also enormous, at least in numerical terms;

- the standards and types of travel demand are widely different between urban and rural Chinese. In 1993, the average spending per urban tourist was about 450 yuan, approaching one-month salary of an average urban worker. Of the whole travel expenditure, 28.2% was spent on transportation, 19.4% on shopping, 18.3% on accommodation, 18.3% on foods, and

---

[10] NTA 1994, p. 9.

[11] Xing and Wang 1991, p. 152.

15.8% on enter-tickets and entertainment.[12] This means that an urban tourist can on average make a 2 to 4–day travel in areas about 600–1,000 km from his or her resident place.[13] The travel demand of rural Chinese is much more moderate in monetary terms. The lower level of their travel budgets (60 yuan per traveler) suggests that travels of rural Chinese are not only low in service demand, but limited in geographical scope and short in travel duration.

- Clearly, China's domestic tourism as a whole is still in its infancy. Besides low demand standard, domestic travels take place most often in a spontaneous manner and on an individual basis. In 1993, the number of the tourists whose travels were organized by travel agencies amounted to 8.2 million, accounting for 2% of the total.[14] It seems that a considerable part of such organized tourists were in fact one-day visitors who participated in those organized tour programs. Nevertheless, there is a tendency for the domestic tourism to become more 'organized'. From 1987 to 1993, the number of 'Third Category' travel agencies had grown from 551 to 2,371.[15] On the whole, such 'organized' travel demand appears mainly in those wealthy areas in the coastal provinces.

(3)  Travel motives and demand groups

The so-called 'floating population' is a newly coined term in migration studies in China.[16] 'Floating population' refers to those non-locals

---

[12]1994, p. 9.

[13]This estimate is made on the following assumptions: 1) a tourist spends 20–40 yuan per day on accommodation; 2) 80% of the transport expenditure is spent on inter-regional transportation; 3) a 'hard-seat' one-way train ticket costs 30–40 yuan at a distance between 6,00 to 1,000 km. *Zhongguo tielu keyun shikebiao* (China Rail Passenger Transportation Timetable), 1992–1993).

[14]NTA 1994, p. 9. According to a survey of 2,440 travel agencies, in 1992 around 28 million travelers were accounted as 'organized tourists', making up 8.5% of the total (Zhen 1993, p. 1). It remains unclear how did such a big difference arise from 1992 to 1993.

[15]NTA 1988, p. 59; 1994, p. 107. According to China's industrial regulations, 'First Category' travel agencies are authorized in doing business directly with overseas tour operators and receiving international tourists; 'Second Category' travel agencies are permitted to receive international tourists who are organized by the 'First Category'; whereas 'Third Category' only domestic tourists. In fact, according to author's fieldwork, many 'Second Category' and some 'First Category' travel agencies have been also involved in domestic tourism businesses since the late 1980s.

[16]For a discussion of the 'floating population' phenomenon, see Taubmann 1991, pp. 161–78, 1993a, pp. 163–85; Li et al., 1991.

who have no official status of urban citizen (*fei chengshi hukou*), but stay or live in a city for a certain period of time, and participate in various social and economic activities. According to Chinese sources, the 'floating population' may approach 60–80 million.[17]

In Chinese literature, only those who stay in a city more than 3 days are included in 'floating population'.[18] Thus, 'floating population' covers only a very small part of domestic tourists. A rough differentiation of 'floating population' gives us some hints about the major types of travelers (Tab. 5–2). Apparently, the 'floating population' should be viewed mainly as a phenomenon of economically-oriented population movements. The largest part of 'floating population' have little to do with tourism. Instead, they are temporary job-seekers from China's vast countryside.

### Table 5–2: Travel Motives of 'Floating Population' in Selected Chinese Cities (%)[1]

|  | Beijing (1988) | Shanghai (1988) | Guangzhou (1989) | Hangzhou (1989) | Chengdu (1989) |
|---|---|---|---|---|---|
| Population Size (mn)[2] | 5.6 | 7.2 | 2.9 | 1.1 | 1.7 |
| Floating Population (mn)[2] | 1.3 | 2.1 | 1.3 | 0.5 | 0.4 |
| Tourism-related (%) | 32.1 | 46.5 | 21.5 | 32.6 | 40.5 |
| . Sightseeing | 9.0 | 5.7 | 2.6 | 14.9 | 3.2 |
| . Meeting & Business | 14.3 | 21.5 | 12.7 | 11.0 | 25.1 |
| . Family-visit, etc. | 8.8 | 19.3 | 6.2 | 6.7 | 12.2 |
| Non-tourism (%) | 67.9 | 53.5 | 78.5 | 67.4 | 59.5 |
| Temporal Job-hunting | 63.2 | 41.1 | 54.7 | 61.3 | 47.1 |
| Others | 4.7 | 12.4 | 23.8 | 6.1 | 12.4 |
| Total | 100.0 | 100.0 | 100.0 | 100.0 | 100.0 |

[1] This survey was done during 1989–1990, and included 8 big cities. Obviously, the largest part of 'floating population' have little to do with tourism. Nevertheless, according to the definition employed in the surveys, 'floating population' covers all non-locals who stay in a city for a certain period of time, including all guests received by hotels and guest houses. Thus, such survey data also included a small part of domestic tourists;

[2] mn = million.

Source: Author's calculation based on information from Li and Hu (eds.), 1991, pp. 8–11 and 97–98.

_____

[17] Li and Hu 1991, pp. 117–118; ZNJFB 1992, p.145; *Renmin Ribao* (People's Daily), 24 February 1996.
[18] Li 1991, pp. 5–9.

Nevertheless, tourism-related travelers have also played an important part in making up 'floating population'. This applies not only in famous tourist cities in the coastal region such as Beijing, Shanghai and Hangzhou, but in a city like Chengdu which is located in the western part of the country. Obviously, the compositions of 'tourism-related' differ from one city to another, depending on their socio-economic functions.

The demand structure of China's domestic tourism is especially noteworthy. On the whole, pleasure-seeking tourists who stay more than one day in destination areas and whose travels are privately financed, tend to make up only a small fraction of the total demand. A much larger part of the roaring domestic tourist demand arises from public institutions, enterprises, and other types of *danwei*. This involves various forms of 'travel meetings', or *gongfei lüyou* as it is called in China.

## (4) Travel meetings

*Gongfei lüyou*, or publicly-financed tourism, has a long tradition in China. It involves a range of travel activities which are financed by Chinese *danwei*.

- In the pre-reform period, the prevailing form of *gongfei lüyou* was endless administration meetings, which were and perhaps still are part and parcel of the Chinese bureaucracy. The size and scope of such meetings have not been damped in the post-reform period, though checking bureaucracy has been declared as one of the goals of the Chinese reforms.

- The rapidly rising demand of business meetings are relatively recent. Among others, the so-called 'business transaction meetings' are especially noteworthy. In the course of economic liberalization, commercial meetings or business conferences at famous tourist cities have been regarded as an effective marketing tactics by many Chinese enterprises, especially big SOEs. In order to attract more business partners and expand business size, large-size business transaction meetings take place at different tourist cities from one year to another. In most cases, meeting travelers are not only group tourists at the meeting places, but individual visitors at other destinations on their ways to or from meeting places.

- A still larger part of publicly-financed tourism activities result from individual business travelers. The surge of individual business travels has several stimuli. Decentralization, free enterprise and intensified competitions have led to an increasing need for marketing and business contacts at the enterprise level. This is true of both the state and non-state sectors. In addition, the under-development of the country's communication systems often makes such face-to-face transactions a necessity. Like meeting tourists, most business travelers are not only visitors at those places where their business partners are located, but tourists in other tourist areas on their ways to and from business destinations. It is a commonplace in China that most managerial personnel, public servants as well as part of *danwei* staff make use of public finance (*gongfei*) to make such additional travels.

(5)  Geographical patterns

In the post-reform era, the spatial mobility of the Chinese people has been rising significantly.[19]  On the whole, domestic travel activities are highly concentrated and city-oriented.  In 1991, while the 479 city-regions accounted for about 30% of the country's territory and 63% of the population, they generated 90% of all passenger traffics in the public transportation systems.[20]

The largest part of passenger traffic between urban centers and their rural hinterlands rely on the road transport systems. In 1992, 85% of all passenger traffics (in persons) were road traffics, with an average transport distance of only 44 kilometers (Tab. 5–3).

**Table 5–3: Average Passenger Transportation Distance in China, 1978–1992**

|               | 1978  | 1984  | 1988  | 1992   |
|---------------|-------|-------|-------|--------|
| Railroad      | 134   | 181   | 266   | 316    |
| Interregional | 742   | 1,013 | –     | 1,078[1] |
| Road          | 35    | 34    | 39    | 44     |
| Waterway      | 44    | 59    | 58    | 75     |
| Airway        | 1,209 | 1,507 | 1,505 | 1,407  |

[1] figure of 1990.

Sources: *Statistical Yearbook of China* 1992–93; *Railroad Transportation Statistics* 1988–92.

---

[19]From 1978 to 1992 China's passenger traffic had increased by more than 6 billion persons or 520 billion person kilometers. The average travel frequency per Chinese per year had increased from 2 to 7 times during the same period. ZTN 1993, pp. 516–57.

[20]ZCTN 1992, pp. 22–27.

Obviously, the largest part of such rural-urban traffics have little to do with tourism. Instead, they result principally from the expanding urban functions of Chinese cities and towns in the sense of Christaller's central place.

It is the railroad that serves as the backbone of inter-regional passenger transportation. Railroad traffics are still more concentrated. In 1991, 31 city-regions whose urban centers were of more than one million inhabitants generated about 45% of all railroad traffics (in persons).[21] The highest traffic densities appear in the eastern part of the country, especially along three major transportation axes. They are Beijing-Shanghai, Beijing-Guangzhou, and Beijing-Shengyang.[22]

On the whole, it can be argued that at present the largest part of domestic tourism activities are concentrated in the wealthy coastal region, especially in the metropolitan areas in the Zhujiang delta, Changjiang delta and Beijing-Tianjin area. Underpinning such a basic pattern of domestic tourist demand are the disparities in living standard at both regional and household levels. It is perhaps still a bit too early to claim that the Chinese society is polarized, but it is in polarizing. Obviously, it is the 'haves' of the Chinese reforms who make up the major part of domestic tourists in the strict sense.

On the one hand, the metropolitan areas of the coastal region are the major tourist sending areas. The booming regional economies, rising standard of living as well as changes in life styles have stimulated enormous pleasure-seeking travel demand.

On the other hand, these metropolitan areas are also the most attractive destinations not only for many earth-bound rural Chinese, but for the urban Chinese themselves. In addition, the changing inter-regional economic relationships have also pulled the principal arrows of business and meeting travel traffics from traditional destinations such as political centers and resource regions toward the booming economic areas in the coastal region. Thus, it is in these coastal metropolitan areas that various travel motives such as sightseeing, cultural activities, businesses, shopping as well as transitions overlap one with another.

The study areas of Guilin, Suzhou and Beidaihe are located in the eastern part of China. Since the early 1980s, they have all witnessed a rapid growth of domestic tourism. Due to apparent differences in primary attractions and geographical location, however, each of them has shown its own characters in the development of domestic tourism.

---

[21] *Ibid.*
[22] ZTN 1993, p. 527.

## 5.2   Natural Sightseeing Tourism in Guilin

Over the past decade, the major attraction and justification for the inflow of large-scale FDI and sizable state investment in Guilin is its leading position in international tourism in the whole country. Nevertheless, parallel to international tourism, domestic tourism has also grown to an enormous size. By the early 1990s, about 15 times as many domestic tourists as international tourists visited this city per annum (Fig. 5–1).

**Figure 5–1: Domestic Tourist Arrivals in Guilin, 1978–1991**

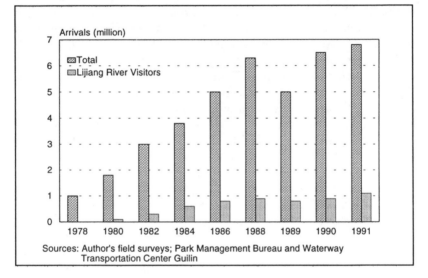

Sources: Author's field surveys; Park Management Bureau and Waterway
Transportation Center Guilin

### 5.2.1   (Inter-regional) Individual Tourism

(1) Dominance of inter-regional travelers

Guilin's tourist attraction is nationwide. As to international tourists, the primary attraction of Guilin to domestic tourists is rooted exclusively in the natural beauty of the karst landscape in and around the city. It is a place which is most typical of natural sightseeing tourism in China.

The travel motive of most domestic visitors to Guilin is single in nature. According to local surveys done in the late 1980s, 70–75% of all passengers came to Guilin primarily for sightseeing purposes.[23]

---

[23] GLERC 1989, pp. 167–174.

Author's field surveys show that such a high share of pleasure-seeking domestic tourists remained basically unchanged in the early 1990s.

With respect to China's major metropolitan areas, Guilin is a remote destination for domestic visitors. By railroad, it is about 850 km from the *Zhujiang* delta (Guangzhou), 900 km from the metropolitan area in Central China (*Wuhan*), 1,600 km from the *Changjiang* delta (Shanghai), and 2,000 km from Beijing-Tianjin area. Except the city *Liuzhou* (0.6 million population), there are no other cities of more than 0.5 million population (non-agricultural) within 400 km from the city Guilin. One-day excursions from the major metropolitan areas to Guilin are hardly possible.

Therefore, domestic tourism in Guilin is dominated by sightseeing tourists from outside the region of Guilin. According to author's field surveys, in recent years 60–65% of all tourist arrivals fall into the category of 'pure' tourists who stay at guest houses or hotels to overnight, and have extensive demand on local tourist services. Another 20% of tourist arrivals appear as family-visitors who do not use accommodation facilities, but generate considerable sightseeing activities at major tourist spots.

**Table 5–4: Breakdown of Park Visitors in Qixin Park, Guilin, 1991**

|  | (1,000) | % |
|---|---|---|
| Total | 2,213.7 | 100.0 |
| International | 251.8 | 11.4 |
| Foreigners | 62.6 | 2.9 |
| *Compatriots*[1] | 189.2 | 8.5 |
| Domestic | 1,961.9 | 88.6 |
| Non–local[2] | 1,652.0 | 74.6 |
| Local | 309.9 | 14.0 |
| Holiday | 111.4 | 5.0 |
| Non-holiday | 198.5 | 9.0 |

[1] Including overseas Chinese;

[2] visitors from outside the city.

Source: Management Office of Qixin Park.

The dominance of the outside tourists manifests itself evidently in the compositions of park visitors. Take the *Qixin* Park (Seven-Star Park) for example. The *Qixin* Park, with an area of more than 40 hectares, is one of the largest sightseeing spots within the city proper, and most famous for a huge karst cave. It combines fantastic hills, rivers, caves and rocks. According to visitor numbers accounted by tickets sold at this, non-locals made up about 75% of all park visitors, or 85% of domestic visitors in 1991 (Tab. 5–4). Parallel surveys in other major tourist spots have shown that the composition of visitors at the *Qixin* park is representative of many tourist places in Guilin.

Compared to Suzhou, Guilin is located in an economically less developed area. Pleasure-seeking travel demand of the inhabitants from Guilin's surrounding areas remains under-developed. Though one-day travelers make up about 15–20% of all passenger arrivals in Guilin, their travel motives are in the first place non-tourism in nature. The majority of one-day visitors are rural inhabitants. Though a small number of one-day travelers also visit scenic spots within the city, most of them have nothing to do with tourism.

(2)  Travel organization

Domestic tourism to Guilin takes place exclusively on an individual basis. According to author's survey of 19 'Third Category' travel agencies, in 1991 they received about 80,000 tourists, accounting for merely 1.2% of all tourist arrivals in Guilin.[24] Though many 'First' and 'Second Category' travel agencies are also engaged in domestic tourism, the size of such businesses remains small. Another group is those tourists who are on packaged tours organized by the travel agencies in their origin areas. However, the number of such organized tourists seems also small. As a whole, no more than 3–5% of domestic tourist arrivals in Guilin fall into the 'organized' category.

The packaged travel demand to Guilin is generated exclusively by the wealthy areas in the coastal region. In 1991, over 80% of all tourists on package tours received by the 19 surveyed travel agencies came from Guangdong, 10% from Fujian, and 5% from Shanghai, Jiangsu and Zhejiang provinces.[25]

(3)  Generating areas of domestic visitors

Two factors are decisive in determining the sending areas of domestic tourists, namely, geographical distance and the level of regional economic development (Fig. 5–2). In recent years, 25–30% of all tourist arrivals in Guilin are generated by the Guangzhou-centered Zhujiang delta area. As one of the fastest growing economic regions

---

[24] For definitions of the classification of travel agencies, see footnote 15.
[25] Author's field surveys 1992.

in China, the Zhujiang delta area enjoys a highest level of regional prosperity, and has become a most important sending areas of domestic tourists in the whole country. Author's field surveys show that the travelers from Guangdong province not only make up the major part of organized tourists, but tend to account for the lion's share of all privately-financed individual tourists.

Shanghai, Jiangsu and Zhejiang provinces are another leading tourist-generating area, making up 10–15% of all tourist arrivals. Besides meeting and business travelers, the share of privately-financed individual tourists from the Changjiang delta area is also high. Travelers from within the province Guangxi (15–20%) and neighboring provinces Hunan, Hubei and Jiangxi (10–15%) appear to be large in number. However, their demand on local tourist services is comparatively smaller in monetary terms. In addition, most of them travel to Guilin with a combination of various motives of economic, business as well as administrative kinds.

**Figure 5–2: Sending Areas of Domestic Tourists in Guilin**

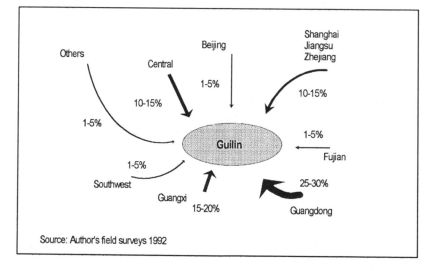

4) Tour activities

As for international tourists, the most attractive tour activity for domestic visitors is the one-day cruise on Lijiang river. The number of domestic tourists who participated in cruise had increased from

135,000 in 1979 to over 1.1 million in 1991. In the early 1990s, domestic tourists made up about 70% of all river arrivals. However, the share of domestic tourists participating in river tours is low, or about 15–20% of all tourist arrivals. Such a low participation rate seems attributable to three main factors:

1. limited environmental capacity of tourist activities on the Lijiang river;
2. low monetary and time budgets of most domestic visitors; and,
3. the fact that many domestic tourists tend to place more values on their travel experience to Guilin than in Guilin.

Obviously, river cruise businesses are among the most lucrative in Guilin's tourism sector. By 1991, 18 tourist transport firms had been engaged in the cruise businesses. The number of tourist boats increased to 114 with 9,162 seats, of which 63 boats (4,966 seats) were engaged in domestic tourism. For both international and domestic tourists, Lijiang river cruise is arranged in a single form. That is to say, all river tours cover the whole river range between Guilin and Yangshuo, and most tourist boats start from Guilin nearly at the same time in the morning.

Local studies showed that, due largely to such rigid tour arrangements, the river environmental capacity for tourist activities between Guilin and Yangshuo tended to be saturated by the mid–1980s.[26] This was also verified by the growing complaints of many tourists about the decreasing qualities of river cruise during that time.

Partly as a character of a seller's market, and partly as a measure to protect tourist resources, the price of river tour services has been soaring since the mid–1980s. According to the information from local tourism bureau, the average river tour price rose from 6–10 yuan in the early 1980s to 60–80 yuan in the early 1990s. A large number of domestic travelers reported that such high costs impeded their desire to take part in river excursions, since their travels are low-budgetary in nature.

As a result, river cruise has become an affordable activity only for a small part of domestic travelers. Among the major participate groups are 1) individual tourists from the wealthy coastal provinces such as Guangdong, Fujian, Shanghai, Jiangsu and Zhejiang, making up about 50% of all river visitors; 2) individual business and meeting travelers (30%) and, 3) group meeting tourists (20%).

---

[26]GLERC 1989, pp. 83–113.

For a larger part of domestic visitors, sightseeing activities take place mainly at scenic spots in and around the city. In 1992, while one million tourists participated in river cruise, about 7 million visitors were accounted at 8 parks and tourist spots in Guilin. And, around 60% of all park visits took place at three spots, namely, the *Qixin*, *Ludi* and *Xiangshan* Park.[27] On the whole, domestic tourist arrivals in Guilin tend to be concentrated in May, August and, specially, in October (Fig. 5–3).

### Figure 5–3: Monthly Distribution of Domestic Tourist Arrivals in Guilin, 1991 According to Entrance Tickets Sold

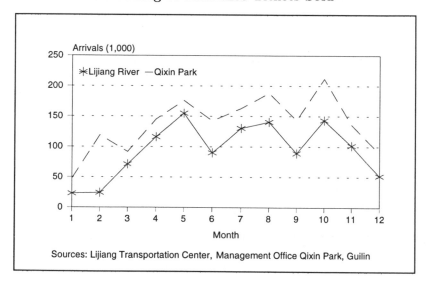

Sources: Lijiang Transportation Center, Management Office Qixin Park, Guilin

## 5.2.2 Travel Meetings

(1) Type and size

As discussed in section 5.1.2, travel meetings involve a range of tourism activities, and are growing rapidly in the course of Chinese reforms. Because of its special attractions, Guilin is not only an ideal place for meeting tourism, but a most favored destination for many individual business travelers, though Guilin is not a business destination in its own right.

---

[27] Guilin Park Management Bureau.

According to author's surveys, in recent years Guilin has accommodated around 1,000 meetings of various kinds each year. Most meetings are small in size, with 100 to 150 participants. Such small meetings are usually organized directly by individual international hotels or sponsor institutions and enterprises. It was estimated that since the late 1980s Guilin has accommodated about 150,000 to 200,000 meeting tourists per annum.[28] Business transaction meetings, which are sponsored by large trade organizations or enterprises from other regions, tend to account for the lion's share of all meetings in Guilin.

The demand of individual business travelers in Guilin is also buoyant. In the late 1980s, it was estimated that about 38% of all domestic hotel arrivals were accounted as individual business and meeting travelers. This figure excluded the group meeting participants, because most of them usually stayed overnight at international hotels. About 50–55% of all domestic hotel arrivals were generated by privately-financed individual tourists, and 3–8% by others.[29] Local tourism bureau estimated that such compositions of hotel arrivals remained basically unchanged in the early 1990s.

Meeting tourism is a very lucrative business. Meeting participants and individual business travelers appear to be among the 'richest' of all domestic demand groups. Compared to privately-financed tourists, meeting and business travelers have much higher demand on such tourist facilities such as high-standard hotels, air transportation, luxury local transport vehicle, and so on. Especially, they are much less price-elastic than most average individual tourists.

Thus, an expanding meeting tourism is obviously in the interest of Guilin's local economy. Plagued by the problems resulted from the over-capacity of international hotels, the local government tends to see a prospect in the meeting tourism to improve the performance of the hotel sector, at least partly.

(2) Commercialization of meeting tourism

Formerly, as a concomitant of the now largely defunct centrally planning regime, most travel meetings in China used to be organized by various administrative institutions. As business and commercial conferences have become an important form of travel meetings, an increasing part of business meetings begin to be organized by commercial organizations and trading centers. In Guilin, the businesses of

---

[28]Interviews at the Office for Meeting Management, Guilin.
[29]GLERC 1989, p.170.

travel meetings have developed a new dimension. That is, an increasingly discernible tendency of commercialization of meeting tourism.

Besides many individual international hotels, a kind of meeting organizer quasi travel agency but specialized in meeting tourism has emerged in Guilin. In April 1991, a so-called 'Office of Meeting Organization and Management' was established in Guilin, which was the first of its kind in the whole country. This Office is specialized in providing packaged services for large-size meetings. Though, administratively, this Office is a *shiye danwei*, or a public institution under the city government, it works as a commercial tourism firm quasi a travel agency. But, it is more than a travel agency.

Because of its special position, this Office has developed a wide range of networking and influences in the local tourism industry. By 1992, this Office had incorporated a number of tourism firms including 13 international hotels, major tourist boat and vehicle firms and, perhaps most important, the railroad and air transportation bureaus. Its target market is large- and medium-size meetings and conferences. The commercial meeting services provided by this Office take two forms, namely, 'packaged' and 'elementary' services. 'Packaged' arrangements cover the provision of accommodation, meeting rooms, tour arrangements, inter-regional transportation, and so on. 'Elementary' arrangements provide single services such as accommodation, tour arrangements, transportation, etc.

With few exceptions, the business coverage of this Office is nationwide.[30] That is to say, as far as meeting tourism is concerned, geographical distance tends to play no significant roles in determining the demand size. According to the Office's reports, large-size travel meetings with more than 1,000 participants are usually sponsored by the ministries in Beijing, making up 1/3 of its all businesses.

Business transaction meetings are in most cases sponsored by big enterprises from the economically booming areas such as Shanghai, Jiangsu and Zhejiang Provinces, making up another 1/3. The remaining 1/3 meeting business demand comes virtually from all over the country, though more often from neighboring provinces such as Hunan and Hubei.

Large-size travel meetings usually last 3 to 5 days, of which at least one day is arranged for sightseeing activities. In most cases, the largest part of meeting costs including tour service costs are taken

---

[30]One exception is perhaps the province Guangdong. Due to the restrictive policy of the provincial government, the demand of travel meetings from Guangdong to Guilin has been kept small.

over by sponsor organizations or enterprises. Though travel meetings should take place principally in the off-seasons of international tourism (before May and after November), this principle tends to be most often neglected when meeting businesses arise.

Obviously, competitions for such lucrative meeting businesses between this Office and other individual travel agencies or international hotels are keen. Nevertheless, for many meeting sponsors, this Office is the ideal meeting organizer. This is simply because most individual hotels or travel agencies have very limited capacity in providing packaged meeting services, especially such adequate and timely interregional transportation services as are provided by this Office.

Thus, the tourism firms centered at this Office stand gaining from their stronger competitiveness, and have achieved sizable returns from the buoyant meeting demand in recent years. The director of this Office reported that from April to December 1991, this Office organized 37 travel meetings, and received over 26,000 participants. The performance of all firms within this 'group' was reportedly much better than that of most individual travel agencies or international hotels.

The business size of this Office tends to be in rapid expanding. In May 1992, this Office organized 'China 1992 Spring Commercial Meeting of Light Industrial Products'. This conference was sponsored by a Beijing-headquarted trade organization. The meeting organizer received over 7,000 participants not only from China's large and medium-sized SOEs, but from numerous joint-ventures and rural enterprises from the coastal region. This meeting lasted 4 days, and resulted in a total volume of business transactions of 2.4 billion RMB yuan. The spending per participant averaged about 1,000 yuan. The transportation demand of this conference was so huge that, with the help of the Ministry of Railroad Transportation, two special trains (to Beijing and Shanghai) had to be organized.[31]

## 5.3   Cultural Sightseeing Tourism in Suzhou

Suzhou is one of the areas which lead the country in the development of domestic tourism. Already in the late 1970s, Suzhou received 2–3 million visitors per annum. The number of domestic visitors expanded to 6–7 million in the mid–1980s. Due to the re-structuring of tourist demand, tourist arrivals seemed numerically stagnant in the

---

[31]The Office for Meeting Management, Guilin.

second half of the 1980s (Fig. 5–4). As a domestic tourism destination, Suzhou's attraction is multifold. On the whole, Suzhou is a
place which is typical of cultural sightseeing tourism in China.

**Figure 5–4: Domestic Tourist Arrivals in Suzhou, 1978–91**

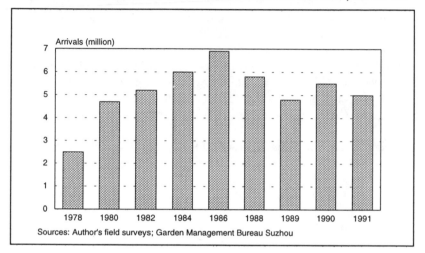

Sources: Author's field surveys; Garden Management Bureau Suzhou

### 5.3.1 One-day Excursions

Domestic tourism started in Suzhou in the late 1970s, and began with
an enormous expansion in sightseeing activities of one-day visitors
from neighboring urban centers. According to the estimates made
by local garden management bureau, one-day visitors made up over
80% of all park visitors in the early 1980s. The majority of such one-
day visitors came from Shanghai. It was estimated that in the early
1980s around 60% of all railroad passenger arrivals in Suzhou were
from the direction of Shanghai.[32] In these early years, local tourism
planners often spoke of Suzhou as a 'suburban park' of the metropolis
Shanghai.

The share of one-day visitors from neighboring cities has declined
significantly since the mid–1980s. As more and more tourist infrastructure has been developed at both regional and national levels,
urban travelers from this delta area begin to have a wider range of
possibilities in choosing travel destinations. They no longer confine

---

[32]Wu 1985, p. 54.

themselves to local and regional destinations. It seems that, after 2 or 3 visits to Suzhou, an increasing part of the one-day visitors have dropped their interests in visiting more or less the same sights in Suzhou.

During author's field surveys, a large number of park visitors reported that they had made or planed to make travels to such destinations as Mt. Huangshan (Anhui), Hangzhou (West Lake) and other scenic spots in Zhejiang province, or even to Guilin, Beijing and Xi'an, etc. According to some reports, from 1985 to 1986 the number of travelers to Suzhou, whose travels were organized by Shanghai's travel agencies, decreased by 30%, while the demand on long-distance travels to Zhejiang, Guilin and Beijing increased by 35%.[33]

**Figure 5–5: Sending Areas of Domestic Tourists in Suzhou**

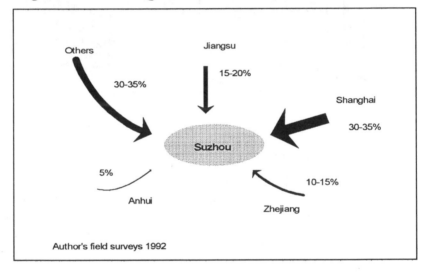

Author's field surveys 1992

By the early 1990s, the share of one-day visitors from neighboring cities had declined to about one-half of all part visitors in Suzhou. On the other hand, however, the number of one-day visitors from the delta's rural areas has been on rapid increase, leading to an expanding size of urban tourism (see the following section). On the whole, one-day visitors come from the areas within 150 to 200 kilometers around Suzhou. According to author's surveys of 240 tourist buses at 6

---

[33]Wang 1987, p.74.

major gardens and parks in 1991, about 45% of non-local tourist vehicles were from Shanghai, northern Zhejiang province, southern and central Jiangsu province as well as eastern Anhui province (Fig. 5–5).

One-day tour activities are usually organized either by big Chinese *danwei* or individual families. In the course of economic reforms, *danwei*-sponsored travel activities tend to become a new item on the welfare list of many Chinese *danwei*, though some 'traditional' ones begin to be cut off. *Danwei*-sponsored one-day outing or short-term sightseeing travels take place on a regular basis. *Danwei*-organized visitors usually travel in group, and often use buses hired by their work units.

Individual visitors appear in the form of family travels. 'To let children see the world' seems to be one of the most popular motives of such trips. One-day visitors usually arrive in Suzhou in the morning, visit 2–3 gardens and parks, then return home late in the afternoon. Both *danwei*-sponsored and individually-organized one-day outings usually take place at weekend or on traditional holidays, resulting in a clear-cut periodicity of tourist flows at major sightseeing spots.

Due to their huge size, one-day visitors exert enormous pressures on tourist spots as well as on urban transportation facilities. Such pressures are intensified by the spatial and seasonal concentration of tourist activities (Tab. 5–5, Fig. 5–6). According to local statistics , in 1991 about 70% of all part visits (12 million) took place in 4 parks and gardens, i.e. the Tiger Hill, the Humble Administrator Garden, the Lion Grove Garden, and the Linger-here Garden.

## Table 5–5: Concentration of Domestic Tourist Activities in Suzhou, 1991

| Tourist Spots | Tickets sold (1,000) | % |
|---|---|---|
| The Tiger Hill | 3,309.6 | 26.9 |
| The Humble-Admin- istrator's Garden | 2,178.6 | 17.8 |
| The Lion Grove Garden | 1,641.9 | 13.3 |
| The Linger-here Garden | 1,449.2 | 11.7 |
| Others | 3,760.5 | 30.3 |
| Total | 12,339.8 | 100.0 |

Source: Suzhou Garden Management Bureau.

**Figure 5–6: Distribution of Domestic Tourist Activities by Month, Suzhou, 1991**

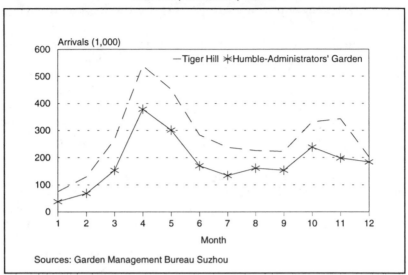

Sources: Garden Management Bureau Suzhou

The concentration of tourist activities in Spring tends to result from a tradition in Southeast China. That is, many families make 'outgoing in Spring' (*chenyuo*). It seems that, though domestic tourist activities tend to distribute over a wider range of tourist spots, travel demand of domestic and international tourists coincides with each other both spatially and temporarily.

Certain undesirable consequences of the influx of mass domestic visitors, especially ever-growing pressures on Suzhou's garden facilities, had become discernible by the mid–1980s. During peak tourism seasons, major tourist spots such as the Humble Administrator Garden and Linger-here Garden received as many as 20,000 to 30,000 visitors per day.[34]

Obviously, most one-day visitors have hardly any demand on local services outside transportation. Thus, in the interest of both garden protection and local revenues, Suzhou's garden and tourism bureaus have to resort to raising the price of entrance tickets at major tourist spots. In the case of the Humble Administrator Garden, a single entrance ticket price has risen from 0.5 yuan in the early 1980s to 15 yuan in recent years.

---

[34]Wu 1987, p. 53.

## 5.3.2  Urban Tourism

With respect to domestic tourism, it is not a cliché to remind that the Chinese society remains largely a peasantry one, not only demographically but perhaps socio-psychologically as well. This seemingly routine fact is responsible for another nationwide and increasingly important form of domestic tourism. That is, urban tourism of rural Chinese.

In the course of economic liberalization, the decade-long earthbound rural Chinese have not only the desires but the possibilities to *jinchen,* or visit the cities. It seems that the skylines, modern industrial and commercial activities as well as the life atmosphere of big cities present strong attractions to many travelers from rural areas. Though a dominant part of rural Chinese travel to the booming metropolitan areas for seeking their better fortunes, the travel motive of rural inhabitants differs significantly form one region to another.

The *Changjiang* delta area leads the country in regional economic prosperity. Traditionally, inhabitants in this delta area tend to have a high mobility, though not necessarily in the sense of modern tourism. Recently, the rural population of the *Changjiang* delta area enjoys much higher living standard than the national average, generating a rapidly rising travel demand. For many inhabitants in the rural hinterland, Suzhou is not only a big city of modernity, but a shopping center full of commercial activities. Travel experience of city visits, especially to big cities, tends to be widely viewed as a prestige not only by travelers themselves but by their community fellows.

Thus, while the number of one-day visitors from neighboring cities tends to stagnate, travel demand of the rural population is on the rapid increase, leading to a growing size of urban tourism. According to author's field surveys, visitors from rural areas made up about 15–20% of all park visitors in Suzhou in the early 1990s. The majority of rural visitors are from the *Changjiang* delta area, especially the central and southern parts of Jiangsu province and the northern part of Zhejiang province.

It is noteworthy that the 'floating population' from outside the delta area also plays a part in urban tourism. Those 'peasantry workers' who stay months or years in Suzhou occasionally appear as visitors at certain tourist spots. In addition, they play an important role in spreading knowledge of modern cities into rural communities, stimulating travel desires of their village fellows as well as family members. Many temporary peasantry workers in Suzhou reported that they regularly bring their families to visit the city, especially during holidays or school vacations.

At the national level, some reports have evoked the impression that the pleasure-seeking travel demand of the Chinese peasantry makes up a considerable part of domestic tourism.[35] However, according to author's field surveys, the share of pleasure-seeking rural travelers at inter-regional level is very low. Furthermore, travels of rural inhabitants to big cities usually take place with a combination of various motives including sightseeing, shopping, family- and relative-visits, etc. As a rule, tour activities of rural visitors are very limited. They often appear to be more interested in downtown areas than in cultural or scenic sights. Their travel expenditure tends to be low. They usually spend more on purchasing daily-use goods than on tourist goods and services.

It should be pointed out that, though the term 'urban tourism' is employed in this study to refer to the travel demand of rural Chinese, a large part of tourist activities of urban Chinese described in the preceding sections can also be viewed as a sort of culturally-motivated urban tourism. It can be observed in many parts of the country that there is a 'vertical' and 'horizontal' population movement of pleasure-seeking kind among the Chinese urban systems. While many inhabitants of smaller cities are motivated to visit big modern cities, inhabitants of big cities are increasingly interested in visiting cities in other parts of the country.

### 5.3.3 Pilgrimage

Religious activities have staged a comeback in the post-reform era, giving a rebirth of pilgrimage tourism to many traditional destinations. Though Suzhou is not a pilgrimage destination in the first place, religious activities also play a part in domestic tourism in Suzhou. This is mainly due to the fact that most tourist spots in and around Suzhou combine historical, cultural and scenic sights in themselves. On the whole, pilgrimage in and around Suzhou is a local phenomenon. Travelers from surrounding rural areas make up the largest part of visitors at religious sites. In this regard, the boom of religious activities at *Lingyan* (Miraculous-rock) Hill is a case in place.

The *Lingyan* Hill, about 15 km west of the city of Suzhou, is a typical suburban tourist spot which combines historical and cultural relics with rural scenery. Because of the numerous religious construc-

---

[35]Sun 1984, pp. 17–18; Wang 1987, p. 74; Zhang 1992, p. 18; NTA 1994, p. 9.

tions like *Lianyan* Temple and Pagoda, the *Lingyan* Hill is a traditional pilgrimage destination at the local level. Since the mid–1980s, the religious sites at this place have witnessed a boom of pilgrimage.

Local tourism planners estimated that in recent years around 350,000 people visit this spot each year, and most of them practice certain religious activities. Pilgrims are principally rural inhabitants from southern Jiangsu and northern Zhejiang province. Most pilgrims are female farmers at age of 40–50. They usually travel in a group of 30–40 persons.

The travel experience of some local young people has played an important role in stimulating the travel desires of rural pilgrims. Take a pilgrim group from the *Pinhu* county (Zhejiang province) for example. This group reported that most of them had little knowledge of Suzhou, and were formerly afraid of making such a trip alone. Their pilgrimage trip to Suzhou became possible because of the services provided by a local young people, who was said to have good knowledge about Suzhou after his several visits to Suzhou over the past years. The pilgrims reported that this local organizer provided such a pilgrimage travel arrangement at a 'packaged' price, for which he was responsible for guide of visits, food (usually self-prepared), transportation and accommodation (by renting a boat). Thus, this local organizer staged a role of 'travel agency' of primitive kind.

Local pilgrims usually have very limited range of activities. Besides visits to religious sites, they usually go shopping in the downtown area. Sightseeing activities are of secondary importance. Such a trip usually lasts 2 to 3 days. This group reported that this young people organized such trips on a regular basis, especially in Spring or during traditional festivals.

Pilgrimage is largely a matter of the rural Chinese, but not exclusively. Some visitors from neighboring cities also appear at religious sites in and around Suzhou, though conducting religious activities are not their travel motive in the first place. In the city, the most frequently visited religious sites include the Temple of West Garden, the Cold Mountain Temple, the Temple of Mystery, Suzhou Confucian Temple. In addition, urban travelers also often visit the religious sites in the surrounding areas.

### 5.3.4 (Inter-regional) Individual Tourism and Travel Meetings

As outlined in preceding sections, Suzhou is first and foremost a regional destination of domestic tourism. Nevertheless, Suzhou's attraction is also nationwide. Famed as a typical *jiangnan* city, or a typical city south of the *Changjiang* river, Suzhou is traditionally connected not only with the cultural characters and sophisticated commercial traditions of Southeast China, but with the picturesque landscape typical of the areas south of the *Changjiang* river. Both historical-cultural sights and modern industrial and commercial activities make Suzhou a famous travel destination in the whole country.

Since the mid–1980s, pleasure-seeking travelers from outside the *Changjiang* delta area have played an increasing part in Suzhou's domestic tourism. In recent years, they make up 20–30% of all visitors. Obviously, it is the inter-regional travelers who generate intensive demand on local tourist service sectors including transportation, catering, and accommodation.

Inter-regional tourists fall into three types. First, privately-financed individual tourists. They make up 30–35% of all inter-regional visitors. Well-to-do urban workers tend to account for the lion's share of this group. For a large part of individual tourists, Suzhou is not always the primary destination. Instead, it appears as a stop-over on the way to or from other destinations, especially Shanghai.

Second, individual business travelers. They make up the largest part of inter-regional visitors (40–45%). Individual business travelers include not only those businessmen who have their business partners in Suzhou, but business travelers who make a stop-over in Suzhou on their way to or from other business destinations.

Third, meeting tourists. Suzhou is an attractive place for meeting sponsors at the regional level, and occasionally at the national level. Travel meetings in Suzhou are commercial in nature, which is obviously attributable to the city's modern commercial and industrial development. As in the case of individual business travelers, meeting travelers include not only participants of those meetings taking place in Suzhou, but individual meeting travelers who attend meetings at other destinations. As a whole, meeting travelers play a small part in Suzhou, or about 10% of all inter-regional visitors.

As in Guilin, sightseeing activities of meeting participants are usually organized by meeting sponsors. For the privately-financed tourists and individual business travelers, one of the most favored tour arrangements is the packaged one-day sightseeing programs. Such programs are organized by local travel agencies. One-day bus tours usually start from the major transportation stations, and include major tourist spots.

Take the 'one-day garden tour' for an example. This packaged tour program is organized by the Suzhou Travel Service. The tour starts from Suzhou's Railroad Station, and includes visits to 6 famous gardens and parks. Sightseeing activities usually take 6 to 8 hours. Such a tour costs 20 to 30 yuan per tourist, which are affordable for many domestic tourists. Because of the convenience in organization, such tour services appear to be favored by many individual tourists. According to the reports of local travel agencies, in recent years around half a million tourists participated in such one-day tour programs per annum.

## 5.4   Seaside Resort Tourism in Beidaihe

As discussed in section 3.4, Beidaihe is traditionally the most important seaside resort of China. It was opened to the mass of domestic tourists in the early 1980s. To certain extent, the opening of a place like Beidaihe, which was formerly only accessible to the political prominent and party functionaries, reflects the pragmatic approaches of the Chinese reform policy.

**Figure 5–7: Domestic Tourist Arrivals in Beidaihe, 1984–1991**

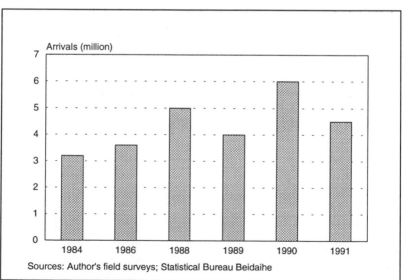

Sources: Author's field surveys; Statistical Bureau Beidaihe

Since its opening, Beidaihe has developed rapidly into a destination of mass domestic tourism in North China. Already in the

early 1980s, millions of domestic visitors began to flood into Beidaihe. Since the mid–1980s, the development of the neighboring
Nandaihe and Changli beaches has diverted a considerable part of
tourist flows, leading to a stagnation of tourist arrivals in Beidaihe
(Fig. 5–7). Roughly, domestic tourism in Beidaihe appears in two
forms, namely, *danwei*-financed tourism and individual tourism.

### 5.4.1  *Danwei*-financed Tourism

*Danwei*-organized recreational activity has a long tradition in Beidaihe, and used to be the only form of resort tourism in this place.
Today, due to the enormous increase of individual visitors, *danwei*-
financed holiday-makers make up only a small part of all tourist demand. In recent years, the state-run recreational facilities receive
about 0.2 million holiday-makers per annum, accounting for 5% of
all visitors, or 20–25% of hotel arrivals.

Publicly-financed holiday-makers are exclusively senior staff of
government bodies, public institutions or various big Chinese *danwei*. Obviously, party leaders, governors at various administration
levels as well as leaders of various *danwei* as ever enjoy privilege in
making holidays in Beidaihe. This is evidently reflected in the high
share of 'officials' in tourist compositions (Tab. 5–6).

### Table 5–6: Occupations of Domestic Tourists in Beidaihe Area (in %)

| Occupation | Beidaihe (1991) | Changli (1992) |
|---|---|---|
| Officials | 59.9 | 41.5 |
| Worker | 30.0 | 15.9 |
| Technician[1] | 4.0 | 31.3 |
| Student | 3.3 | 6.9 |
| Farmer | 0.5 | 2.8 |
| Others | 2.3 | 1.6 |
| Total | 100.0 | 100.0 |

[1] Including educational, scientific and technical occupations.
Sources: Statistical Bureau of Beidaihe and Changli.

*Danwei*-financed tourism is separated apparently from the mass
tourism. *Danwei*-financed holiday-makers stay at the holiday quarters of their own *danwei* (Fig. 5–9). Such facilities, though still

simple, are comparatively much better equipped than private and collective ones.[36] They provide holiday-makers with more comforts unparalleled by those simple facilities which are used by individual tourists. Services provided by *danwei* holiday quarters are not accessible to individual holiday-makers. In general, publicly-financed holiday-makers have little demand on local services. They usually stay longer than individual tourists, ranging from one to two weeks. The entire costs are taken over by their *danwei*. Besides recreational activities in Beidaihe, they make tours to sightseeing spots in and around Shanhaiguan.[37]

### 5.4.2 Individual Tourism

Since the opening of Beidaihe, tourist activities in this place have been dominated by individual holiday-makers. In recent years, around 4 million individual travelers visit Beidaihe per annum, accounting for 95% of all visitors. As in Suzhou, one-day visitors make up the largest part of all tourist arrivals in Beidaihe. In 1991, around 4.5 million tourists visited Beidaihe, of which 0.87 million were accounted as hotel arrivals, making up 20% of all visitors.[38] Most individual holiday-makers are urban inhabitants from Beijing-Tianjin metropolitan area (Fig. 5–8). In general, one-day visitors come from the areas with a travel time of 2–3 hours to Beidaihe.

In Beidaihe, one-day tours are organized principally by individual families. Many visitors reported that, during school vacations, it has become a commonplace for families to make one-day visits or short holidays in Beidaihe. They usually combine recreational and sightseeing activities in a single trip. Besides Beidaihe, most of them visit the Great Wall and other historical sights in and around Shanhaiguan. In recent years, Shanhaiguan received around 6 million visitors per annum. One-day visitors generate much traffics in and around Beidaihe, but have little demand on local services.

From the point of view of local economy, the most important demand group is the individual holiday-makers who stay more than one day in Beidaihe. The number of such tourists tended to lie between 0.6 to 0.9 million in the early 1990s. Most individual holiday-makers are urban inhabitants from North China. In recent years, the number of holiday-makers from Southeast China tends to be on the increase.

---

[36] Compare section 7.2.
[37] Compare section 3.4.2.
[38] BDHTN 1992, pp. 370–371.

The average length of stay of individual holiday-makers was 5 days in 1991.

### Figure 5–8: Sending Areas of Domestic Tourists in Beidaihe

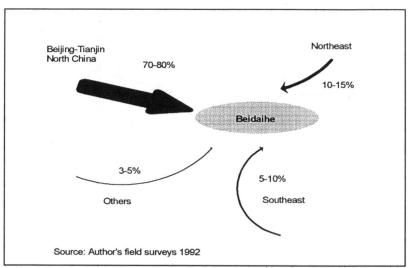

Source: Author's field surveys 1992

As will be discussed in section 7.4, in Beidaihe more than one-half of accommodation capacity is provided by the private sector. Many private households have quickly got adapted to the rising demand, and achieved sizable returns. Many families which were engaged in accommodation business reported that, because of their better service, many tourists prefer to stay at family guest houses, instead of state or collective ones (Fig. 5–9). During peak seasons, their facilities are fully occupied.

Over the past years, many private guest houses have even developed a sort of reservation system. Since a large part of their guests make holidays in Beidaihe each year, they are most likely to stay at the same guest houses. Therefore, such guests usually make reservations before tourism season comes. Since telephones are still rare in many parts of the country, such reservations are usually done by writing to private guest houses. In addition, individual tourists have also played an important role in spreading information about accommodation services provided by the private sector.

## Fig. 5-9: Tourism Infrastructure in Beidaihe

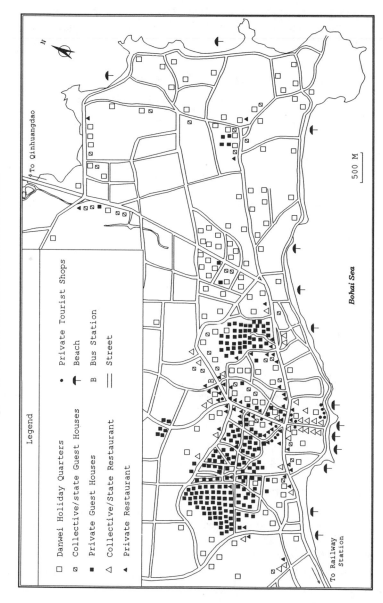

103

For climatic reasons, tourism activities in Beidaihe are strongly season-conditioned.[39] Local tourism planners estimated that over 90% of all visitors are concentrated in the three months from July to September, especially from mid-July to mid–August (about 70% of all visitors).

## 5.5  Summary: A Descriptive Model of Domestic Tourism in China

The domestic travel demand of the Chinese people in the post-reform era is enormous. Mass domestic tourism has been rising at a time when the average income and living standard of most Chinese people still remained low, and the expenditure structure of individual households under-developed. On the whole, domestic travel demand is low-budgetary in nature. This basic development context has played a decisive part in shaping domestic tourism in contemporary China.

China's tourism industry is characterized by a sharp discontinuity in both service demand and supply between international and domestic tourism. Such a dualistic structure is apparent and pervasive. Consequently, the substitutability between these two parts is marginal. Under certain circumstances, such a dualistic structure may lead to instability of China's entire tourism industry.

Direct contacts between international tourists and domestic visitors are limited. As the case studies have shown, such contacts take place principally at scenic and cultural sites, though part of international hotels as well as air transportation facilities are increasingly used by domestic meeting and business travelers.

Furthermore, the case studies of Guilin, Suzhou and Beidaihe have shown that, even on the part of domestic tourism, divisions among various market segments are apparent too (Tab. 5–7).

Travel motives, destinations, expenditure and the range of demand on local tourist services are widely different between average (low-budgetary) individual travelers and 'handsome' meeting and business travelers, between urban and rural travelers, and so on. The complex form of domestic tourism is multiplied by the variety of tourist destinations. Underpinning such a diversity are the appalling regional disparities, urban-rural divisions, the widening gap of personal income as well as the socio-political structure of the contemporary Chinese society.

---

[39]Compare section 3.4.2.

## Table 5–7: Types and Forms of Domestic Tourism in Suzhou, Guilin and Beidaihe

| | Type and Form | Demand Groups |
|---|---|---|
| Guilin | Inter-regional landscape-sightseeing Tourism (35–40%) | Well-to-do urban workers, teachers and students, etc. |
| | Travel meetings | Officials and businessmen |
| | . Groups (5–10%) | |
| | . Individuals (35–40%) | |
| | One-day travels (10–20%) | Peasants, etc. |
| Suzhou | One-day excursions (45–50%) | Urban inhabitants from neighboring cities |
| | Urban tourism (15–20%) | Well-to-do peasants |
| | Pilgrimage | Peasants, in combination with urban tourism |
| | Travel meetings | Officials and businessmen |
| | . Groups (5%) | |
| | . Individuals (10–15%) | |
| | Inter-regional cultural sightseeing tourism (5–10%) | Well-to-do urban workers, teachers and students etc. |
| Beidaihe | Individual resort tourism | Urban inhabitants from neighboring cities, well-to-do urban workers, teachers and students, etc. |
| | . One-day excursions (55–60%) | |
| | . More than 1 day (20%) | |
| | *Danwei*-financed resort tourism (5–10%) | Officials; senior staff of *danwei* |
| | Travel meetings (5%) | Officials and businessmen |

In summarizing the main findings, we can make following arguments regarding the nature of today's domestic tourism in China (Fig. 5-10):

(1) Demand groups
Domestic travel demand arises not only from well-to-do individual households but, even in a larger measure, from such 'social groups' as public institutions, enterprises and the like. In many important respects, Chinese *danwei* play a big part in domestic tourism. *Danwei*-financed travel meetings make up a significant part of the entire domestic tourism. On the part of individual travel demand, the participating groups have far out-ranged their traditional dimensions.

(2) Travel motives
As the demand groups have expanded to a much wider basis, travel motives have become multiplied. Domestic travels often take place with a combination of various motives. Nevertheless, domestic tourism as a whole is sightseeing in nature. This makes a big difference to the modern recreational and tourism activities dominated by holiday-making in the industrialized countries.

**Figure 5–10: A Descriptive Model of Domestic Tourism**

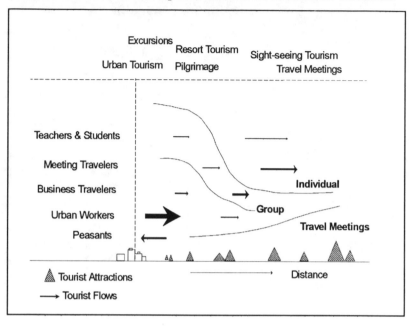

(3) Types and forms

Because of the diversity in travel demand and the wide variety of tourist destinations, domestic tourism has developed a wide range of forms including one-day excursions of urban Chinese, urban tourism of rural Chinese, sightseeing tourism of natural and cultural kinds, seaside resort tourism, pilgrimage tourism, and so on. On the whole, domestic travels take place on an individual basis. Packaged tour arrangements remain unknown to most domestic travelers.

(4) Pattern of travel destinations

China's domestic tourism is urban-biased in nature, and short in travel distance. Such an urban-biased pattern of tourist flows is not exclusively due to the city-centered public transportation networks or the absence of personal transport means, but due to the fact that the Chinese society remains largely a peasantry one, both demographically and socio-psychologically. It seems that the skylines, modern commercial activities as well as the life atmosphere of big cities present strong attractions not only to the decade-long earth-bound rural Chinese, but to many urban Chinese as well.

(5) The dominance of one-day travels

On the whole, domestic tourism is apparently dominated by one-day travels. Such form of domestic tourism is most typical of the densely populated areas in the eastern coastal region. One-day trips usually take place in the areas with a radius of 150 to 200 km from an urban center. Two major directions of tourist flows are discernible:

- first, from urban to rural areas. That is, urban inhabitants to tourist spots in surrounding rural areas, taking the form of one-day excursions;

- second, from rural to urban areas. That is, rural inhabitants to big cities, taking the form of urban tourism.

While one-day trips of urban Chinese to surrounding areas are pleasure-seeking in nature, travels of rural Chinese to big cities usually combine various motives. In general, one-day trips generate large-size urban-rural traffics and exert enormous pressures on local tourist infrastructure, but they have little demand on local services.

(6) High cost- and distance-elasticity of travel demand

Domestic travel demand is highly cost- and distance-elastic. This is especially true of the privately-financed individual tourists. On the whole, the share of pleasure-seeking individual tourists at the inter-regional level remains low. Urban workers from the wealthy coastal provinces and the educated tend to account for the lion's share of this part of tourist demand. With increase in distance from origin areas, the share of privately-financed travelers drops significantly.

On the other hand, the travel demand of meeting and business travelers appear to be much less cost- and distance-elastic. This explains why the meeting and business travelers make up a considerable part of all domestic tourist demand in a destination like Guilin which is far away from China's major metropolitan areas.

# Part III

# Tourism Infrastructure Development

# 6

# International Hotel Industry

Obviously, the rapid expansions of international tourism and the rise of mass domestic tourism are generating huge demand for and enormous pressures on local infrastructure in Guilin, Suzhou and Beidaihe. At the initial stages, insufficient provision of transportation and accommodation was the most apparent bottleneck which restrained tourism expansions. 〔主体 开头〕

Though considerable efforts have been made in improving transportation facilities, most transportation projects require not only huge investments which are far beyond local financial capacity of individual destinations, but also inter-regional cooperation. Especially, decisions of large transportation constructions, such as the new airport project in Guilin, are usually made by the central government.

It is the accommodation sector which constitutes the core part of tourism-specific infrastructure at the local level, and has drawn much attention in discussions of tourism investment policies at both national and local levels. Over the past decade, the international hotel sector has attracted not only considerable domestic (state) investments but large-size FDI as well.

At the same time, the rapidly rising domestic tourism has also simulated considerable investment made by local small investors in building simple accommodation facilities. Thus, the accommodation sector seems to be one of the major areas in which different types of investors and considerable local participation can take place.[1] For

---

[1] For discussions on China's tourism investment policies and FDI in tourism development, compare sections 2.2 and 2.3.3.

these reasons, following two chapters will focus on the recent development and associated problems of the hotel sector in the study areas.

The recent growth of the international hotel industry in the study areas, especially in Guilin, is impressive, but problematic, too. Due to extreme hotel shortage at the beginning of tourism development, a small but growing amount of domestic capital began to flow into the hotel sector in the early 1980s, leading to the first (small) wave of hotel investment in Guilin and Suzhou.

In the mid–1980s, with the inflow of large-size foreign direct investment (FDI) and extra-budgetary domestic capital raised by local governments, the second (big) wave of hotel investment 'fever' took place in Guilin, Suzhou and Qinhuangdao (Beidaihe).[2] Since then, the hotel sector has been expanding at a pace unknown before. As a result, unlike other infrastructure 'bottlenecks', the problem of hotel supply shortage has been solved unexpectedly within only a short period of time.

Such rapid expansions have undoubtedly contributed a decisive part to the booming of international tourism in Guilin and Suzhou. Unfortunately, however, this is only part of the story. Recent discouraging performance of the hotel sector suggests that international hotels, especially high-standard hotels, are costly over-developed, in particular in Guilin.

## 6.1   Growth in Hotel Capacity

### 6.1.1   Guilin

The international hotel industry of Guilin grew nearly from ground-up. When tourism industry came into being in 1973, Guilin had only one low-standard hotel, i.e. the Ronghu Hotel (248 beds) which was built in 1953. Though two domestically-invested hotels, the Lijiang Hotel (778 beds) and Jiashan Hotel (660 beds), were opened in 1976 and 1980, the whole city had only a hotel capacity of 2,056 beds by 1980.

Due to the rapidly rising demand, the problem of hotel shortage became more serious in the following years. From 1980 to 1985, tourist arrivals grew at 20% per annum, whereas hotel capacity

---

[2]This seems also true of many other tourist areas in the country. Cf. Chen 1990, pp. 22–28.

(rooms) at a much lower rate of 7.3% per annum. Insufficient provision of hotel facilities was one of the most apparent bottlenecks restraining the growth of international tourism. Low service qualities were often sharply criticized and even refused by international tour operators as well as tourists. In extreme cases, tourists had to be sent to nearby cities to overnight.[3]

However, the problem of hotel shortage in Guilin was largely a matter of the first half of the 1980s. Due to the 1984/85 liberal tourism policy discussed in section 2.3, large-scale foreign hotel investment began to flow to Guilin in the mid–1980s, leading to an enormous expansion in hotel capacity (Fig. 6–1).

### Figure 6–1: The Growth in International Hotel Capacity in Guilin, 1985–1993

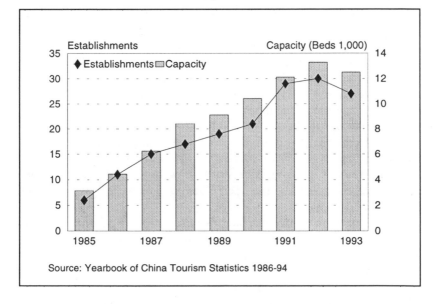

Source: Yearbook of China Tourism Statistics 1986-94

During 1986–87, 9 new international hotels (3,100 beds) began to receive tourists. Thus, Guilin's hotel capacity was doubled within only two years. All these new hotel complexes are of international standards, and 4 of them are 4–star hotels. This investment 'fever' continued in the following years. Besides follow-on projects of some existing hotels, another 15 new hotels had been completed by 1992.

---

[3]Zhen 1989, pp. 78–80.

Thus, from 1988 to 1992 Guilin's hotel capacity had another increase of 7,000 beds, or more than doubled on the 1987–basis. By the end of 1992, 30 international hotels had already been in operation, providing a total capacity of 6,694 rooms (13,290 beds). The decline in hotel capacity in 1993, though moderate (about 800 beds), indicates that the international hotel sector has been costly overdeveloped in Guilin.

## 6.1.2 Suzhou

Compared to Guilin, international hotel expansions in Suzhou took place much later and in a much less spectacular manner. As late as in 1983, Suzhou still had no modern hotels of international standards, though international tourist arrivals had grown to a considerable size by that time.[4] In these early years, accommodation of international tourists relied merely on the relatively bigger guest houses of the municipal government, such as Lexiang, Nanlin, Suzhou, Nanyuan and Tonwu. These facilities had been steadily modified or renovated in the course of tourism development. Even by 1985, Suzhou had only 5 hotels (1,050 beds) of middle standard.

Substantial expansions of the hotel sector began to take place in Suzhou in the second half of the 1980s (Fig. 6–2). However, hotel constructions in Suzhou have followed a way which is apparently different from that of Guilin. That is to say, a large part of the capacity expansions were contributed by those existing big guest houses. From 1986 to 1988, though only two new hotels (about 400 beds) were built, Suzhou's hotel capacity had increased by 830 rooms or 1,845 beds.

The expansion of existing facilities has taken two forms, namely, renovation of former guest houses and, more importantly, continuing expansions of these guest houses. In the later case, new hotel buildings are usually constructed just beside the old guest houses. Since individual buildings of a hotel complex are constructed in different years, they vary widely not only in their standards but in architectural styles. As a result, today's hotel landscape in Suzhou is characterized by a couple of apparently different buildings standing side by side within virtually a same hotel plot. The Suzhou Hotel and Nanlin Hotel are most representative of such a continuous development process.

---

[4]Compare section 4.1.

## Figure 6–2: The Growth in International Hotel Capacity in Suzhou, 1985–1993

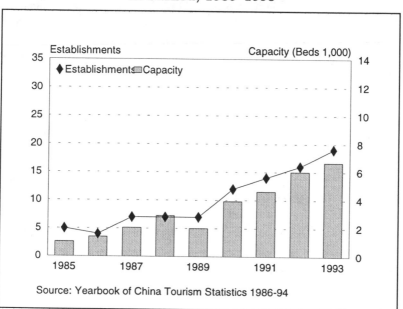

Source: Yearbook of China Tourism Statistics 1986-94

Since the late 1980s, hotel development in Suzhou has entered into a new stage.

- First, Suzhou's hotel sector has been expanding at a much faster rate, and the growth in capacity has resulted principally from new hotel constructions. From 1989 to 1992, 9 new hotels were opened, expanding the capacity by 1,600 rooms (3,120 beds).

- Second, besides small- and medium-sized domestically-invested hotels, big joint-venture hotels began to emerge. Two newly built joint-venture hotels, the Yadu Hotel (410 rooms) and Zhuhui Hotel (400 rooms), contributed over one-half of the total increase in hotel capacity during this period. Such a tourist facility like the Yadu Hotel, which is the highest construction in Suzhou (29–story), has not only changed the city's skylines but, in effect, become a new 'tourist attraction' for many domestic visitors.

### 6.1.3 Qinhuangdao (Beidaihe)

It seems arguable that the second hotel investment 'fever' has not confined to the 'key tourist cities' like Guilin and Suzhou, but spread to many parts of the country where international tourist demand is insignificant. The rapid rise of the international hotel sector in Qinhuangdao, under which Beidaihe is administrated, is a case in place.

Up till 1993, international tourist arrivals in Qinhuangdao had never reached 18,000, of which 2,500 in Beidaihe. However, since the mid–1980s, the international hotel sector in this city has also been expanding at an astonishing pace, though hotel expansions in Beidaihe remain moderate (by 1992, 5 hotels with 1,275 beds).

In 1985, Qinhuangdao had only 3 international hotels (about 700 beds). Yet, from 1986 to 1989, as many as 23 new international hotels (9,280 beds) were opened and, thus, the hotel capacity increased by over 14 times (Fig. 6–3)! By 1993, there were 33 international hotels (13,380 beds) in operation.

### Figure 6–3: The Growth in International Hotel Capacity in Qinhuangdao (Beidaihe), 1985–1993

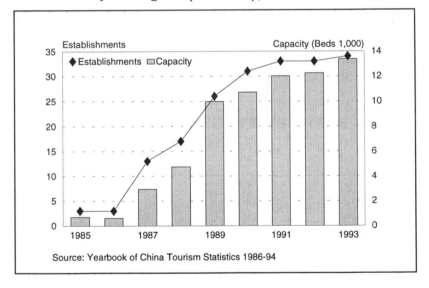

Source: Yearbook of China Tourism Statistics 1986-94

Thus, in terms of international hotel capacity, Qinhuangdao had even surpassed a 'key tourist city' like Guilin which receives around one half million international tourists.

Still more puzzling is the seemingly quite good performance of the hotel sector in Qinhuangdao, at least statistically. According to official statistics, during 1986–1993 the average occupancy rates of international hotels in Qinhuangdao reached 50% to 73%, which were at least as high as those in Suzhou, and much higher than those in Guilin during the same period.[5]

Obviously, such seemingly good performance can be only explained by the buoyant demand of domestic travelers. Though we do not have reliable data on the structure of hotel arrivals in Qinhuangdao, the demand structure of the whole province (Hebei) gives us some hints. In 1990, for instance, domestic travelers accounted for 80% of all hotel arrivals (overnights) in province Hebei.[6]

### 6.1.4 Structure of Hotel Standards

Besides rapid growth in capacity, the recent hotel expansions in Guilin and, to a less extent, in Suzhou have been dominated by high-standard hotels. The largest part of hotel investment has been concentrated in the top-class categories. By 1992, while above 3–star hotels made up 28% of all hotel capacity in the country, this percentage reached 64% in Suzhou, and 71% in Guilin (Tab. 6–1).

### Table 6–1: Standards of International Hotels in Guilin and Suzhou, 1992

| | Hotel | | Capacity (Beds) | | | | |
| | | | Absolute | | % | | |
| Standards | Guilin | Suzhou | Guilin | Suzhou | Guilin | Suzhou | China[1] |
|---|---|---|---|---|---|---|---|
| Star | 27 | 13 | 12,500 | 5,372 | 94.1 | 89.3 | 53.4 |
| 5-star | – | – | – | – | – | – | 3.5 |
| 4-star | 4 | – | 3,450 | – | 26.0 | – | 7.3 |
| 3-star | 11 | 6 | 6,000 | 3,860 | 45.1 | 64.2 | 17.7 |
| 2-star | 9 | 7 | 2,590 | 1,512 | 19.5 | 25.1 | 19.6 |
| 1-star | 3 | – | 460 | – | 3.5 | – | 5.3 |
| Non-star | 3 | 3 | 790 | 640 | 5.9 | 10.7 | 46.6 |
| Total | 30 | 16 | 13,290 | 6,012 | 100.0 | 100.0 | 100.0 |

[1] This data set is listed for comparative purposes. NTA 1993, pp. 104–105.
Sources: Author's field surveys; Tourism Bureau Guilin and Suzhou.

Obviously, in the 'key tourist cities' Guilin and Suzhou, a certain level of higher proportion of high-standard hotels than the national average is economically rational. However, tourist demand on high-standard hotels has been much over-estimated in both places. Unfor-

---

[5] Compare Fig. 6–4.
[6] NTA 1991, pp. 94–95.

tunately, only very recently have the local tourism planners come to realize such a structural problem.

This structural problem has become especially acute as the entire hotel sector turns out to be over-developed. Because most international tourists have little possibilities in choosing hotel services among different standards, one of the direct outcomes of such a structural problem is the unbearable pressures on many middle- and low-standard hotels which, in most cases, are (local) state-owned. In Guilin, according to local regulations, since 1993 hotels ranked under 3-star have no longer been allowed to receive international tourists.

## 6.2 The Role of Foreign Direct Investment (FDI)

### 6.2.1 The Surge of Joint-venture Hotels

The rapid rise of China's international hotel sector can be ascribed in large measure to the inflow of FDI. From 1980 to 1990, around 30 billion RMB yuan had been invested in the country's hotel industry, of which 2/3 foreign capital (about 5–6 billion US$). 85% of the foreign hotel investment has come from the capital market of Hong Kong and Macao. And over 60% of all joint-venture hotel projects were concentrated in the 'key tourist cities'.[7]

Among dozens of problems, the first and foremost barrier to tourism development in an economically less developed area like Guilin is capital scarcity. Though Guilin received certain preferential policy treatments including financial subsidiaries, tourism-specific grants-in-aid from the central government seemed more symbolic than adequate in alleviating, let alone solving the problem of capital shortage.[8] Since domestic investment is limited, the large-scale hotel constructions in Guilin have placed heavy reliance upon foreign finance, leading to a rapid surge of joint-venture hotels.

Already in the first half of the 1980s, all increase in hotel capacity in Guilin resulted from the construction of 3 joint-venture hotels. Much more spectacular were the expansions of joint-venture projects

---

[7]Zhao and Wei 1990, pp. 225–38; Meng 1992, pp. 7–12.

[8]By the late 1980s, the central government had granted a total amount of 300 million RMB yuan subsidiaries to the 4 'key tourist cities' of Guilin, Xi'an, Hangzhou, and Suzhou. Such financial resources were invested principally in urban infrastructure development (Zhou 1990, p. 20). However, this kind of tourism-specific grants-in-aid almost disappeared in the early 1990s when China started a new round of reforms in areas such as center-local resource-sharing, investment, banking, and so on.

in the following years. It was estimated that, from May 1985 to November 1987, about 287 million US$ had been invested in Guilin's hotel sector, of which 75% were foreign investment.[9]

From 1986 to 1992, 13 newly constructed joint-venture hotels (7,225 beds) contributed more than 70% of total increase in capacity. By 1992, 16 joint-venture hotels had been in operation, making up 63% of all hotel capacity in Guilin (Tab. 6–2). Most joint-venture hotels are big modern complexes, and belong to the top categories (Tab. 6–3). As a result, today's hotel landscape of Guilin is dominated apparently by the joint-venture hotels.

Over the past one and half decades, many tourist cities in China have seen a rapid penetration of international hotel groups. However, the extent of such penetration differs widely from one region to another. Unlike in Guilin where international investment groups appear in strength, the use of FDI in Suzhou's hotel sector has been kept much lower.

Till the late 1980s, foreign hotel investment had played a small part in this place, though in such a hotel project like the Gusu Hotel, foreign capital was used in importation of hotel facilities and equipment. By 1992, Suzhou had two joint-venture hotels (1,600 beds), making up 26% of total capacity. The comparatively stronger regional economy, and more sophisticated commercial and industrial traditions seem to be the decisive explanatory factors to the lower share of foreign hotel investment in Suzhou.

### Table 6–2: Sources of Growth in International Hotel Capacity in Guilin, 1973–1992

|                | 1973–80 | 1981–85 | 1986–87 | 1988–92 | by 1992[1] |
|----------------|---------|---------|---------|---------|------------|
| Hotel Total    | 2       | 3       | 9       | 15      | 30         |
| Joint-ventures | 0       | 3       | 7       | 6       | 16         |
| Beds Total     | 1,808   | 1,095   | 3,098   | 7,041   | 13,290     |
| Joint-ventures | 0       | 1,095   | 2,328   | 4,897   | 8,320      |
| % of total     | –       | 100.0   | 75.1    | 69.5    | 62.6       |

[1] In 1992, joint-venture hotels made up 25% of total hotel capacity in China. NTA 1993, pp. 100–101.

Source: Author's field survey; Tourism Bureau Guilin.

---

[9]Tang 1990, p. 303.

**Table 6–3: Standards of Joint-venture Hotels in Guilin, 1992**

| | Hotels | | Beds | | |
|---|---|---|---|---|---|
| | Total | J–V[1] | Total | J–V[1] | % |
| China[2] | 2,354 | 476 | 737,600 | 186,100 | 25.2 |
| Guilin | 30 | 16 | 13,290 | 8,320 | 62.6 |
| Star | 27 | 16 | 12,500 | 8,320 | 66.6 |
| 4-star | 4 | 4 | 3,450 | 3,450 | 100.0 |
| 3-star | 11 | 8 | 6,000 | 3,940 | 65.7 |
| 2-star | 9 | 3 | 2,590 | 810 | 31.3 |
| 1-star | 3 | 1 | 460 | 120 | 26.1 |
| Non-star | 3 | – | 790 | – | – |

[1] All international hotels with FDI;
[2] For comparative purposes, NTA 1992, pp. 100–101.
Sources: Author's field surveys; Tourism Bureau Guilin.

## 6.2.2  Incentive Factors

The underlying forces pushing the large-scale hotel investment in the study areas are manifold. And, the motives of foreign and domestic hotel investment are different. In the case of Guilin, the following factors are especially noteworthy.

(1) Early short-run monopolist profits and over-optimistic expectations
The extreme hotel shortage in the early 1980s had led to a short-run monopoly situation in which early hotel investors tended to reap large capital gains. Before 1985, the 3 joint-venture hotels in Guilin achieved an occupancy rate of around 85%.[10] Even in the mid–1980s, Guilin's hotel sector remained by and large a seller's market. Partial treatment of the high returns on earlier investments had led to an over-optimistic expectation.

To many foreign and domestic investors, it seemed quite sure that hotel investment in Guilin could earn high and quick returns on their capitals without much risk. According to the feasibility studies of 8 hotel projects constructed during 1985–88, 6 of them were designed

---

[10]Meng 1992, pp. 7–12.

at expected occupancy rates of 75–80%, and 2 at 60–65%[11]. Such
expectations may seem justified from the standpoint of individual
projects.[12] However, issues of overall balance in hotel supply have
been neglected.

(2) Hotel industry legislation
As pioneer industry legislation, the incentives provided by national
hotel industry policies are extensive, favoring FDI in joint-venture
hotel projects. Such incentives are concentrated on reducing liability
for import duties and income taxes (Tab. 6–4).

### Table 6–4: Differences in Policy Treatments between Joint-venture and State-owned Hotels

|  | Joint-venture | State-owned |
|---|---|---|
| Income Taxation | zero-rate income tax for the first two years; 50% income tax relief for another 3 years | full taxation |
| Importation | licensed for importation and partial duty-free imports | no rights for importation and full payment of import duties |
| Foreign Exchange | legitimated in use of foreign exchange, no need to settle accounts in the Bank of China regarding foreign exchange receipts | no rights in use of foreign exchange, all FEC receipts (except circulating capital) must be settled in the Bank of China |
| Pricing | legitimated in seasonal pricing | subject to state price regulations |
| Labor Hiring | autonomy in labor hiring | subject to state arrangements |
| Salaries and wages | flexibility in determining the rates of salaries and wages, and tax relief on bonus | state-determined rates of salaries and wages, income tax on bonus |

Source: Various Chinese documents.

In view of the emerging tourism boom in China, the policy effects of incentive legislation on foreign hotel investment are enormous,
though such fiscal concessions are applicable to many other sectors
of the Chinese economy. Furthermore, in many cases, various concessions seem to be extended at the local level. Obviously, negotiation
in joint-venture projects requires local investors to have specialized
knowledge of ongoing terms in international tourism businesses and
of the firm negotiated with. Such expertise is anything but sufficient
in most Chinese tourist cities including Guilin.

---

[11] GLERC 1989, p. 190.
[12] In 1986, Guilin's entire hotel sector still achieved an occupancy rate of 82.6%.
Compare Fig. 6–4.

The incentives for domestic investors to participate in joint-venture projects are also enormous. Capitals, marketing know-how and business networking brought by joint-ventures are the most desperately needed inputs for tourism development at the local level. The flexibility legitimated for joint-venture hotels in construction, management as well as in day-to-day decision-makings is also very appealing to individual hotel firms. In addition, non-monetary advantages granted to managerial personnel such as duty-free importation of cars tend to have also played certain part. Thus, hotel projects, whenever possible, try to be labeled as joint-ventures.

(3) Distortion of tourism development objectives

In a transitional economy, former 'gross and quantitative' development thinking seems still at play, though its incidence tends to be in declining. Numerous documents on local tourism policies, development strategies as well as project planning suggest that local authorities in Guilin and Suzhou have pursued a goal of 'quantitative maximization' in tourism development.

Objectives set in tourism promotion have confined themselves exclusively to few gross incremental parameters such as 'total tourist arrivals', 'international hotel capacity' and, perhaps as a most economic performance-like indicator, 'gross tourist receipts'. Logically, such development thinking puts heavy emphasis on quantitative expansions of tourist infrastructure such as international hotels. Extensive expansions of the joint-venture sector tend to be enhanced by two further factors, namely,

- particular emphasis of national tourism schemes on the 'key tourist cities', and

- the difficulties in checking 'investment hunger' at the enterprise level.[13]

## 6.3   Over-investment

### 6.3.1   The Problem

Since the mid–1980s, the hotel supply in Guilin and Suzhou has been growing at much faster rates than tourist arrivals. This seemed desirable in those years when tourism development still suffered from hotel shortage. However, in quantitative terms, the problem of hotel

---

[13] For discussions on enterprise behaviors in a transitional economy, see Jefferson and Xu 1991, pp. 45–64; Perkins 1994, pp. 23–46; Jefferson et al 1994, pp. 47–70.

shortage in Guilin and Suzhou had been solved by no later than the late 1980s.[14] Since then, the major 'bottleneck' constraining tourism growth has shifted to the inadequate provision of transportation services.

Unfortunately, necessary adjustments in investment structure have not taken place. Hotel expansions have continued into the 1990s. As a result, the discrepancies in growth rates between hotel expansions and tourist arrivals have become increasingly apparent (Tab. 6–5). In Guilin, it was estimated that by 1992 the 30 international hotels (13,300 beds) could accommodate at least 1.3 million tourists, whereas tourist arrivals in 1992 were 508,000.[15] In Suzhou, the still high growth rate in hotel capacity seems attributable to its relatively later start-up in extensive hotel investment.

**Table 6–5: Annual Growth Rates of Hotel Capacity and Tourist Arrivals (%)**

|        | 1985–1988 | | 1988–1992 | |
|--------|-----------|----------|-----------|----------|
|        | Capacity  | Arrivals | Capacity  | Arrivals |
| Guilin | 27.9      | 8.1      | 9.5       | 2.0      |
| Suzhou | 28.8      | 8.8      | 15.7      | 3.0      |
| China  | 14.0      | 15.5     | 6.1       | 3.7      |

Source: Author's calculation based on the data from NTA 1986–1994.

### 6.3.2 Consequences of Over-capacity

The cost of over-development of the hotel sector is high, especially in Guilin. As hotel supply has changed from a seller's market to a typical buyer's market, serious problems have become increasingly apparent. Recent poor performance of the hotel sector suggests that local efforts in tourism development in the past years tend to be inconsistent to the declared local goals (Tab. 6–6).

(1) Disastrous drop-offs in occupancy rates
It should be especially underscored that in Guilin and Suzhou the dramatic declines in occupancy rates are the direct result of overinvestment, though the political incidents of 1989 had undoubtedly negative impacts. In Guilin, the average occupancy rate of the entire

---

[14]Interviews with tourism planners in Guilin and Suzhou.
[15]Compare section 4.1.

hotel sector dropped from 82.6% in 1986 to 46.7% in 1988, and then fell further to 41% in 1993. Similar tendencies have also appeared in Suzhou (Fig. 6–4).

### Table 6–6: Consequences of Over-investment in the International Hotel Sector

| Problem area (I): Over-capacity |
| --- |
| * dramatic declines in occupancy rate |
| * excessive competitions, price-cutting, and poor performance |
| * unfavorable terms of payments and chains of debts |
| * existence problems of SOEs |
| Problem area (II): Over-involvement of foreign capital (Guilin) |
| * heavy foreign debts |
| * extensive leakage of foreign exchange |

### Figure 6–4: Declines in Occupancy Rates in Guilin and Suzhou, 1985–1992 (%)

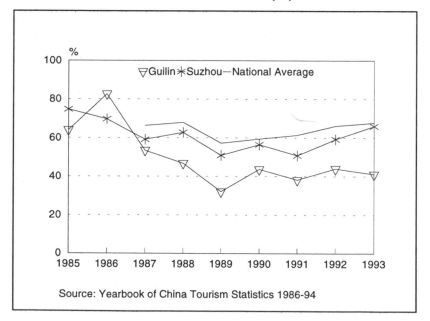

Source: Yearbook of China Tourism Statistics 1986-94

The less dramatic declines in Suzhou seem attributable to the considerable demand of domestic business and meeting travelers, which are clearly associated with the industrial and commercial dynamics of this area. Nevertheless, in both places the average occupancy rates have since 1987 remained below the national averages. Obviously, such poor performance does not match the expected leadership of the 'key tourist cities' of Guilin and Suzhou in the national tourism schemes.

(2) Excessive competitions, widespread price-cutting, and poor performance

As over-supply of hotel capacity in Guilin and Suzhou appears more and more apparent, competitions among individual suppliers have become progressively intensified, which in turn have exerted substantial downward pressures on room rates. Though some middle- and low-category hotels began to turn to domestic tourism, tourist demand remains far from sufficient.[16] As a result, all hotels have to compete savagely by offering lower prices to tour operators, and price-cutting has become a commonplace. According to author's surveys, the 4–star Guishan Hotel and Wenhua Hotel in Guilin, for instance, had to cut their standard room rates from 60–70 US$ to below 40 US$ in the early 1990s. Room rates of some 3–star hotels went even down to 10 US$.

The net outcome of such excessive competitions is the deterioration of performance of the entire hotel sector. According to the information from the Tourism Bureaus Guilin and Suzhou, in 1991 the entire hotel sector in Guilin operated at a profit rate of minus 13.2%, or minus 6.9% in Suzhou. The performance of joint-venture hotels seemed even much poorer. In Guilin, 15 of the 16 joint-venture hotels have been run with substantial losses in recent years.[17]

As such problems became very serious in the early 1990s, the state had to stand out to interfere into the supply market. Since 1990, there have been nationwide campaigns for price-maintenance arrangements, which try to discipline individual hotel firms and to develop coherent and common price strategies to deal with transna-

---

[16]From 1986 to 1990, the share of domestic guests in total hotel overnights increased from 46% to 48.5% in Guangxi province, and from 45.4% to 49.5% in Jiangsu province. NTA 1986, pp. 42–43, 1991, pp. 94–95.

[17]Interviews with personnel in tourism bureaus in Guilin and Suzhou. This problem seems applicable to the entire hotel industry in China. By 1991, over 20% of state-run hotels and 60% of joint-venture hotels remained in substantial losses (NTA 1992, p. 12.)

tional corporations.[18]   Such strategies involve the arrangements of desirable levels of standard room rates in various hotel categories, and the extent of price concessions granted at the enterprise level.

However, author's investigations in Guilin and Suzhou suggest that the implementation of such price-maintenance arrangements have met enormous difficulties.   It seems that the knowledge of individual hotels about the sensitivity of tourist flows to price changes has developed to a quite admirable level.   Many hotel managerial staff reported that some tour operators have switched their clients to other hotels in response to upward price changes in individual hotels. Thus, as a matter of fact, once price-cutting had been introduced in one hotel or even in another area, many hotels found themselves forced to follow suit.

(3) Unfavorable terms of payments

Another consequence resulted from over-capacity is the 'chain of debts'.   As competitions become steadily intensified, most individual hotels, as weak bargaining partners, have to accept unfavorable terms in negotiating with tour operators, such as long delays in payment as well as more price concessions.   Such practices have led to dozens of problems which have been described by the recently-coined phrase *sanjiaozhai*, or 'chain of debts', i.e. liabilities from foreign tour operators –> domestic travel agencies –> individual hotels.

The Tourism Bureau of Guilin reported that in 1989 local travel agencies in this city had to accept a total amount of 32.5 million FEC 'outstanding payments' from foreign tour operators or other domestic travel agencies.   And Guilin's international hotels in turn had to accept over 20 million FEC delayed payments from local travel agencies.   In 1990, such outstanding payments amounted to 42 million FEC in Guilin.[19]   Some hotels in Guilin even reported that the payment from some parts of this 'chain' is in fact out of the question.

(4) Existence problems of state-owned hotels

Compared to most of the newly constructed joint-venture hotels, the state-run international hotels in Guilin and Suzhou are characterized by lower standards and unsophisticated managerial skills.   Neverthe-

---

[18]This is the so-called 'lowest price maintenance' policy. Cf. *Lüyou jingji* (Tourism Economy) (1991) 3:54.

[19]This problem is nationwide. In 1990, China's leading travel agencies had a total amount of 250 million US$ of delayed payments from foreign tour operators. Cf. Gu 1992, pp. 62–68.

less, in both places the state-run hotels once played a decisive role in the early 1980s. Today, however, even survival of many state-run hotels has become a pressing problem.

Take two state-owned hotels in Guilin for example (Fig. 6–5). Rongchen Hotel was the first and single hotel which was engaged in international tourism, and almost always fully occupied in the early 1980s. In 1985, its occupancy rate still remained at 76%, and even reached 91% in 1986. However, the heyday of this hotel was definitely gone when joint-venture hotels began mushrooming from 1986 onwards. By 1988, Rongchen's occupancy rate had already dropped hopelessly to 28%. As a result, this hotel had to be partly closed down after 1989.

**Figure 6–5: Declines in Occupancy Rates of Different Types of Hotels in Guilin, 1985–1993**

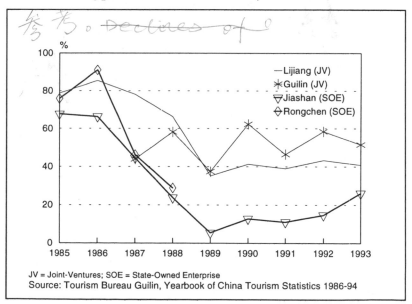

Similar fortunes have also happened to the Jiashan Hotel (built in 1980). From 1985 to 1988, its occupancy rate had slid from 67% down to 23%. In 1989, it fell to an incredibly low level of 5%. Even by 1993, Jiashan's occupancy rate had recovered only to 26%. Author's field surveys suggest that, unfortunately, the cases of Rongchen and Jiashan are not the exceptions in Guilin.

The existence problem of many state-run hotels arises from several grounds. Besides the built-in problem of lower service standards, one decisive factor in explaining the decline of the state-run sector seems to be the 'unevenness' in policy treatment at the enterprise level. As discussed in section 4.2.2, differences in policy treatment between state-run and joint-venture hotels are explicit and substantial. It seems that such incentive legislation has been devised for three purposes. That is, first, to help eliminate early supply shortage; second, to help hotels acquire management know-how and, thirdly, to exert pressures on state-run hotels so as to push them marketwards.

However, while supply shortage has been eliminated, the expected spread effects of joint-ventures' managerial know-how have not taken place. On the contrary, as is reported by most state-run hotels in Guilin and Suzhou, the explicit 'unequal' policy treatments have made them much less competitive. And such an unfavorable situation has drastically deteriorated since the late 1980s when over-capacity became more and more apparent.

Obviously, on such policy issues the Chinese policy-makers are caught in a dilemma. It is by no means a simple exercise to offer incentives strong enough to attract more FDI while creating a sound policy environment for the growth of domestic firms. From the point of view of local economic development, the issues of survival of local state-owned hotels are especially critical, because the performance of such locally-run hotels is, among others, most decisive in determining the share of economic returns directly distributed to the local economies.

### 6.3.3   Consequences of Over-involvement of FDI (Guilin)

Unfortunately, until the early 1990s the long-term effects of numerous joint-venture projects in Guilin had hardly been taken into account. Obviously, the use of large-scale FDI and the offer of fiscal concessions are simply due to the lack of development resources at the local level. However, in order to keep low the erosion of benefits to the local economy, at least the extent and the way of using FDI can be partly manipulated by local governments. However, such issues have not received sufficient attentions from local tourism planners. On the contrary, manipulation of incentive legislation at the local level turns out to be self-defeating in many cases. In this sense, the incentives offered to joint-venture undertakings have represented a cost to the local economy in Guilin, though it remains unclear whether a substantial proportion of the hotel investment would have also taken place with substantial reduced incentives.

(1) Heavy foreign debts

The first result of extensive joint-venture hotel constructions is mountain-high foreign debts. By 1989, 10 joint-venture hotels in Guilin had a total amount of 88 million US$ foreign debts. It was estimated that Guilin has to pay around 150 million US$ when the foreign debts are due to return.[20] According to the repayment contracts, Guilin has to pay 15 million US$ foreign debts per annum, which re much more than the (annual) gross revenues of these ten hotels altogether in recent years.[21] In 1993, the gross revenues of Guilin's entire hotel sector were 236 million RMB yuan (about 41 million US$).[22]

Still more serious is the discouraging performance of most joint-venture hotels. According to author's investigations, 10 of the 11 international hotels which had foreign debts still remained in substantial losses of about 50 million FEC in 1991. Even by 1993, the occupancy rates of most joint-venture hotels had hardly reached 40%. It has become clear that in many cases the repayment of foreign debts is far beyond the financial capacity of individual hotels involved, at least within the terms of contract arrangements. Thus, a considerable part of such liabilities have in fact shifted to the local government, relying principally on continuing extensions of bank credits, local financial budgets and the like. During author's field surveys, local tourism planners reported that from 1990 to 1993 the city government of Guilin (via banks and local revenues) had to take the responsibility in repaying 6-7 million US$ foreign debts per annum, making up 60–70% of total repayments.

One additional factor tends to further the seriousness of foreign debts. That is, the continuing devaluation of RMB yuan. From 1985 to 1990, RMB yuan was devaluated by 62%, resulting in an increase in foreign debts by around 2/3. By 1995, domestic currency had another devaluation of about 60%.[23]

---

[20]Meng 1992, pp. 7–12.

[21] *Ibid.*

[22]NTA 1994, p. 125.

[23]ZTN 1992, p. 640; *Renmin Ribao* (People's Daily), December 1995.

(2) High leakage of foreign exchange revenues

The erosion of economic benefits resulted from extensive use of FDI seems astonishing. First, the import-content of hotel investments is very high. Local managerial staff and tourism planners reported that nearly all key raw materials and equipment for hotel construction have been imported. Importation arising from hotel extensions and equipment replacement is also substantial. This is attributable not exclusively to the negotiation arrangements, but partly to the dissatisfying qualities of domestic investment goods, especially in construction of high-standard hotels.

Second, the strong penetration of multi-nationals in hotel businesses has exerted substantial upward pressures on the operation costs of joint-venture hotels, especially those directly managed by international hotel groups. Such costs arise from several areas, such as 'foreign management costs', i.e. a certain contracted proportion of total revenues (instead of profits), and personnel costs of foreign managerial staff filling key positions in joint-venture hotels. In Guilin, 9 of the 10 joint venture hotels, which not only had foreign debts but were run with losses, were managed by multi-national hotel chains, though in differing ways and degrees. In 1990, these 9 hotels employed about 140 foreign managerial staff, and paid a total amount of 10 million FEC personnel costs including wages and salaries.[24]

---

[24]Wang 1991, p. 63; Meng 1992, pp. 7–12.

# 7

# Domestic Accommodation Sector

## 7.1 Discontinuities in Service Standards

²With respect to its supply system, China's tourism industry is dualistic in nature. Sharp cleavage in service standards between international and domestic tourism is pervasive. Such a dualistic structure is most apparent in the accommodation sector.

While large-size FDI and considerable state investments have been concentrated in the international hotel sector, many small domestic investors have participated actively in building domestic accommodation facilities. As the 1984/85 tourism policy created a favorable policy environment, and the boom of domestic tourism opened plentiful market opportunities, provision of accommodation services has become a lucrative business for many local investors. Over the past decade Guilin, Suzhou and Beidaihe have witnessed substantial expansions of the domestic accommodation sector.

Today, in the study areas big modern hotel complexes are surrounded by numerous small accommodation facilities. However, between these two parts exist insurmountable discontinuities in service standards and room rates. Though some domestic travelers, such as meeting and business travelers, well-to-do individual tourists and the like, tend to have above-average demand for accommodation services, yet, on the whole such demand remains a tiny proportion of the total demand. In this sense, a dualistic structure in accommodation supply is de facto an economic rationale. On the other hand, however, extremely limited substitubilities between these two parts tend to build an extra instability factor in the tourist supply system.

According to China's hotel regulations, the distinctions between international and domestic accommodation facilities are clear and simple. That is, whether or not a hotel is officially allowed to receive international tourists. Domestic accommodation facilities cover a wide spectrum from temporary or simplest private guest houses to big hotels of high standards. In Chinese language, however, the name of an accommodation facility often tells little about its standard. This is especially true of such phrases as *fandian, lüguan,* and partly *zhaodaisuo.* A *fandian,* for instance, can be an international hotel, a domestic hotel of high standard, or a small guest house providing simplest services.

## 7.2 Types and Forms

Roughly, domestic accommodation facilities in the study areas fall into three categories: domestic hotels, guest houses, and *danwei* holiday quarters (Tab. 7–1).

**Table 7–1: Types of Domestic Accommodation Facilities in the Study Areas**

| Type | Standard | Ownership | Demand Group |
|------|----------|-----------|--------------|
| Hotels | relatively higher standards | state; collective | business and meeting travelers; well-to-do individual tourists, etc. |
| Guest houses | low in standards; simple in services | | most individual tourists; business travelers |
| *zhaodaisuo* [1] | | state; collective | business travelers; individual tourists |
| *lüshe/kezhan* [2] | | collective; private | individual tourists and travelers |
| *linshi zhaodaisuo* [3] | | state; collective | individual tourists |
| *Danwei* holiday quarters | well-equipped | state | holiday-makers of big *danwei* |

[1] *Danwei* guest houses; [2] collective or private guest houses/inns;
[3] temporary guest houses

## 7.2.1  Domestic Hotels

Domestic hotels are facilities of relatively higher standards but only accessible to domestic travelers. They play a larger part in Guilin than in Suzhou (Tab. 7–2). Besides international hotels, this type of accommodation facilities are most noticeable, since they are not only big in size, but often located in the downtown areas, around major transportation stations or along main streets within tourist cities.

High-standard domestic hotels are usually owned and run by state and collective *danwei*. They have developed partly from formerly simple guest houses. In Guilin, however, newly built hotels tend to make up a considerable part of the capacity in this category. Today, domestic hotels have become fairly well-equipped (e.g. 2–3 beds, color TV sets, bathrooms, etc.), and big in size (on average 185 beds per hotel in Guilin, 190 in Suzhou). Consequently, room rates are relatively high, ranging from 20 to 60 yuan per day. Business travelers, meeting tourists, private businessmen and well-to-do individual tourists make up the major part of their guests.

**Table 7–2: Structure of Domestic Accommodation Sector in Guilin and Suzhou, 1991**

| | Guilin | | | Suzhou | | |
|---|---|---|---|---|---|---|
| | $E^1$ | Beds | $B/E^2$ | $E^1$ | Beds | $B/E^2$ |
| | | 1,000 | % | | 1,000 | % | |
| Total | 444 | 41.1 | 100.0 | 92 | 346 | 26.8 | 100.0 | 77 |
| Hotels | 76 | 14.0 | 34.2 | 185 | 23 | 4.4 | 16.4 | 190 |
| *Zhaodai-suo* [3] | 190 | 20.1 | 48.9 | 105 | 167 | 13.3 | 49.5 | 80 |
| *Lüshe* [4] | 178 | 7.0 | 16.9 | 39 | 156 | 9.1 | 34.1 | 58 |

[1] Establishments; [2] beds per establishment; [3] *danwei* guest houses; [4] inns
Source: Author's field surveys, Statistical Bureau Guilin and Suzhou.

## 7.2.2  *Danwei* Guest Houses

*Danwei* guest houses not only have a long tradition, but play an active part in today's domestic tourism. They make up about one-half of total accommodation capacity in Guilin and Suzhou (Tab. 7–2). *Danwei* guest houses are owned and, in most cases, still run by either state or big collective *danwei*.

*Danwei* guest houses cover a wide spectrum of facilities. *Danwei* guest house has an average size of 100 beds in Guilin, and 80 beds in

Suzhou. Room rates are usually between 5 to 20 yuan per day, which are widely affordable for average tourists. There seem practically no price regulations, as the standards of services are widely different.

Although most guest houses are simple in facilities and low in service qualities, the standards of service provided by *danwei* guest houses vary remarkably from one to another. A big guest house of a municipal government, for instance, can be an equivalent of a 1 or 2–star international hotel. But a guest house of a factory can be as simple as a *lüshe* (inn).

In many important respects, the guest houses of Chinese *danwei* have developed a hierarchy of service standards, reflecting the underpinning social and political structure.

### 7.2.3  *Lüshe/Kezhan* (inns)

*Lüshe* and *kezhan* (inns) are the simplest facilities which are frequently used by domestic travelers, especially average tourists. They make up 34% of total capacity in Suzhou, and 17% in Guilin (Tab. 7–2). In Beidaihe, the majority of accommodation facilities (80%) outside the state-run sector fall into this category (Tab. 7–3).

**Table 7–3: Structure of Domestic Accommodation Sector in Beidaihe, 1991**

|  | E[1] | Beds | | B/E[2] |
|---|---|---|---|---|
|  |  | 1,000 | % |  |
| Total | 927 | 61.4 | 100.0 | 66 |
| Holiday Quarters[3] | 88 | 24.2 | 39.4 | 275 |
| *Zhaodaisuo*[4] | 70 | 8.0 | 13.0 | 114 |
| *Lüshe*[5] | 769 | 29.2 | 47.6 | 37 |

[1] Establishments; [2] beds per establishment; [3] *danwei* holiday quarters; [4] *danwei* guest houses; [5] inns
Source: Author's field surveys; Statistical Bureau Beidaihe.

*Lüshe* and *kezhan* (inns) differentiate themselves from *danwei* guest houses in three important respects, namely,

1. the dominance of small collective and private ownership;
2. very small size and lowest standard of services; and
3. primitive ways of marketing and management.

*Lüshe* and *kezhan* (inns) used to be owned and run exclusively by *xiaojiti danwei*, or 'small collective units'. In Chinese cities, typical small collective *danwei* are the so-called *jiedao*, or 'street committees'. Therefore, such facilities are also called *jiedao lüshe*, or 'street committee's guest houses'. In the early 1990s, small collective *danwei* still provided around one-half of the capacity of *lüshe* in Guilin (Tab. 7–4).

### Table 7–4: Ownership and Size of *Lüshe* Guest Houses in Guilin, 1991

|            | E[1] | Beds  | %[2]  | B/E[3] |
|------------|------|-------|-------|--------|
| Total      | 178  | 6,963 | 100.0 | 39     |
| State      | 10   | 681   | 9.7   | 68     |
| Collective | 48   | 3,473 | 50.0  | 72     |
| Private    | 120  | 2,809 | 40.3  | 23     |

[1] Establishments; [2] % of total bed capacity; [3] beds per establishment
Source: author's field surveys; Statistical Bureau Guilin.

As will be discussed in following sections, quasi 'small privatization' such as 'leasing' contracts or arrangements have taken place in the operation of many collective guest houses in recent years. In Beidaihe, the mushrooming of such simplest facilities is a relatively new phenomenon, and most of them are privately owned and run. Therefore, they are often called *geti lüshe* or *kezhan*, or private guest houses.

Most *lüshe* and *kezhan* guest houses are very small in size. A *lüshe* or *kezhan* has an average size of 40 beds in Guilin, and 60 in Suzhou. Private boarding-houses are still smaller (about 20 beds). As a rule, this kind of guest houses can only provide simplest services. Rooms are very simply equipped, usually with 4–6 beds in a room, black-white TV sets, shared sanitary facilities, etc.

### 7.2.4 *Danwei* Holiday Quarters

*Danwei* holiday quarters are specific to Beidaihe. They are in fact a special type of *danwei* guest houses. *Danwei* holiday quarters are invested exclusively by the governments at various levels, big enterprises and organizations, universities, research institutions or other *danwei*, from almost all over the country.

Such facilities are not only big in size (on average 275 beds per establishment) but well equipped. In 1991, 88 *danwei* holiday quarters had a capacity of 24,200 beds, making up 40% of the total capacity in Beidaihe (Tab. 7–3). However, recreational services in this sector are not accessible to individual holiday-makers. They are provided for the staff of big Chinese *danwei* as a welfare item.[1]

## 7.3 Commercialization in the Early 1980s

The rise of domestic accommodation sector in the study areas began with a commercialization of limited accommodation services. In the pre-reform period, domestic travels in China used to be tightly controlled, and provision of very limited accommodation services were non-independent and non-commercial in nature. Such 'socialist' travel services were supplied principally by various Chinese *danwei*.

Among many routine services provided by *danwei* were also accommodation possibilities for travelers from 'brother' *danwei*. Such accommodation facilities were and are called *danwei zhaodaisuo*, or *danwei* guest houses. Virtually every big Chinese *danwei* had and has at least one guest house of differing size and standard. Room rates of *danwei* guest houses were symbolic at that time.

As broad-based domestic tourist demand began emerging in the late 1970s, the supply of accommodation services soon gained commercial colors. Stimulated by the country's new policy of economic liberalization, former *danwei*-owned accommodation facilities had been commercialized by the early 1980s. In these early years, *danwei* guest houses played a decisive part in meeting the rapidly rising demand. Then existing *danwei*-run guest houses were all opened to individual private travelers, and capacity expansions also took place.

On the other hand, as provision of accommodation services gradually became a lucrative business, other types of facilities such as *lüshe and kezhan* (guest houses or inns) also restored their commercial functions and began expanding. This kind of simple guest houses had a long tradition, and were run principally by collective units.

Despite of such expansions, the capacity of domestic accommodation facilities remained far from adequate in the early 1980s, as demand had been on rapid increase. While already over one million domestic travelers visited Guilin per annum by the early 1980s, this city had only about 110 simple guest houses (7,700 beds).

---

[1] Compare section 5.4.

In Beidaihe, though there existed quite a number of well-equipped recreational facilities, they were not accessible to individual visitors. Accommodation demand of individual holiday-makers had to be met by a newly rising sector. By 1983, about 90 guest houses (9,800 beds) emerged in Beidaihe, of which 60 (4,450 beds) were temporary facilities. Obviously, most of them were very simple facilities with a large number of beds.

In Suzhou, accommodation supply shortage seemed comparatively less apparent. This was due to two main facts. First, the nature of domestic tourism in Suzhou, i.e. the dominance of one-day visitors;[2] second, the comparatively better development of urban infrastructure. By 1982, Suzhou had already 130 guest houses with 17,000 beds.

Thus, by the early 1980s, inadequate provision of accommodation services was one of the 'bottlenecks' constraining the growth of domestic tourism in the study areas. Most domestic travelers were invariably confronted with difficulties in finding appropriate accommodation possibilities. In Guilin, many tourists complained that 'while Guilin's scenery is unparalleled under heaven, tourists had to overnight underground'.[3]

## 7.4 Rapid Expansions and Restructuring

### 7.4.1 Rapid Growth in the Mid–1980s

Substantial expansions of domestic accommodation facilities first took place in the mid–1980s, when the decentralization policy of tourism development came into force in 1984/85. Since then, besides the state, collective and individual private investors have been not only legitimated but greatly encouraged to participate in building local tourism infrastructure. A large number of small investors quickly got their ways into domestic accommodation businesses, leading to a significant growth in accommodation capacity in the study areas (Fig. 7–1, 2, 3).

---

[2] Compare section 5.3.

[3] In most big Chinese cities, there exists an underground canal system which was built mainly during the 1960s and 1970s, and originally conceptualized to serve as 'defense works' in event of a 'nuclear war'. Since the late 1970s, a considerable part of this underground canal system has been re-constructed into accommodation facilities in many cities.

## Figure 7–1: Growth in Domestic Accommodation Capacity in Guilin, 1980–1991

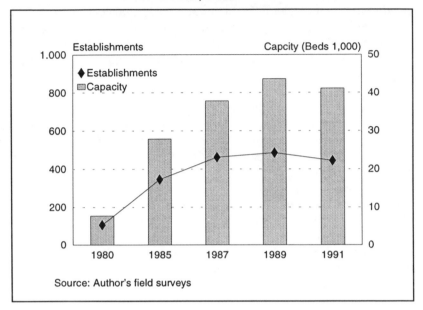

Source: Author's field surveys

## Figure 7–2: Growth in Domestic Accommodation Capacity in Suzhou, 1980–1991

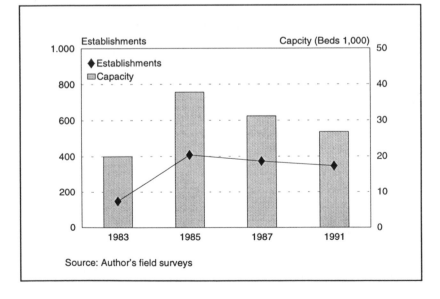

Source: Author's field surveys

**Figure 7–3: Growth in Domestic Accommodation Capacity in Beidaihe, 1980–1991**
(Excluding *Danwei* Holiday Quarters)

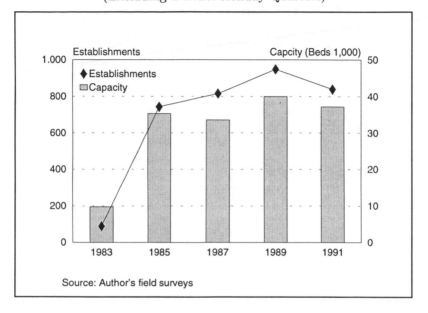

Source: Author's field surveys

From 1985 to 1988, the capacity of domestic accommodation facilities in Guilin had an increase of 15,700 beds, accounting for 47% of the total increase during 1980–1991. The expansions of the accommodation sector in Beidaihe were still more impressive. Besides steady expansions of recreational facilities, especially remarkable was the mushrooming of small guest houses whose number rose rapidly from 89 in 1983 to 843 in 1988, or a capacity expansion of 27,400 beds. In Suzhou, the major part of capacity expansions had already taken place prior to 1985. This seemed due largely to the more liberal 'local policies' in advance of the 1985/85 national tourism policy.[4]

The growth of domestic accommodation sector in the mid–1980s was quantitative in nature. Besides establishment of new guest houses, one of the widespread practices in expanding capacity was simply to put more beds in those already existing facilities. Another measure was to open temporary facilities, especially in Beidaihe. During 1983–85, 654 guest houses (25,440 beds) were established in Beidaihe, of which 557 (16,800 beds) temporary establishments, or 66%

---

[4]Information from various government departments in Suzhou.

139

of the total increase. Obviously, such a development was determined largely by the high concentration of resort tourism activities in summer seasons.

In Beidaihe, the largest part of temporary guest houses are owned and run by individual households. Another type of temporary facilities are owned by various *danwei* such as factories, government bodies, small collective units, etc. Local tourism planners reported that even many middle schools in Beidaihe once got involved in such businesses during vocations.[5] Because they are in operation only in tourism seasons, temporary facilities are in most cases not officially registered.

Such practices were tolerated or even implicitly promoted by local authorities, since they served at least partly as a short-cut solution to the early supply shortage. In Guilin, there were about 110 temporary facilities (2,700 beds) still in operation in 1987 In Suzhou, 18 guest houses (1,425 beds) were seasonally in operation in 1985.

## 7.4.2 The Role of Different 'Actors'

The major source of growth in accommodation capacity was different from one area to another. In general, there has been a tendency for the non-state sector to play an increasing role in domestic tourism supply. Two factors tended to especially favor such non-state initiatives:

- first, limited financial resources available to local governments and SOE in Guilin and Suzhou had flown first and foremost into international tourism sector. In Beidaihe, state investment had been concentrated exclusively in expanding recreational facilities. Thus, the local governments were and are obviously not in the position to provide necessary infrastructure for domestic tourism;

- second, due to low barriers to entry and exit, domestic accommodation business is an economic area in which a wide variety of investors can play an active part.

The rapid rise of small, non-state tourist firms was most apparent in Beidaihe (Fig. 7–4; Tab. 7–5). From 1983 to 1986, over 70% of the total increase in accommodation capacity outside *danwei* holiday

---

[5] According to author's fieldwork, a considerable part of the middle schools in Beidaihe still remain in receiving domestic tourists during vacations, which is regarded as a practical way to increase teachers' income.

quarters was contributed by the privately-owned facilities. Private
guest houses are usually very small in size and simple in services.

### Figure 7–4: The Growth of the Private Sector in Accommodation Supply in Beidaihe, 1983–1991
(Excluding *Danwei* Holiday Quarters)

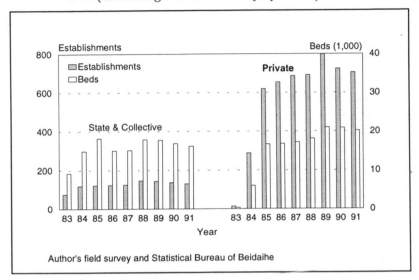

Author's field survey and Statistical Bureau of Beidaihe

### Table 7–5: Source of Growth in Accommodation Capacity in Suzhou and Beidaihe

|  | State | Collective | Private | Total |
|---|---|---|---|---|
| *Suzhou*<br>1982-85 increase in |  |  |  |  |
| Establishments | 11 | 205 | 60 | 276 |
| Beds | 1,586 | 17,963 | 1,307 | 20,856 |
| % | 7.6 | 86.1 | 6.3 | 100.0 |
| *Beidaihe*[1]<br>1983-87 increase in |  |  |  |  |
| Establishments | 45 | 9 | 673 | 727 |
| Beds | 4,498 | 2,370 | 16,883 | 23,751 |
| % | 18.9 | 10.0 | 71.1 | 100.0 |

[1] Excluding *danwei* holiday quarters
Source: Author's field surveys, Statistical Bureau Suzhou and Beidaihe.

The largest part of private establishments took the form of temporary guest houses. In 1985, there were 619 (16,650 beds) privately-owned guest houses in operation, of which 565 (14,440 beds) temporary ones, i.e. 87% of the total capacity in the private sector. By 1991, the private sector accounted for 54% of the accommodation capacity outside *danwei* holiday quarters in Beidaihe. Indeed, the rapid proliferation of small private guest houses in Beidaihe exemplifies an early triumph of private initiatives under China's new policy of economic liberalization.

Two factors are decisive in explaining the rapid rise of the private sector in Beidaihe:

- first, till the early 1980s local tourist infrastructure for mass domestic tourism outside the state-owned recreational sector was almost non-existent in Beidaihe, therefore, competitions from the supply-side remained nearly empty;

- second, land-use possibilities for the construction of private guest houses were and are plentiful. Beidaihe is an urban district which is surrounded directly by several rural villages. There are even two villages within the urban district.[6]

Not only are the privately-owned houses of the rural inhabitants much more spacious than those of their counterparts in the city, but the construction of rural settlements is subject to a set of regulations which are widely different to urban land-use planning, and more flexible in nature.

Obviously, such plentiful land-use possibilities are not available in the big tourist cities Suzhou and Guilin. Moreover, housing of the urban inhabitants themselves is a pressing problem. Thus, the growth of a private sector in domestic accommodation business has been apparently impeded by the shortage of business space.

In Suzhou, by 1987 there had been only 54 (1,140 beds) privately-owned guest houses in operation. And the share of the private sector has been even in decline since the late 1980s. The leading part in domestic accommodation supply in Suzhou was played by collective units, especially the so-called *dajiti danwei*, or big collective units (Tab. 7–5). From 1982 to 1985, 164 of the 205 newly established guest houses (or 74% of capacity) were owned by such big collective *danwei*.

---

[6]Compare Fig. 5–9.

The dominance of collectively-owned guest houses in Suzhou was attributable to two factors:

- First, collective ownership has a strong tradition in the local economy, which is one of the central elements of the so-called *Sunan Model*.[7]
- Second, plagued by pressing problems of under-employment in collective *danwei*, expansions of accommodation sector were regarded as one of the instruments in alleviating such employment problems.

In the case of Guilin, data on the source of growth in accommodation capacity are not existent. Nevertheless, one argument can be made. That is, neither the private sector nor the collective sector had played a big part in domestic accommodation supply in Guilin (Tab. 7-6).

**Table 7-6: Ownership of Domestic Accommodation Facilities in Guilin, Suzhou and Beidaihe, 1991**

|  | State | Collective | Private | Total |
|---|---|---|---|---|
| *Guilin* |  |  |  |  |
| Establishments | 188 | 136 | 120 | 444 |
| Beds ('000) | 24.7 | 13.6 | 2.8 | 41.1 |
| % | 60.0 | 33.1 | 6.8 | 100.0 |
| B/E[1] | 131 | 100 | 23 | 92 |
| *Suzhou* |  |  |  |  |
| Establishments | 75 | 223 | 48 | 346 |
| Beds ('000) | 9.6 | 16.1 | 1.0 | 26.8 |
| % | 35.8 | 60.2 | 4.0 | 100.0 |
| B/E[1] | 128 | 72 | 22 | 77 |
| *Beidaihe*[2] |  |  |  |  |
| Establishments | 57 | 78 | 704 | 839 |
| Beds ('000) | 7.3 | 9.7 | 20.1 | 37.2 |
| % | 19.8 | 26.0 | 54.2 | 100.0 |
| B/E[1] | 129 | 124 | 28 | 44 |

[1] Beds per establishment; [2] excluding *danwei* holiday quarters
Source: Author's field surveys, Statistical Bureau Guilin, Suzhou and Beidaihe.

---

[7]Since the early 1990s, the private sector has been playing an increasingly important role in *Sunan* area (the southern part of Jiangsu province). Cf. Cai and Chen 1992, pp. 14–15.

In 1987, 152 (3,000 beds) privately-owned guest houses were in operation in this place, accounting for 8% of the total capacity. And the share of the private sector tends to be also in decrease. Thus, in Guilin the state-owned guest houses were the major contributors to the expansions of accommodation services. In most cases, such guest houses resulted from restructuring of existing facilities of some SOEs, and are very low in standard.

It should be pointed out that, despite the low share of privately-owned facilities in Suzhou and Guilin, individual participation in accommodation supply is not insignificant. One of the recently widespread practices in these two places is the so-called *chenbao jinying*, or 'leasing' of collective- or state-owned guest houses to individual businessmen.

Author's field surveys suggest that a considerable part of publicly-owned, especially small collectively-owned guest houses have been run by individuals, explicitly or implicitly. Such individual private businessmen are usually the former workers of various *danwei* in question. They are responsible for the 'gains or losses' of such businesses, and committed to transfers to their *danwei* (owners of facilities) a fixed amount of returns which are defined on a negotiation basis. Such 'leasing' contracts have gained ground, as China's enterprise reform schemes encourage the 'separation of ownership from management'.

### 7.4.3 Restructuring Since the Late 1980s

Since the late 1980s, domestic accommodation facilities have been quantitatively in decrease in the study areas (Fig. 7–1, 2, 3). Such quantitative decrease, however, does not imply a decline of domestic tourism. Instead, it signs a structural change in the local tourist markets from both demand and supply sides.

On the supply side, it seems that by the late 1980s the expansions of domestic accommodation sector in Guilin, Suzhou and Beidaihe had arrived at a point where the capacity supply had quantitatively met the demand. Competitions among individual suppliers have thereafter become intensified. As a result, less competitive facilities, such as locationally-disadvantaged, simple and small guest houses, had to be closed down. Some relatively bigger facilities also began to change their functions partly. The People's Hotel in Suzhou, for instance, changed its 1st and 2nd floors into a department store in 1990.

Changes on the demand side have been also significant. It can be argued that during the mid–1980s the issue of standard and quality of accommodation services had hardly been taken into account by the supply or demand side. Since the late 1980s, however, as the standard of living of some Chinese began to rise, a growing part of domestic tourists have become unsatisfied with low-quality services. Guest houses with more than 4–6 beds in a room began to lose their competitiveness. Thus, improvement in facility and service soon became a necessity.

The responses of many guest houses to the new demand seemed quite prompt. A considerable part of accommodation facilities began to be renovated and modernized. The number of beds in a room became smaller, and more 'comforts' such as sanitary installations, color TV sets and the like are added. Thus, the need for improvement in service quality has led to a quantitative decline in capacity (beds).

In addition, two factors are responsible partly for the quantitative declines since the late 1980s, namely,

- first, the political incidents of 1989. Clearly, small privately-run firms were especially sensitive to changes in the political climate. In Beidaihe, about 100 small guest houses (860 beds) were closed down during 1989–1991. On the whole, the private accommodation sector in the study areas tends to be in decline after 1989;

- second, urban renovation programs have made some accommodation facilities disappeared. In Suzhou, local city planning bureau reported that, from 1985 to 1991, Suzhou's renovation projects involved some 40 guest houses (about 3,000 beds) in the inner city alone.

### 7.4.4 Ways of Functioning

The early commercialization and the substantial growth in the mid–1980s has given birth to a significantly expanded and diversified domestic accommodation sector in the study areas. With respect to its ways of functioning, the accommodation sector has both underdeveloped and transitional features. It is underdeveloped because modern marketing techniques find little applications in accommodation businesses. And, it is transitional because the issue of property rights of a large number of facilities remains unclear, and the accommodation services supplied by various *danwei* are not apparent in the markets.

Big domestic hotels of relatively higher standards usually have favorable locations, and their businesses seem rather lucrative. Though the market tends to play an increasing role in demand and supply of services in this category, active marketing remains seldom. It seems that, due to the buoyant demand for better services, big domestic hotels tend to feel less compelled than smaller ones in doing active marketing.

The way of management of *danwei* guest houses has changed a lot. Originally, they served principally visitors and travelers from counterpart *danwei* in the same administration spectrums. Today, nearly all domestic travelers know this part of services. However, they can hardly be noticed in the supply markets, because most of them are usually located 'inside' a '*danwei's* wall'.

On the whole, *danwei* guest houses are a major supplier of accommodation services for business travelers. Typically, business travelers always try first to find accommodation possibilities in their partner *danwei*, or even make some kind of reservations, especially in peak tourism seasons. In fact, travelers from government departments, social organizations, enterprises, and universities and research institutes can virtually always find their counterpart *danwei* in almost every part of the country, either 'vertically' or 'horizontally'.

Accommodation for travelers from higher administration levels is usually 'arranged' by their sub-branches. Travelers from a certain administration spectrum of a province, say, a municipality-level 'economic research center', can always find their counterparts in other provinces either at the same, or at a higher or lower level. In this way, *danwei* guest houses interweave closely with each other. They have in effect developed a sort of business networking via the intricate administrative systems, instead of an intermediate market.

Small collective *lüshe and kezhan* guest houses are traditionally open to all domestic travelers. In contrast to *danwei* guest houses, *lüshe and kezhan* often appear apparently to individual travelers, because they occasionally do certain 'advertising', however primitive. In an effort to demonstrate their existence, a commonplace of small guest houses in doing 'advertisement' is to hang plates carrying their names and indicating their locations (or simply writing on a wall) along main streets or at places where travelers pass by or visit.

As in many other Chinese cities, a widespread practice of 'active' advertising has become increasingly observable in the study areas. That is, 'recruiting' of guests directly at major transportation stations. Such practices originate from the initiatives of 'active marketing' of some private guest houses which aimed at raising their market shares.

As some guest houses achieved sizable pay-offs, such activities have become popular since the mid–1980s. Today, this kind of practice involves not only private guest houses, but a number of collective- and state-owned but privately-run guest houses, especially those with disadvantaged locations. It works approximately in following ways.

A *lüshe or kezhan* guest house hires one or two salesmen or women to recruit guests at transportation stations. Such salesmen or women in turn get certain fixed amount of 'commissions' for each 'recruited' guest, staging the role of a market intermediary, though primitive. In many cases, such intermediaries are temporary job-seekers from rural areas. They tend to have the gift of the gab in persuading travelers to stay at 'their' guest houses by emphasizing their accessibility or their services in booking train tickets.

Obviously, promises to provide tickets for return or further trips are especially attractive to many travelers, especially those who have neither local contacts nor good knowledge of the city. In addition, free-of-charge transportation from railway stations to guest houses is often provided.

It seems that such a way of direct meeting of supply and demand sides usually works smoothly. However, conflicts arise when 'intolerable' cheating practices appear. This involves big words or partial information about the accessibility and/or the quality of services of guest houses, big differences in price asked before and after arriving at guest houses and so on. Conflicts also arise when guest houses break their words to take care of a guest's tickets, etc.

# Part IV

# Economic Effects

# 8

# Tourism Revenues and Their Distribution

As discussed in section 2.4, the prime motive of tourism promotion at both national and local levels is to earn foreign exchange. Up to now, most discussions on the economic effects of tourism in China have confined to gross foreign exchange receipts and their contributions to the 'balance-of-payments' at the national level.[1] This chapter tries to explore the growth and structure of tourism revenues, and identify those factors which are decisive in determining the local shares of tourism revenues.

## 8.1 The Growth of Foreign Exchange Receipts

Due to the significant expansions of international tourism, Guilin and Suzhou have achieved a substantial growth in foreign exchange receipts over the past decade. From 1980 to 1993, gross foreign exchange receipts increased from 13.9 to 80.7 million US$ in Guilin, and from 9.4 to 37.4 million US$ in Suzhou (Fig. 8–1). Taking the period of 1980–93 as a whole, tourism receipts grew at an average rate of 13.4% per annum in Guilin and 10.4% in Suzhou, while international tourist arrivals at 10.4% and 11.2% in Guilin and Suzhou respectively.[2]

Foreign exchange receipts are not the entire revenues of international tourism. At the local level, revenues generated by international

---

[1]Qui et al. 1990, pp. 21–27; Zheng 1990, pp. 78–90.

[2]In the same period, the national average growth rate of tourism receipts was 15.6%, and tourist arrivals 15.2%. NTA 1994, p. 30 and p. 118.

tourism are reported in both FEC and RMB yuan. In Guilin, the share of FEC receipts in total revenues declined from 70% in 1980 to 61% in 1992.[3] Non-FEC revenues have two major sources.

The first source is the expenditure of domestic travelers received by international hotels and other international tourist service sectors. The second source is the expenditure of international tourists (especially *compatriots*) paid in RMB yuan at hotels, tourist shops and so on. The yuan payments of international tourists, who exchange foreign currency with relatives or friends (in the case of *compatriots*) or through local 'black' markets, are one of the principal 'loopholes' of foreign exchange leakage in China.[4] Officially, FEC was expired in 1994.

### Figure 8–1: The Growth of Foreign Exchange Receipts Guilin and Suzhou, 1980–1993

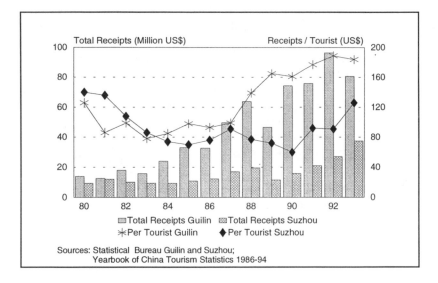

Sources: Statistical Bureau Guilin and Suzhou;
Yearbook of China Tourism Statistics 1986-94

### 8.1.1 Yuan-based Price System and Its Consequences

The major source of growth in foreign exchange receipts before and after the mid–1980s is different. On the whole, the growth of tourism receipts in the first half of the 1980s was quantitative in nature. That

---

[3]GLTN 1993, p. 258.
[4]Cf. Wei 1988, pp. 93–94.

is to say, such growth resulted primarily from a faster increase in tourist arrivals. From 1980 to 1986, while international tourist arrivals grew at an average rate of 18.2% per annum in Guilin and 13.3% in Suzhou, tourism receipts increased at a much lower rate of 13.0% and 3.9% respectively.

In Suzhou, total tourism revenues were stagnant in the first half of the 1980s. Average receipts per tourist dropped sharply from 140 US$ in 1980 to 76 US$ in 1986. The root cause of such drops was the remarkable declines in dollar receipts per tourist on local souvenir goods, which were the most important source of all tourism revenues.[5] In Guilin, despite of the growth in total revenues, average receipts per tourist first declined from 126 US$ in 1980 to 78 US$ in 1983, and then stagnated. Besides the declines in average length of stay, two major factors were responsible for the drops/stagnation in average receipts per tourist: (1) the continuing devaluation of domestic currency RMB yuan,[6] and (2) the deficient price system in international tourism sector.

The pricing system of international tourist service prior to 1987 was problematic. Though RMB yuan was (and still is) not a freely convertible currency, tourist service prices at the enterprise level were quoted in domestic currency in the period prior to 1987. As a matter of fact, the yuan price of packaged tour services had been raised nearly every year since 1980. However, due to continuing devaluation of RMB yuan, the dollar price of packaged tour services had de facto declined in the first half of the 1980s.

From 1980 to 1986, the national average of packaged service price per tourist per day, excluding inter-city transportation fees, had climbed from 65 to 104 RMB yuan (or an increase of 60%), but its dollar price dropped from 43 to 28 US$, or a decrease of 35%.[7] Inter-city transportation fees were raised first in February 1986 by 54–78% on five busiest routines.[8]

The net outcome of this problematic price calculation method was a remarkable decline in dollar receipts per tourist, as was documented in Guilin and Suzhou. It seems that, at both national and local levels, the focus of tourism promotion in these early years was merely on getting more tourists to come to the country or to their cities, rather

---

[5] Compare section 8.2.

[6] From 1980 to 1986, RMB yuan was devalued from 1 US$:1.49 yuan to 1 US$:3.70 yuan. Li 1991, p. 49.

[7] Li 1991, pp. 47–51; Ma 1991, pp. 42–44.

[8] This round of price increase on other routines followed in April 1987, but at a lower rate of 30%. Ma 1988, p. 43.

than increasing tourist expenditure, let alone maximizing net returns. Pursuit of sales maximization (albeit in an incomplete fashion) had led to the focal concerns on the growth of gross tourism revenues, which had concealed the problem of declining tourism revenues in real terms.

### 8.1.2   Dollar-based Price System and Its Effects

A decisive step in price reforms in the tourism sector was taken in 1987. The kernel element of this reform scheme is a floating price system which is based on the official exchange rates between dollar and RMB yuan.[9] Since then, tourist service prices at the enterprise level have been quoted in both yuan and US$. And, the yuan prices are floating up- or downward in pace with changes in official exchange rates. Thus, the effects of further devaluation of RMB yuan in the following years have been offset fully by proportional increases in yuan prices.

Furthermore, soaring inflation and unfolding reforms in areas such as banking, taxation, and wages and salaries have exerted substantial upward pressures on tourism supply costs in the second half of the 1980s. Recent studies have shown that at the national level the increases in tourist service price have surpassed the pace of yuan devaluation since the mid–1980s.[10]

The effects of this dollar-based price system and the price-raising measures turned out to be substantial in Guilin. From 1986 to 1993, Guilin achieved a much higher growth rate of tourism receipts (11.9% per annum) than tourist arrivals (2.6%), leading to an increase in average receipts per tourist to 184 US$. The slight decline in average receipts per tourist in 1990 appeared to be the result of price concessions made after the political incidents. Since the average length of stay of international tourists in Guilin remained in decline, or from 2.5 days in 1986 to 2.1 days in 1993, it can be concluded that the growth of gross tourism revenues and the increase in average receipts per tourist since 1987 have resulted principally from the price increases.

In Suzhou, the growth of foreign exchange receipts takes a different picture. From 1986 to 1993, the average length of stay of international tourists in Suzhou increased slightly from 1.2 to 1.4 days.[11]

---

[9]This price reform scheme was called *baozhi cuoshi* (value maintenance measures).

[10]Li 1991, pp. 47–51; Ma 1991, pp. 41–44; Wang and Shen 1990, pp. 73–76, Sun 1991, p. 66; Wang 1991, p. 51.

[11]Compare Tab. 4–2.

In the same period, the growth of gross tourism receipts (14.9% per annum) was faster than that of tourist arrivals (7.9% per annum). However, the average receipts per tourist (126 US$ in 1993) had not reached the 1980–level. Two factors seem responsible for such an undesirable performance.

First, the significant shifts in the composition of tourist arrivals. As discussed in section 4.2, Suzhou had seen a rapidly rising market share of *compatriots* in the second half of the 1980s. Local travel agencies in Suzhou estimated that, in general, the average spending power of *compatriots* on local services and goods is much lower than that of foreign tourists.[12]

Thus, while the new pricing system tended to push the curve of average receipts upward in 1987, such effects had been offset by the declining average expenditure per tourist in the following years. First since 1991, average receipts per tourist have been on the increase, which seems attributable to the recovery of foreign tourist arrivals. It is noteworthy that in Guilin the effects of the shifts in tourist market compositions on the average receipts per tourist seemed insignificant, because tourist spending on local goods makes up only a very small fraction of total expenditure.

The second explanatory factor is the extremely low share of inter-city transportation receipts. China's air transport remains a seller's market. Since the mid–1980s, the price increases in air transport have outpaced the devaluation of RMB yuan. In 1989, while RMB yuan was devalued by 21%, air transportation fees increased by nearly 30%.[13] However, such price-raising measures had no effects on the average receipts per tourist in Suzhou, since inter-city transportation of international tourists to this place depends exclusively on railroad. And inter-city transportation receipts makes up only 3–4% of all tourism revenues.

Thus, since the mid–1980s, Guilin has achieved a much higher growth rate of tourism receipts (compared to tourist arrivals), and a much higher level of average receipts per tourist than Suzhou. However, this does not necessarily imply that international tourism has yielded proportionally larger returns to the local economy in Guilin than in Suzhou. Determining the local share of tourism revenues requires an analysis of the structure of tourism receipts.

---

[12]This seems also true of the national average. Cf. Liu et al 1990, pp. 35–38; Lew 1995, p. 166.

[13]Wang et al. 1990, p. 75; Li 1991, p. 49.

## 8.2 Local Shares of Foreign Exchange Receipts

The question whether tourism industry has yielded sufficient economic returns commensurate with the considerable inputs of development resources at the local level has to date received little attentions. Obviously, from the local standpoint, a mere emphasis on gross returns without structural analysis is insufficient and often misleading. Unfortunately, most local tourism planners have hardly asked: to what extent have their local economies benefited from hitherto tourism development?

The paucity of previous approaches to the distributional issues of tourism receipts seems attributable to two major factors. First, subject to the priorities of national goals, local claims on foreign exchange revenues tend to get marginalized. Second, to make a clear differentiation of local revenues from total tourism receipts is difficult. Apparently, in a country in which the state sector remains the dominant owner of key tourism infrastructure and service sectors, it is rather vague what part of tourism receipts is 'local'.

### 8.2.1 Ownership Structure and Revenue Distribution

In the light of China's industrial legislation, international tourism is a component of the country's export sector. With respect to the distribution of foreign exchange revenues, enterprises engaged in international tourism enjoy favorable treatments as those producing export goods.

In an effect to stimulate local initiatives in promoting international tourism, a contract regarding the central-local sharing of foreign exchange receipts was made in 1979. According to the revenue-contract, all local enterprises engaged in international tourism were legitimated to retain 30–50% of foreign exchange revenues they generated. In 1980, this share was fixed at a uniform rate of 40%.[14] Since then, it remains unchanged. Because such a contract applies equally to Guilin and Suzhou, the key factor affecting the local share of foreign exchange revenues is the structure of tourism enterprises. At the local level, tourism enterprises consist of three parts:

1. big SOEs run by the central government (or provincial governments), especially in the transportation and communications sectors;
2. joint-ventures in the hotel sector, and
3. local enterprises.

---

[14]Chi 1993, pp. 14–15.

Local tourism enterprises include locally-run SOEs, collectively-owned enterprises, and small private firms. According to author's fieldwork, the foreign exchange revenues received by small collective and private firms, which are engaged principally in souvenir trading and local transportation, have not been included in official statistics (Tab. 8–1).

### Table 8–1: Ownership Structure and Distribution of Foreign Exchange Receipts

| Distribution of Foreign Exchange | Ownership of Tourism Firms | | |
|---|---|---|---|
| Total Receipts | | SOEs | Non-SOEs |
| - Revenues of Central SOEs | -----> | Central Government | |
| - Revenues of Provincial SOEs | ----> | Provincial Governments | |
| - Part of the Revenues of Joint-ventures | ---> | | Foreigners |
| 40% of the Revenues of Local Firms | --> | Local Governments | Small Collective |
| | | | Private |

Though we do not have precise information on the ownership structure of tourism enterprises in Guilin and Suzhou, the structure of tourism receipts provides some insights into the distributional patterns of foreign exchange revenues between local and non-local economies (Tab. 8–2).

Obviously, the foreign exchange receipts generated by inter-city transportation (air and railroad) and communications sectors do not constitute the source of local revenues. They are the revenues to the public sector run directly by the central government. Thus, a rough differentiation between central and non-central revenues leads to a totally different picture in Guilin and Suzhou. In 1991, nearly 49% of all foreign exchange receipts in Guilin were generated by the transportation and communications sectors. They were definitely not the local revenues of Guilin. This central-revenue share was about 6% in Suzhou. In absolute terms, while international tourism yielded nearly twice as much receipts per tourist in Guilin (176 US$) as in Suzhou (92 US$), there were practically no differences in non-central receipts per tourist.

## Table 8-2: The Structure of Foreign Exchange Receipts in Guilin and Suzhou, 1991

|  | US$ per Tourist | | % | |
|---|---|---|---|---|
|  | Guilin | Suzhou | Guilin | Suzhou |
| Total | 176 | 92 | 100.0 | 100.0 |
|  |  |  |  |  |
| Goods | 26.9 | 50.0 | 15.3 | 54.3 |
| Shopping | 12.3 | 37.1 | 7.0 | 40.3 |
| Food | 14.6 | 12.9 | 8.3 | 14.0 |
|  |  |  |  |  |
| Services | 149.0 | 42.0 | 84.7 | 45.7 |
| Accommodation | 41.0 | 19.0 | 23.3 | 20.7 |
| Transport & Communi- |  |  |  |  |
| cations | 85.5 | 5.3 | 48.6 | 5.8 |
| Local services[1] | 22.5 | 17.7 | 12.8 | 19.2 |
| Non-Central Revenues[2] | 90.5 | 86.7 | 51.4 | 94.2 |

[1] Including travel agencies; [2] all receipts minus the revenues generated by transportation and communications sectors
Sources: Statistical Bureau Guilin and Suzhou.

Of course, non-central revenues are not equal to local revenues. Non-local revenues outside transportation and communications sectors may arise from the participation of non-local domestic investors (e.g. provincial-level governments), and the participation of foreign investors. Author's field surveys have come to the conclusion that the participation of provincial-level governments and enterprises in Guilin and Suzhou's tourism industry is insignificant. Thus, the major source of erosions to local foreign exchange revenues is FDI in the hotel sector. This is particularly apparent in Guilin.

### 8.2.2 FDI and Leakage of Tourism Revenues in Guilin

As discussed in section 6.2, FDI in Guilin's hotel sector is huge, and its later-on costs too. According to the estimates made by the Tourism Bureau of Guilin, in recent years about 90% of all foreign exchange revenues received by the hotel sector in Guilin were generated by joint-venture hotels.[15]

---

[15]In 1992, joint-venture hotels made up 62.6% of all capacity (beds) in Guilin (compare section 6.2). In the same year, 476 joint-venture hotels made up 25.2%

China's joint-venture corporations legislation stipulates that foreign capital should constitute at least 25% of a joint-venture's registered capital. In total hotel investments, domestic and foreign shares should be kept at 51% to 49%. Domestic and foreign investors should share profits or losses according to this ratio.

In the case of Guilin, the real shares of FDI in most joint-venture hotel projects tend to be lower than the legislation requirements.[16] Nevertheless, the degree of erosions of foreign exchange receipts to Guilin's hotel sector is astonishing. According to the information provided by the Tourism Bureau of Guilin, in the early 1990s about 80% of all foreign exchange receipts generated by joint-venture hotels in Guilin were not local revenues.

Thus, it can be concluded that in 1991 only about 30–35% of all foreign exchange receipts were the revenues of the locally-run tourism enterprises of Guilin, or about 50 US$ per tourist.[17] Taking into account the 40 percent-contract, the benefits of foreign exchange revenues distributed directly to the local economy of Guilin is anything but encouraging.

Since the early 1980s, the local government of Guilin has set out almost entirely on the international tourism industry. The local government has taken an active part not only in infrastructure investment, but directly in international tourism businesses via Guilin's tourism bureau. One of its major objectives is to earn hard currency too. The major source of foreign exchange revenues to the local government is the revenues from operation of locally-run SOEs as well as public utilities.

The largest part of local government's participation is in international hotel businesses. Besides locally-run state-owned hotels, the local government has acted as the domestic investors in many joint-venture projects. However, due to the existence problems of most state-owned hotels and the aforementioned serious leakage of tourism receipts in joint-venture hotel sector, the returns of foreign exchange receipts to the local government seem negligible.

Other sources of revenues are government taxation. In China, there is a bewildering array of taxes. Some are highly visible and in the form of state legislation, while others are invisible and, in many

---

of all capacity (beds), and generated over 73% of all foreign exchange receipts in China's entire hotel sector. NTA 1993, p. 104.

[16] Cf. Meng 1992, pp. 7–12.

[17] According to local estimates, this rate was 27.2% in 1988, and only 16% in 1990. Lan et al 1990, p. 251; Tan 1991, p. 44.

cases, only locally-raised. Local government can, for instance, levy surcharges, various fees and fines on tourism enterprises. However, several factors tend to make tax revenues insignificant.[18]

Take income tax on hotel enterprises for instance. Income tax is levied on enterprise profits. Besides tax frauds and evasions, two factors lead to a diminishing tax base in Guilin's hotel industry. First, in the joint-venture hotel sector, exemptions or greatly reduced rates of income tax apply. Second, similar to the deficit-ridden state enterprises in other sectors, a large part of locally-run SOEs in Guilin are loss-making in recent years. Thus, both enterprise revenues and tax yields to the local government are *prima facie* negligible.

Even taking into account all tourism revenues including non-FEC receipts, such a discouraging picture remains unchanged. According to local estimates, in 1990 the international tourism sector of Guilin yielded 13.5 million yuan (including non-FEC receipts) to the local budgetary revenues, accounting for only 2% of total tourism revenues.[19] In this sense, much of the local efforts in pursuit of local development by using large-size FDI seems self-defeating.

### 8.2.3 Enterprise Structure and Souvenir Trading in Suzhou

The structure of the international tourism industry in Suzhou favors its local economy in two ways. First, till the early 1990s, the penetration of international hotel groups in Suzhou had been kept moderate, with joint-venture hotels making up about 26% of all capacity.[20] Two joint-venture hotels just began getting into businesses. Most importantly, Suzhou has several domestically-invested high-standard hotels such as Suzhou, Gusu and Nanlin hotels, which are in good financial shape.

According to the estimates made by the Tourism Bureau of Suzhou, in 1991 the foreign exchange receipts generated by joint-venture hotels accounted for no more than 35% of all hotel revenues, of which about 60% were non-local receipts. Thus, in 1991 about 90% of all foreign exchange receipts were the revenues of locally-owned enterprises, resulting in a higher level of local receipts per tourist in Suzhou (about 80 US$) than in Guilin (about 50 US$).

---

[18]Tax revenues collected at the local level are of course not local tax receipts. During 1984–1992, there were tax-contracts between various administration levels. Since 1993, a new tax code, i.e. tax-sharing between central and local governments, has been implemented. Cf. Yusuf 1994, p. 75.

[19]Tan 1991, p. 44.

[20]Compare section 6.2.

Second, Suzhou has a prosperous souvenir production and trading sector. Over the past decade, souvenir trading remains the largest single contributor of foreign exchange revenues in Suzhou's tourism sector. During 1981–1988, around 50% of all foreign exchange receipts were generated by souvenir trading (Fig. 8–2). Much bigger receipts from souvenir trading explain a large part why in the early 1980s the level of average receipts per tourist was even higher in Suzhou than in Guilin, although in the latter case tourism receipts encompassed a much bigger inter-city transportation revenues, and international tourists stayed there longer.

**Figure 8–2: The Contribution of Souvenir Trading to Local Tourism Revenues in Suzhou and Guilin, 1980–1992**

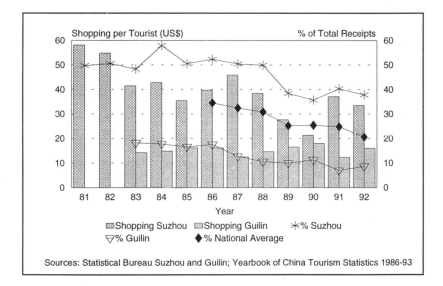

Sources: Statistical Bureau Suzhou and Guilin; Yearbook of China Tourism Statistics 1986-93

Though the share of receipts from tourist shopping has declined remarkably since the late 1980s, still in 1991 the expenditure per tourist on shopping in Suzhou (37 US$) was 3 times as much as in Guilin (12 US$). Furthermore, author's field surveys suggest that, in Suzhou, not only are souvenir trading firms locally owned, but the overwhelming part of souvenir goods are locally produced. The widely differing capacity of local participation in such an economic sector as souvenir production and trading depends largely on the local production traditions, tourism development strategies as well as overall development stages of the local economies.[21]

## 8.3   Domestic Tourism Revenues

### 8.3.1   Size and Structure

(1) Estimating the Size
Information about domestic tourism receipts in the study area is non-existent. Clearly, the average expenditure of domestic tourists is moderate in nature, and differs significantly from one demand group to another. Nevertheless, the information about the national average of tourist expenditure, however incomplete, gives us some rough ideas about the economic effects of domestic tourism in the study areas.

Investigations have shown that, at the national level, the average expenditure per tourist per day lay in the range of 10–20 yuan in 1985, and 60–100 yuan in 1992.[22] According to the reports delivered by the NTA, average receipts per tourist rose from 33 yuan in 1985 to 75 yuan in 1992, then jumped to 211 yuan in 1993 (Tab. 8–3).

**Table 8–3: National Average of Travel Expenditure per Tourist, 1985–1993**

| Year | Yuan per Tourist |
|------|------------------|
| 1985 | 33.3 |
| 1986 | 39.3 |
| 1987 | 48.3 |
| 1988 | 62.3 |
| 1989 | 62.5 |
| 1990 | 60.7 |
| 1991 | 66.7 |
| 1992 | 75.8 |
| 1993 | 210.7 |

Sources: Various reports of the NTA; NTA 1994, p. 9.

Though high inflation is a significant explanatory factor to the rapid increase in tourist expenditure, such a big difference in average spending per tourist from 1992 to 1993 may have resulted from different calculation methods.

---

[21] Compare section 9.3.
[22] Zhen 1993, p. 3.

Author's field surveys suggest that the pre–1993 figures approach approximately the level of average spending per tourist including all one-day visitors. According to the limited survey data provided by the Tourism Bureau of Beidaihe, the average expenditure per tourist (including one-day visitors) in this place was 65, 70 and 85 yuan in 1990, 1991 and 1992 respectively. In other words, it is most likely that at the national level the pre–1993 data had been produced on the basis of all visitors including one-day travelers, while the 1993 figure only those tourists who stayed in destination areas more than one day.

At the local level, three factors are most decisive in determining the size of domestic tourism revenues a destination area can receive, namely, (1) the type and size of domestic tourism, (2) the demand structure and, (3) the range of tourist services and goods a destination area can provide.

In general, it can be argued that the average spending of domestic visitors in the study areas should not be lower than the national average. This is because:

1. Guilin is a most famous tourist city in the country, and the share of inter-regional domestic tourists who stay in destination areas more than one day is much higher in Guilin than in most other areas;
2. in Suzhou, though one-day visitors make up the largest part of all tourist demand, tourist spending on various goods provided by the local market appears large;
3. in Beidaihe, a considerable part of holiday-makers stay there several days, and make intensive use of local tourist services.[23]

Based on these observations, some rough estimates can be made about the revenues generated by domestic tourism in the study areas (Tab. 8–4). Obviously, due to the immense number of domestic visitors, domestic tourism revenues received by Guilin, Suzhou and Beidaihe are huge. In the early 1990s, domestic tourism generated 400–450 million yuan revenues per annum in Guilin, 300–330 million yuan in Suzhou, and 300–360 million yuan in Beidaihe.

Three further notes should be made regarding the estimated size of domestic tourism revenues in the study areas:

- first, because of the very high share of inter-regional tourists and, especially, 'handsome' meeting and business travelers in

---

[23]For discussions on the features of domestic tourism in the study areas, see chapter 5.

Guilin, the revenues generated by domestic tourism in this place tend to be still larger;

- second, taking into account the average inflation rates approaching double-digit levels from after 1985, the increases of tourism revenues in real terms seemed insignificant;[24]

- third, due to such factors as different purchasing powers and the devaluation of domestic currency, comparisons of the size and growth of revenues between domestic and international tourism can be made only in a qualified sense.

**Table 8–4: Domestic Tourism Revenues in Guilin, Suzhou and Beidaihe (Million Yuan), 1985–1991**

| Year | Guilin | Suzhou | Beidaihe |
|------|--------|--------|----------|
| 1985 | 153 | 210 | 133 |
| 1986 | 197 | 275 | 142 |
| 1987 | 261 | 314 | 193 |
| 1988 | 392 | 360 | 312 |
| 1989 | 312 | 300 | 250 |
| 1990 | 395 | 333 | 364 |
| 1991 | 454 | 334 | 300 |

Sources: Author's estimates based on the national average of receipts per tourist.

(2) Structure

Compared to foreign exchange receipts, the most important aspect of domestic tourism revenues is their contributions to the local economies of the destination areas. As discussed in the preceding sections, international tourism tends to in the first place serve the national goals, i.e. pursuit of balance-of-payments objectives. On the contrary, domestic tourism appears to be much more friendly to the local economies.

Rough information about the expenditure structure at both national and local levels shows that the largest part of domestic tourism revenues tend to be distributed directly to the locally-owned tourist enterprises (Tab. 8–5). Similar to foreign exchange receipts, domestic tourist expenditure on inter-regional transportation (20–28%) belongs to the revenues of SOEs run by the central government.

---

[24] For discussions of the macro performance of the Chinese economy in the post-reform period, see Yusuf 1994, pp. 71–92; Perkins 1994, pp. 23–46.

## Table 8–5: The Structure of Domestic Tourist Spending

| | Beidaihe | | | National Average[1] |
|---|---|---|---|---|
| | 1990 | 1991 | 1992 | 1993 |
| Expenditure per tourist in yuan[2] | 343 | 354 | 593 | 445 |
| % | 100.0 | 100.0 | 100.0 | 100.0 |
| Transport | 22.7 | 22.6 | 20.4 | 28.2 |
| Accommodation | 8.4 | 21.2 | 18.0 | 18.3 |
| Food | 22.4 | 14.1 | 18.2 | 18.3 |
| Shopping | 27.1 | 25.4 | 16.4 | 19.4 |
| Others[3] | 19.4 | 16.7 | 27.0 | 15.8 |

[1] Urban tourists; [2] excluding one-day visitors; [3] spending on park visits, local transportation, entertainment, etc.
Sources: Tourism Bureau Beidaihe; NTA 1994, p.9.

On the other hand, however, nearly all tourist services in accommodation, catering, retail sales and local transportation sectors are provided by locally-run enterprises. In these service sectors, many local small private firms play a big part. In general, it can be concluded that about 70% to 80% of all domestic tourism receipts tend to constitute the source of revenues of the local economies in Guilin, Suzhou and Beidaihe.

### 8.3.2 Distributional Effects

Domestic tourism affects the national economy in a number of ways. At the national level, the role of domestic tourism in withdrawing a certain amount of over-supplied domestic currency from circulation has been recognized since the mid–1980s. This is also one of the major motives of the central government's liberal policy toward domestic tourism.

In the course of economic reforms, the accumulative surplus of purchasing power of the Chinese households has risen enormously. From 1980 to 1992, the total household savings had grown from 39.9 billion yuan to 1,154.5 billion yuan.[25] Domestic savings have become the major source of capital accumulation in China's post-reform period.[26] On the other hand, however, such an ever-growing surplus

---

[25] ZTN 1993, p. 285. Cf. Chen 1992, pp. 68–73; ZNZD 1992, pp. 176–83; ZNJFB 1992, pp. 59–80.
[26] Yusuf 1994, p. 80–81.

may under certain circumstances lead to instabilities of the Chinese economy, such as panic buying and its upward pressures on inflation rates in the second half of the 1980s.[27] As a new area of consumption, domestic tourism has thus been considered to be of certain significance in easing pressures on domestic consumer markets.[28]

Domestic tourism has also re-distributional effects on the national economy. Inter-regional transfer of purchasing power brought about by tourist flows is a case in place. From the standpoint of local economies, the influx of a large number of domestic tourists can expand the local consumer markets of a destination area to a significant extent. In Guilin, in 1992 domestic tourist expenditure made up more than 27% of all realized purchasing power (gross retail sales) in its local consumer markets.[29]

Though we do not have firm figures about the structure of gross retail sales in Beidaihe and Suzhou, two arguments can be made.

- First, such re-distributional effects tend to be more significant in Beidaihe, since the ratio between tourists and local residential population in this place is much higher.

- Second, in the case of Suzhou, because of the stronger purchasing power and larger base of local population, such effects seem less apparent in percentage. Nevertheless, due to high tourist expenditure on local souvenir products as well as on non-tourist consumer goods, the role of domestic tourism in expanding local consumer markets in Suzhou should not be underestimated.

With respect to the role of domestic tourism in inter-regional transfers of national income, two issues are noteworthy:

- First, the out-flows of purchasing power from the study areas to other destinations should be taken into account. The issue of balance of domestic travel expenditure appears to be of particular importance in a wealthy area like Suzhou, since the travel demand of the inhabitants from Suzhou to other parts of the country is comparatively larger.

- Second, domestic tourism revenues which resulted from inter-regional transfers of national income are not the net revenues of the local economies of the study areas. To what extent the

---

[27] Chen 1992, pp. 114–17; Yusuf 1994, pp. 86–88.

[28] See Chapter 2, footnote 16. Cf. Tang 1990, pp. 149–151; Zhen 1993, p. 3.

[29] In 1992 the spending of international tourists accounted for 9% of the realized purchasing power in Guilin. GLTN 1993, p. 256.

study areas can really benefit from such expanded consumer demand depends on the capacity of their local economies in supplying local tourist goods and services. In this respect, Suzhou tends to enjoy much more favorable conditions than Guilin and Beidaihe. Obviously, a better understanding about the size and nature of multiplier effects of tourist expenditure in a destination requires a wider range of information on the inter-sectoral linkages within its local economy. This area would justify more research attentions.

# 9

# Tourism Employment and Its Role in Local Labor Markets

In tourism literature, it is generally held that the most obvious and immediate benefit of tourism development is job creation and, thus, the opportunities for people in affected areas to increase their income and standard of living. Yet, scholars are divided regarding three important issues of tourism employment effects, namely, the quantitative significance of tourism employment, the quality of tourism jobs offered to the indigenous, and the capital/labor ratio of tourism jobs.[1]

Information about the size and nature of tourism employment in Guilin, Suzhou and Beidaihe is scant. Statistics on direct employment in hotels, though the best available, are incomplete, with information becoming increasingly sketchy on direct employment outside hotels, indirect employment, and tourism investment-induced employment. This chapter attempts to provide some empirical findings about the role of tourism employment in local labor markets in the study areas.

## 9.1 Direct Tourism Employment

### 9.1.1 The Size

Official statistics on tourism-generated employment in the study areas cover only the international tourism sector. From 1982 to 1993,

---

[1]Cf. Bryden 1973, 71–82; Kadt 1979, pp. 35–44; Gormsen 1983, pp. 608–17; Müller 1983, pp. 89–97; Höfels 1990, pp. 21–26; Vorlaufer 1990, p. 12; Harrison 1992, pp. 14–17 and 24–26.

the number of employees in international tourism rose from 2,700 to 11,700 in Guilin, and from 1,400 to 7,300 in Suzhou (Fig. 9–1). During 1985–1991, international tourism contributed 35% and 15% of all new employment in the urban tertiary sectors of Guilin and Suzhou respectively.[2]

## Figure 9–1: Employment in International Tourism in Guilin and Suzhou, 1982–1993

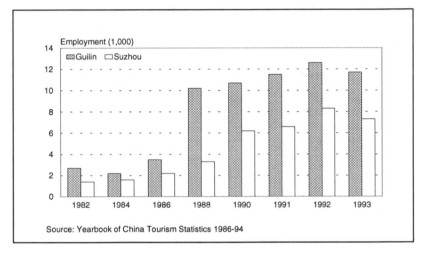

Source: Yearbook of China Tourism Statistics 1986-94

Certainly, such data tell only part of the story of employment in tourism. Statistics at the national level, however incomplete, show that the employment effects of domestic tourism are of even greater significance. In 1993, China's entire tourism industry employed 2.4 million people, of which 0.87 million in international tourism, accounting for 35% of the total.[3]

Unfortunately, even rough employment data covering the entire tourism sector are non-existent in Guilin, Suzhou and Beidaihe. Therefore, the analysis of tourism employment effects at the local level has to restore to direct field surveys. In this study, direct tourism employment includes jobs in those sectors that sell goods and services

---

[2]SZTN 1992, pp. 250–251; GLTN 1992, pp. 274–275. For data on employment in China's urban tertiary sector, see ZCFS 1990, pp. 142–143.
[3]NTA 1994, pp. 108–110.

directly to tourists. Hotels, restaurants, tourist transportation, souvenir trading, and other tourism-specific service sectors are the major surveyed areas.

Apparently, the size and nature of tourism employment depends not only on tourism-specific factors such as the stage and type of tourism development, but also on area-specific factors such as the linkages between tourism and other local economic sectors as well as stage of local economic development. Due to its rapid expansions over the past decade, tourism industry has created a considerable number of jobs for the local labor markets in the study areas.

According to author's field surveys, till 1991 direct tourism activities had generated about 35,100 jobs in Guilin, 24,300 in Suzhou, and 13,200 in Beidaihe (Tab. 9–1). Though differentiation of employment effects between international and domestic tourism can be made only in a qualified sense, it seems that the international tourism sector has contributed no more than one-third of all direct tourism employment in Guilin and Suzhou, while its contribution in Beidaihe is negligible.

## Table 9–1: Direct Tourism Employment in Guilin, Suzhou and Beidaihe, 1991

|  | Guilin | | Suzhou | | Beidaihe | |
|---|---|---|---|---|---|---|
|  | 1,000 | % | 1,000 | % | 1,000 | % |
| Total | 35.1 | 100.0 | 24.3 | 100.0 | 13.2 | 100.0 |
| Accommodation | 19.4 | 55.3 | 6.5 | 26.8 | 9.3 | 70.5 |
| Catering | 4.6 | 13.1 | 6.2 | 25.5 | 1.2 | 9.1 |
| Tourist Transport[1] | 3.0 | 8.5 | 1.3 | 5.3 | 0.5 | 3.8 |
| Tourist Shops[2] | 4.8 | 13.7 | 6.8 | 28.0 | 1.0 | 7.6 |
| Travel Agency & Service | 1.8 | 5.1 | 1.0 | 4.1 | 0.2 | 1.5 |
| Parks & Gardens | 1.1 | 3.1 | 2.0 | 8.2 | 0.2 | 1.5 |
| Others[3] | 0.4 | 1.1 | 0.5 | 2.1 | 0.8 | 6.1 |

[1] Tourist boats & vehicles;
[2] souvenir and film shops, etc.;
[3] administration, photography, bicycle renting, air mattress renting (Beidaihe), etc.
Source: Author's field surveys; Statistical Bureau of Guilin, Suzhou and Beidaihe.

## 9.1.2 The Structure

In all of the study areas, the top-three employment-generating sectors are hotels, restaurants, and souvenir trading. In 1991, they made up about 82% of all direct tourism employment in Guilin, 80% in Suzhou, and 87% in Beidaihe. However, the role of individual sectors in job creation differs widely from one place to another.

**Table 9–2: Employment Effects Generated by Different Types of Accommodation Facilities in Guilin, Suzhou and Beidaihe, 1991**

|  | Employment | | Jobs / Hotel | Job / Bed |
|---|---|---|---|---|
|  | 1,000 | % |  |  |
| *Guilin* |  |  |  |  |
| Total | 19.4 | 100.0 | 41 | 0.36 |
| International | 9.5 | 49.0 | 328 | 0.78 |
| 3-4 star | 1.4 | 38.1 | 490 | 0.84 |
| 1-2 star | 1.7 | 8.8 | 154 | 0.65 |
| Non-star | 0.4 | 2.1 | 140 | 0.60 |
| Domestic | 9.9 | 51.0 | 22 | 0.24 |
| Hotels | 5.6 | 28.8 | 61 | 0.30 |
| Guest houses[1] | 4.3 | 22.0 | 12 | 0.19 |
| *Suzhou* |  |  |  |  |
| Total | 6.5 | 100.0 | 18 | 0.21 |
| International | 3.0 | 46.2 | 214 | 0.65 |
| 3-4 star | 2.0 | 30.8 | 410 | 0.74 |
| 1-2 star | 0.8 | 12.3 | 110 | 0.60 |
| Non-star | 0.2 | 3.1 | 95 | 0.32 |
| Domestic | 3.5 | 53.8 | 10 | 0.13 |
| Hotels | 0.9 | 13.8 | 39 | 0.21 |
| Guest houses[1] | 2.6 | 40.0 | 8 | 0.12 |
| *Beidaihe* |  |  |  |  |
| Total | 9.3 | 100.0 | 10 | 0.15 |
| International | 0.8 | 8.6 | 160 | 0.62 |
| Domestic | 8.5 | 91.4 | 10 | 0.14 |
| *Danwei*[2] | 4.9 | 52.7 | 56 | 0.20 |
| Guest houses[1] | 3.6 | 38.7 | 4 | 0.10 |

[1] Including all types of guest houses; [2] *danwei* holiday quarters
Sources: Author's field surveys; Statistical Bureau of Guilin, Suzhou and Beidaihe.

(1) Accommodation sector

The accommodation sector was the largest single contributor to all direct tourism employment in Guilin (55%) and Beidaihe (70%). Due to the dominance of one-day visitors in Suzhou, the demand of domestic tourists on local accommodation services was smaller, leading to a moderate size of hotel employment in this place.

It is noteworthy that, even in the famous destinations Guilin and Suzhou, the international hotel sector has generated less than one-half of all hotel employment, while in Beidaihe its contribution was less than 9% in 1991. In the latter case, hotel guests are principally not international tourists.

The amount of employment generated by an accommodation facility varies with its size, standard of services as well as ownership and location. Measured in job per bed, employment effect in the accommodation sector rises significantly from low to higher categories, and falls with decreasing size in each category. Furthermore, hotel employment effects differ from one area to another. In general, the hotel sector in Guilin tends to generate more job(s) per establishment or per bed (Tab. 9–2).

As a rule, state–owned facilities and those hotels enjoying advantageous locations tend to generate more jobs. In addition, employment in larger hotels is more stable seasonally, which is attributable to their off–season convention and conference businesses, especially in Guilin.

(2) Souvenir trading sector

As emphasized in various parts of this study, the capacity of the local economies of Guilin, Suzhou and Beidaihe in supplying locally-produced tourist goods is apparently different. This is especially evident in souvenir trading. In Suzhou, souvenir businesses play the largest part in generating tourism employment, contributing 28% of the total in 1991. This share was much lower in Guilin (13.7%) and Beidaihe (7.6%).

In Suzhou and Guilin, souvenir shops fall into two categories.

- First, state- and collective-owned souvenir shops, which are usually large in size. Such facilities are established as shopping places for international tourists, especially those on packaged tours. In addition, international hotels and retail sales shops of souvenir-producing factories are also engaged actively in souvenir businesses. Their targeted market is international tourists.

- Second, small private shops which are large in number but small in size. They make up the largest part of employment in this service sector. As a rule, while larger tourist shops are located in downtown areas, small private shops are concentrated around major sight-seeing spots and hotel areas.

Compared to Suzhou and Guilin, souvenir trading plays a much smaller role in Beidaihe. Souvenir businesses are occupied exclusively by the private sector. Tourist shops with fixed business space are small in number. Souvenir trading most often takes place along the roads leading to major beach areas.

(3) Catering service sector

Catering service is another lucrative business in the big tourist cities. In 1991, it contributed 13% and 25% of all direct tourism employment in Guilin and Suzhou respectively. International tourism in Guilin and Suzhou is dominated by packaged tourism, and most international tourists do not visit restaurants individually. Therefore, it can be argued that the major part of employment in the catering service sector is generated by domestic tourism.

Small restaurants in more peripheral urban areas, which obviously have little to do with tourism, were kept out in author's field surveys. Yet, it is noteworthy that a large part of the surveyed restaurants, especially those in downtown areas, serve not only tourists but the indigenous as well. This is especially true of a big city like Suzhou.

In Beidaihe, two factors tend to make the absolute employment size in restaurant business smaller. First, all *danwei* holiday quarters and most private guest houses provide foods for their guests. Second, the majority of one-day visitors, whose activities are confined to beach areas, usually do not go to restaurants.

(4) Other sectors

Differences also exist in job opportunities in other tourist service activities in the study areas. This tends to result less from the possible incompleteness of the field surveys than from the different nature of tourism. In Guilin, a large number of tourists go on river cruise, resulting in more jobs in the transportation sector (8.5%). In Suzhou, because most tourist activities are concentrated in gardens and parks, the need for management and maintenance of park and garden facilities tends to generate more jobs (8.2%). In Beidaihe, since most tourists need air mattresses to help their swimming or floating on the water, air mattress renting turns out to be a very lucrative business.

Thus, tourist service activities in beach areas also play a certain part in job creation (5.7%).

### 9.1.3 Tourism and Urban Tertiary Sector Employment

Statements about the quantitative significance of tourism employment in local labor markets are affected by two major factors, namely, the area and population size of a destination selected, and the definition of the scope of tourism employment. Different definitions of study areas and the scope of tourism employment often lead to widely different conclusions.

In Guilin, Suzhou and Beidaihe, tourist activities are highly concentrated in their urban areas. And, since the 'boundaries' of secondary tourism employment are fuzzy and data on them rather sparse, following discussions will center on the role of direct tourism employment in the urban labor markets.

On the whole, the contributions of the tourism sector to the urban labor markets in the study areas are significant. The role of tourism in employment generation is reflected first and foremost in the urban tertiary sector. In general, the quantitative significance of tourism employment rises apparently with decreasing size of an urban economy or its labor market (Tab. 9–3).

### Table 9–3: The Significance of Direct Tourism Employment in the Urban Labor Markets of Guilin, Suzhou and Beidaihe, 1991[1]

|  | Guilin | Suzhou | Beidaihe |
|---|---|---|---|
| Absolute (1,000) | | | |
| Labor Total | 294.1 | 520.3 | 32.3 |
| Tertiary Sector | 106.9 | 159.1 | 18.0 |
| Tourism-direct | 36.1 | 24.3 | 14.0 |
| Percent (%) | | | |
| Tertiary / total | 36.3 | 30.6 | 55.7 |
| Tourism / Tertiary | 33.8 | 15.3 | 77.8 |
| Tourism / Total | 12.3 | 4.7 | 43.3 |

[1] All data sets refer to *shi* (city), compare section 1.3 for definitions.
Source: Author's field surveys; SZTN, GLTN and BDHTN 1992.

In a large city with developed and diversified economy like Suzhou, the contribution of tourism employment is not so spectacular, providing some 15 percent of tertiary sector employment, and less than 5% of all employment. In a comparatively smaller city with less developed economy like Guilin, these proportions go up to 34% and 12% respectively. In a still smaller area with a single-structured local economy like Beidaihe, employment created directly by the tourism sector keeps about three-quarters of the tertiary labor force or 43% of all labor force busy.

Tourism industry tends to play a role of catalyst in the urban tertiary sector. In general, there is a tendency for a tourist city to have a more developed tertiary sector. In 1991, tertiary sector employment made up 30–55% of all urban employment in the study areas, which were higher than the national average of 25% in the same year.[4]

### 9.1.4  Estimating the Capital/Labor Ratio

Obviously, many economic sectors may have equal, if not greater, claims on limited development resources at the local level. Therefore, with respect to employment generation, it is of importance to ask what costs have recent tourism expansions presented to the local economies of the study areas.

The employment generated by tourism in the study areas seems sizable. However, little is known of its investment costs. Sketchy investment data suggest that recent tourism investment in the study areas, especially in Guilin, is enormous. Obviously, the largest part of tourism investment has flown into the international tourism sector. In Guilin, according to local estimates, by 1988 some 630 million RMB yuan had been invested in 17 international hotel projects alone.[5] However, information about capital investments in the entire tourism sector is inadequate for a capital/labor ratio analysis.

Fig. 9–2 gives some hints about the average investment costs per job in selected branches of tourism and some industrial sectors at the national level. Three remarks should be made about the data sets employed.

---

[4] Nation-level data included 479 cities. ZCFS 1992, p. 30.
[5] Xie 1990, p. 286.

## Figure 9–2: Capital Intensity per Job in Selected Sectors in China, 1991

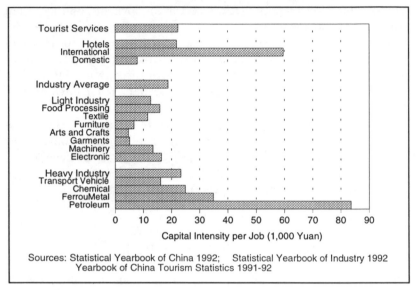

Sources: Statistical Yearbook of China 1992;   Statistical Yearbook of Industry 1992
Yearbook of China Tourism Statistics 1991-92

- First, due to data limits, capital/labor ratio has not been calculated in marginal terms;

- Second, as a relatively new economic sector, China's tourism industry has to rely heavily on extensive capital investment in its start-up stage, leading to a high investment costs per job;

- Third, the high average investment costs per job in tourist service activities outside hotels tends to result principally from the importation of a large number of cars and tourist buses which serve international tourism.

The investment and employment data at the national level indicate three tendencies.

- First, a wholesale judgment about the investment costs per job in tourism is risky. Differences in average capital/labor ratio within tourism and industry per se are significant.

- Second, during its start-up stage, tourism does not seem to be a typical labor-intensive sector, as is held by many tourism advocates. Average investment costs per job in and outside hotels, though lower than those in heavy industry, tend to be even higher than those of the entire industry, and much higher than those in traditional manufacturing branches such as furniture, arts and crafts, textile, etc.

- Third, if account is taken of the heavy hotel investment, the opportunity costs to the local economies in job creation in international tourism are very high. On the contrary, domestic tourism appears to be a cheaper way of job creation. Jobs in the accommodation sector which serves domestic tourism are apparently low-cost in nature. This impression will be enhanced, if some still lower-cost non-hotel employment in domestic tourism is taken into consideration.

Thus, the monolithic argument that tourism is a labor-intensive sector whose development requires little investments seems questionable. Recalling the different nature of tourism development, especially the significantly different size of investments in international tourism in the study areas, we can conclude that the average investment costs per job in tourism tend to be much higher in Guilin than in Suzhou, which in turn are higher than in Beidaihe.

Unfortunately, the issues related to the significant effects of investment strategies on the nature and costs of tourism employment have to date received little attentions from local tourism planners.

### 9.1.5 Income Effects

Information about income effects generated by tourism is extremely scant. Statistics at the national level suggest that the average salaries and wages in tourism tend to be higher than the 'all sectors' average, and those in industry (Tab. 9–4). In 1992, the annual wages of an employee in tourist service activities outside hotels were about 20% higher than those of an industrial worker, while wages in the hotel sector were 3% higher than average industrial wages. The lower wage level in the hotel sector may have resulted from inclusions of all domestic accommodation facilities.

Differences in wage levels between state, collective and private sectors are significant. In general, wage levels in the private and cooperative sectors are higher than those in the state sector, and much higher than those in the collective sector. In 1992, the annual wage level in tourist service activities (outside hotels) in the 'others' ownership category, which includes all types of private, cooperative and joint-venture enterprises, was 50% and 100% higher than those in the state and collective sector respectively. In the hotel sector, these figures went up to 63% and 122% in the same year.

### Table 9–4: Average Annual Salaries and Wages in Selected Sectors (in Yuan), China, 1992[1]

|  | Average | Ownership | | |
|  |  | State | Collective | Others[2] |
|---|---|---|---|---|
| All Sectors | 2,711 | 2,878 | 2,109 | 3,966 |
| Industry | 2,774 | 2,995 | 2,094 | 3,872 |
| Construction | 3,087 | 3,419 | 2,554 | 4,693 |
| Transportation & Communications | 3,261 | 3,553 | 2,200 | 5,680 |
| Commerce, Catering, etc. | 2,221 | 2,483 | 1,859 | 4,008 |
| Estate, Public Util., Services, etc. | 2,891 | 2,987 | 2,214 | 4,555 |
| Services | 2,719 | 2,810 | 2,085 | 4,471 |
| Tourist Services[3] | 3,374 | 3,220 | 2,333 | 4,781 |
| Hotels | 2,851 | 2,735 | 1,995 | 4,445 |

[1] All figures in this table refer to base salaries and wages. If bonus and subsidiaries are included, then the figures in the 'all sectors' category are as follows: average = 3,882, state = 4,202, collective = 2,800, others = 5,323;
[2] including all types of private, cooperative and joint-venture enterprises;
[3] definition of the 'tourist service sector' is unclear, but it seems that official statistics on this category refer to tourist service activities outside hotels and catering services.
Source: ZTN 1993, pp. 122–131.

The wage levels of tourism employees also vary from one area to another. In 1991, annual wages in the state-owned service sector, including accommodation and other tourist service sectors, averaged 2,662 yuan in Suzhou, 2,267 yuan in Beidaihe, but 2,092 in Guilin.[6] At the local level, wage differences also exist between different ownership categories.

---

[6]Bonus and subsidiaries not included. SZTN 1992, p. 248; GLTN 1992, p. 270; BDHTN 1992, p. 315.

Of course, cautions are called in interpreting the purchasing power of money wages of tourism employees in different ownership categories. While staff and employees in the state-owned sector still enjoy state subsidiaries in such areas as housing, healthy insurance as well as *danwei*-based fringe benefits, such non-monetary income for the employees in the private sector seems much lower, if not non-existent. On the whole, the differences in real income of tourism employees in different ownership categories are less significant than the pure wage statistics may have suggested.

## 9.2 Individual and Self-Employment

### 9.2.1 Tourism and Private Sector Employment

A rapidly rising non-state sector has been widely regarded as one of the decisive explanatory factors to the economic prosperity in the coastal region and, perhaps in a less significant measure, to the recent growth of the Chinese economy as a whole.[7] Stimulated by the policy of economic liberalization, there is an increasingly apparent tendency for the non-state sector, especially the private sector, to have an ever bigger part to play in the service sector. In tourist areas, a growing tourism industry seems vital to the development of the private sector.

Private participation in tourism occurs principally in the domestic tourism sector. Because of low entry barriers, and plentiful and lucrative market chances, domestic tourism has opened up a wide array of 'window of opportunity' for local small investors in Guilin, Suzhou and Beidaihe. Obviously, job opportunities, either as job-shifts or job opening, and higher personal income are the first-ranked motive of individual participation.

One of the major justifications for private participation in tourism development lies in its capacity of absorbing a certain amount of labor force, with little direct state investments. Today, the private sector plays a significant part in some tourist service sectors in the study areas (Tab. 9–5, 9–6). According to author's field surveys, in 1991 about 20% of all direct tourism employment in Guilin were in the private sector. This share went up to 33–34% in Beidaihe and Suzhou in the same year.

---

[7]Heberer 1989, pp. 376–93; Jefferson et al. 1994, p. 58–62; Perkins 1994, pp. 26–31; Naughton 1994, pp. 266–70; Rawski 1994, pp.271–75; Putterman 1992, pp. 479–80.

**Table 9–5: Percentage of the Private Sector in Direct Tourism Employment in Guilin, Suzhou and Beidaihe, 1991 (%)[1]**

|  | Guilin | Suzhou | Beidaihe |
|---|---|---|---|
| Accommodation | 1.7 | 1.5 | 21.5 |
| Catering | 59.6 | 50.0 | 58.3 |
| Local Transportation | 15.3 | 10.0 | 30.0 |
| Tourist Shops | 77.1 | 70.6 | 80.0 |
| Others[2] | 6.0 | 5.7 | 68.2 |
|  |  |  |  |
| Total | 20.0 | 34.2 | 33.0 |

[1] % of all direct tourism employment in each job category;
[2] including photography, bicycle renting, air mattress renting (Beidaihe), travel services, administration, etc.
Sources: Author's field surveys, Statistical Bureau of Guilin, Suzhou and Beidaihe.

**Table 9–6: Types of Tourism Businesses and Employment at Selected Tourist Spots in Suzhou, 1991[1]**

|  | Establishments | | Employment | |
|---|---|---|---|---|
|  | Absolute | % | Absolute | % |
| *Types* |  |  |  |  |
| Total | 534 | 100.0 | 765 | 100.0 |
| Restaurants | 85 | 15.9 | 262 | 34.2 |
| Tourist Shops | 356 | 66.7 | 390 | 51.0 |
| Bicycle renting, etc. | 93 | 17.4 | 113 | 14.8 |
| *Ownership* |  |  |  |  |
| Total | 534 | 100.0 | 765 | 100.0 |
| State | 19 | 3.5 | 75 | 9.8 |
| Collective | 23 | 4.3 | 90 | 11.7 |
| Private | 492 | 92.2 | 600 | 78.5 |

[1] Surveyed tourist spots including *Shiquan* Street, Tiger's Hill, Humble Administrator's Garden, North Pagoda, and Linger-here Garden.
Source: Author's field surveys.

In general, there is a tendency for the private sector to account for the lion's share of direct employment in restaurant and souvenir businesses, ranging from 50% to 80%. Subject to tourism- and area-specific factors, however, the major business areas of the private sector vary from one place to another.

In Suzhou and Guilin, two most lucrative business areas for the private sector are souvenir trading and catering service, which created about 90% of all individual employment. The largest part of small private shops and restaurants appear in and around three major areas, namely, (1) sight-seeing spots, (2) hotel areas and, (3) downtown areas. In Guilin, a 'night-market' of souvenir trading, with some 400 selling stands, has been opened along the Binjiang road in recent years. At many places in Guilin and Suzhou, the main manifestation of tourism there is the large number of souvenir shops and restaurants which line the streets leading from bus stations or parking places to major tourist attractions.

Business space of private shops and restaurants has two sources.

- First, temporary facilities which are built by the city or district governments, and rented to individual businessmen. For a large number of private dealers, such simple establishments usually serve as vendors most often standing along streets leading to major tourist spots.

- The second source is rent rooms which were former residential houses. Some have been fully re-constructed, while others only partly. The rents for a room of 20–40 sq.m. lie in the range of 400–600 yuan. Thus, such house owners, though small in number, have become the secondary beneficiaries of tourism development. In the case of family-owned shops or restaurants, ground floors are often used as business rooms, while the second floor as living-rooms.

Beidaihe represents a different case. As discussed in section 7.4.2, due to spacious private living conditions and more house construction possibilities, small private boarding houses have mushroomed in the course of tourism development. Provision of accommodation services to domestic tourists has become a major business area of small private investors. In 1991, 46% of all private sector employment in Beidaihe was in the accommodation sector. And, the private sector made up about 22% of all employment in the accommodation sector inclduing *danwei* holiday quarters.

In Beidaihe, tourism activities in beach areas also generate a certain number of temporary jobs in the summer time (Tab. 9–7). This explains why the share of the private sector in the 'others' job category in Tab. 9–5 is very high in Beidaihe.

**Table 9–7: Temporary Job Opportunities in Beach Areas in Beidaihe, 1992**

| Service Activities | Employment |
|---|---|
| Air Mattress Renting | 360 |
| Photography and Film Shops | 80 |
| Camera Renting | 30 |
| Boat Renting | 30 |
| Bicycle Renting | 6 |
| Others | 30 |
| Total | 536 |

Source: Author's field surveys.

### 9.2.2   The Forms of Private Sector Employment

Private tourist shops, restaurants and guest houses (Beidaihe) are large in number, but very small in size, employing 1–4 person/s. As a rule, a restaurant generates more jobs (3–4 jobs) than a guest house or a tourist shop (1–2 jobs). Most individual employment in tourism is full-time jobs. Part-time employment appears principally in souvenir businesses near hotel areas. Such a form of employment seems widespread in Suzhou. Part-time businesses are usually run by moonlighters who are no longer satisfied with fixed wages in state or collective-owned enterprises.

Job-shifts from low-paid positions in state and collective sectors to self-employment in private tourism businesses are a commonplace. In many cases, there are close relations between former occupations and later-on types of business pursued by private businessmen. Former workers of a souvenir factory, for instance, are most likely to get into souvenir businesses, while those of collective-owned restaurants to catering services. In some cases, the losses of skilled workers of state and collective firms resulted from such job-shifts are not insignificant, especially in the souvenir production industry of Suzhou.[8]

---

[8]Information provided by Suzhou Economic Research Center.

Moreover, some private businessmen tend to have close business contacts and transactions with their former *danwei*. Through private relationships with former work-colleagues or via family ties, some private dealers can, for instance, buy souvenir goods from their former units at lower prices. In some cases, they even entrust state-owned shops to sell 'their' souvenir goods on a commission basis. In general, smaller and collective firms tend to deal more with the private sector than do larger ones.

Small private tourist firms are owned and run exclusively by individual families. As a rule, labor hiring exists most often in restaurant businesses. Typically, a private restaurant employs 2–3 young rural migrants as waiters and kitchen helpers. In Beidaihe, those relatively bigger private guest houses which provide both accommodation and foods also hire non-family laborers. In both cases, a sort of flexible wages and bonus system, based on firm performance, is applied in labor hiring.

In souvenir businesses, however, labor hiring is seldom. Many private businessmen reported that hiring outsiders in running tourist shops may lead to losses of business opportunities, because shop-keepers have to be involved in case-to-case price bargaining. Though given certain room of price concessions, hired shop-keepers often appear to be not flexible enough in doing business. In addition, to the private owners of those tourist shops around hotel areas, the cost of hiring full-time non-family laborers seems high, since day-time businesses are usually sluggish.

In all types of private tourism businesses, engagement of family members is a commonplace. However, it is found seldom for a whole family to get involved in the private sector. In this respect, considerations of spreading risks and widening family income sources as well as on social prestige and housing tend to have played a decisive role.

### 9.2.3 Income Effects

Because of its flexibility in operations, such as longer business hours, more friendly business atmospheres, more price concessions as well as offers of rewards to guides, the private sector seems far more competitive than the state and collective sectors in many business areas. The apparent conflicts between the private and state sector in providing cruise services on the Lijiang river in Guilin has showcased such increasing competitions.[9]

---

[9]Compare section 4.4.1.

As the data at the national level have shown, employees in the private sector receive much higher income than their counterparts in the state- and collective-owned sectors. Understandably, while most private businessmen were ready to provide information about their investments, labor hiring and ways of doing business, they appeared very cautious in talking about their business size and turnovers and, especially, personal or family income. Nevertheless, it is no doubt that most private business activities in tourism have achieved sizable returns.

Apparently, personal income in the private tourism sector varies between different service activities, and from one area to another. According to interviews with private businessmen and individual employees, in general, personal income in the private tourism sector tends to lie in the range of 2 to 4 times as much as that of an average urban worker (Tab. 9–8).

**Table 9–8: Annual Income of Small Private Investors in Tourism Businesses in Guilin, Suzhou and Beidaihe, 1992[1]**

| Business Types | Annual Income (Yuan) |
| --- | --- |
| Souvenir trading | 8,000-12,000 |
| Restaurant | 6,000-10,000 |
| Accommodation | 8,000-16,000 |
| Local Transportation | 7,000-15,000 |
| Bicycle renting, photography, etc. | 5,000-9,000 |

[1] Income data were obtained from author's interviews with about 200 private businessmen in Suzhou, 150 in Guilin, and 120 in Beidaihe. In many cases, the annual income of a private businessman also included the part which was generated by implicit labor inputs of his/her family members. Part-time engagement of family laborers is widespread in souvenir trading and accommodation businesses. The wide range of annual income figures within each business category resulted from the significantly different size of investments and businesses of individual investors.
Source: Author's field surveys.

In Beidaihe, local statistics show that the share of the private sector in all tourism revenues has increased significantly since the mid–1980s. Especially, its higher share in net revenues suggests that the private sector has achieved much better performance than the state and collective sectors (Tab. 9–9).

**Table 9–9: Tourism Income Effects in the Private Sector in Beidaihe, 1984–1991[1]**

|  | 1984 | 1986 | 1988 | 1989 | 1990 | 1991 |
|---|---|---|---|---|---|---|
| Gross Revenues | | | | | | |
| Total (million yuan) | 31.5 | 74.6 | 108.6 | 113.7 | 147.0 | 154.8 |
| Private Sector | | | | | | |
| (million yuan) | 2.8 | 14.9 | 20.6 | 25.0 | 38.7 | 40.7 |
| %[2] | 8.9 | 20.0 | 19.0 | 22.0 | 26.3 | 26.3 |
| Net Revenues | | | | | | |
| Total (million yuan) | 2.5 | 6.7 | 10.3 | 11.2 | 13.0 | 13.2 |
| Private Sector | | | | | | |
| (million yuan) | 0.5 | 3.6 | 5.6 | 6.1 | 7.2 | 7.2 |
| %[2] | 20.0 | 53.7 | 54.4 | 54.5 | 55.4 | 54.5 |

[1] All figures in this table refer to the aggregates of local retail sales, catering and accommodation sectors; [2] % of the private sector in total revenues.
Source: BDHTN 1984–1992.

## 9.3 Employment Spill-overs in Souvenir Manufacturing

In many studies, it has been argued that, besides direct employment, tourism can generate secondary employment effects via its increased demand for a range of goods and services in other sectors. Tourism-related or tourism investment-induced employment may involve such sectors as agriculture, food processing, handicrafts, light manufacturing, wholesale distribution, construction and capital goods industries, etc. The existence of such employment spill-overs seems little disputable. However, little is known of their quantitative significance. Estimates about additional job opportunities in tourism-related sectors have been often made only in qualitative terms.[10]

Obviously, expanding the supply of local goods and products is one of the potential ways to generate more employment and income in the local economies of destination areas. Among many light industrial sectors, the links between souvenir manufacturing and tourism is self-evident. Since tourist expenditure on souvenir shopping tends to be of high elasticity, souvenir manufacturing is thus a sector in which tourist multiplier effects are most likely to take place. However, local capacity in taping potential employment spill-overs in the souvenir production sector is widely different.

---

[10]Cf. Kadt 1979, 35–44; Harrison 1992, pp. 14–17 and 24–26.

## 9.3.1   The Prospering Souvenir Industry in Suzhou

As discussed in sections 8.2.3 and 9.1.2, souvenir trading plays a decisive part in revenue and employment generation in Suzhou. With respect to secondary spill-over effects, the most critical element of Suzhou's success is the high market share of locally-produced souvenir goods. According to author's field surveys, in the major part of souvenir markets in Suzhou, the share of local products tends to lie in the range of 80–90%, depending on the sorts of goods.

Souvenir manufacturing and trading has a long tradition in Suzhou. The effects of recent tourism expansions on its local souvenir industry are threefold:

- First, the increased demand for souvenir goods brought about by an expanding tourism has enlarged market capacity for local souvenir producers in a significant manner. Local souvenir manufacturing has obtained a big boost since the late 1970s. By 1991, 40 large souvenir factors had developed into an enterprise group called Suzhou Arts and Crafts Corp. In 1991, besides retail sales, about 36% of their products supplied directly the local markets, while 64% were exported.[11]  Since the largest part of souvenir demand arises from international tourists who pay foreign currencies, such factories are in effect exporting their products locally.

- Second, not only does international tourism help raise the reputation of Suzhou's souvenir products, but the influx of a large number of international tourists has brought to Suzhou valuable market information from many parts of the world. Some leading souvenir-producing factories reported that international tourism has become a 'window' of testing 'going' trends in the international market, which enables them to adjust product-design and decision-making in new market development promptly. Such non-material effects appear to be of certain significance in promoting local souvenir industry.

- Third, tourist expenditure on local souvenir products tends to have certain multiplier effects in the local manufacturing sector. Take Suzhou's No.1 Silk Factory for example. As one of the leading silk-producing factories in China, the No.1 Silk Factory produces more than 40 varieties of silk products, and employs

---

[11]Information provided by Suzhou Arts and Crafts Corp.

about 1,200 workers. Since the mid–1980s, it has become a most favored visit place of international visitors in Suzhou. In recent years, 25–30% of its final products supply local markets via wholesales and retail sales.

This factory has extensive for- and backward linkages with local silk- and souvenir-producing plants. Besides the raw materials supplied mainly by the agricultural sector of Northern Jiangsu province, about 80% of its intermediate inputs are supplied by local plants. This factory in turn supplies several local manufacturing plants with a large amount of intermediate silk products, which are processed further into various souvenir articles or other products such as garments, handkerchief, etc. Similar results, though in varying manner or degree, have been found in other factories such as Silk Printing Factory (1,000 workers), Embroidery Research Institute (300 workers), Sandalwood Fan Factory (550 workers) and Jade Carving Factory (400 workers).

Today, souvenir industry plays an important part in the entire export sector of Suzhou. In 1991, a wide variety of souvenir goods produced by Suzhou's arts and crafts sector contributed about 10% of all export revenues, and the contribution of silk products reached 32%.[12]

The role of Suzhou's souvenir manufacturing in expanding local labor markets is significant. In 1991, Suzhou's silk industry (25 plants) employed 31,000 persons, and the arts and crafts sector (40 plants) 12,586 workers.[13] Though a large part of the employment in the silk industry is not tourism-induced, local estimates suggest that in 1991 the number of employees directly engaged in souvenir-producing activities lay in the range of 14,000–16,000. Thus, in the case of Suzhou, for each employee in souvenir trading more than two jobs are generated in souvenir manufacturing.

### 9.3.2 Underdevelopment of Souvenir Industry in Guilin and Beidaihe

Souvenir businesses play a much smaller role in Guilin and Beidaihe than in Suzhou. The largest part of souvenir markets in Guilin are occupied by non-local products. According to author's survey of 22

---

[12]For the entire Suzhou area (including 6 counties) these rates were 9% and 27% respectively. SZTN 1992, pp. 220–221.
[13]SZTN 1992, pp. 70–71.

big tourist shops in the downtown area of Guilin, in 1992 locally-manufactured tourist goods accounted for 8–10% of all goods sold at these shops, contributing 6–8% of their revenues. Similar results have been found in interviews with 80 private dealers in souvenir businesses at the 'night-market' along the Binjiang road in the same year. According to local estimates, Guilin's souvenir manufacturing sector employed no more than 3,000 workers in 1992.[14]

Souvenir trading plays a still smaller role in Beidaihe. Besides some small, low-in-value souvenirs typical of a seaside resort, such as articles made of shell, conch and seaweed, most goods purchased by domestic tourists in this place are daily-use articles. Local souvenir manufacturing remains fully underdeveloped, providing some 800 jobs in 1992.[15] Souvenir manufacturing activities are concentrated in the suburban of Beidaihe. Job opportunities in souvenir production are generated exclusively in the private sector, typically in small family-run workshops. Besides family laborers, the majority of employees in such small firms are rural migrants from surrounding counties.

The extent to which local communities can tap the employment potentials in tourism-related manufacturing industries depends on several factors. Besides differences in local production skills and traditions of commerce, following barriers to local participation in souvenir production in Guilin and Beidaihe seem critical.

(1) Lack of market access. Obviously, tourist demand for souvenir products also exists in Guilin and Beidaihe. However, due to the absence of a stimulating entrepreneurial and commercial climate, the ability of individual firms and households in catching such business chances seems limited. Local responses to the emerging market chances tend to be handicapped further by the deficits in diffusing tourist demand information to potential local producers. Seldom can such information reach individual firms or households regarding what are most in demand and their perspective market capacity, how big are the initial inputs required and the expected returns, or how can such products get access to market and find a good sale, etc. Thus, the absence of market access makes potential local producers ignorant of new market opportunities.

---

[14]Information provided by Guilin Economic Research Center and Guilin Economic Planning Committee.

[15]BDHTN.

(2) Lack of start-up investment. The financial resources at disposal of individual firms or households in adopting new techniques and implementing innovations in production are limited. In many cases, individual producers find it extremely difficult to start up a new production system without outside financial supporting at its initial stages.

(3) Lack of basic technical assistance. In many branches of souvenir industry in Suzhou, production and commercial skills have passed down largely via family milieu at earlier stages and, lately, through locally-organized programs of technological transfers and training. Innovative community organization in production and marketing is particularly vital to the success of broad-based local participation. However, such ways of diffusion of appropriate technological know-how are found non-existent in Guilin and Beidaihe.

(4) Lack of demonstration effects. Under the condition of lower level of economic development, the readiness, willingness and capacity of individual producers to the changes of economic or technical kind is restrained. Concerns about possible losses of existing gains, uncertainties of future returns justifying new investments, deficiencies of distributive mechanisms and the like have also played their part. To many potential producers, the opportunity costs of starting or changing to a new production seem high. Therefore, success stories at an early stage would be critical in enlightening market chances and evoking wider initiatives of local participation.

Needless to say, the increased demand brought about by tourism covers a broader range of goods than handicrafts. Each branch supplying goods to tourism businesses requires different kinds and levels of skills. And the potential for local production of foodstuffs is subject additionally to area-specific factors like natural conditions. Nevertheless, author's field surveys suggest that the underdevelopment of other tourism-oriented sectors in Guilin and Beidaihe seems attributable in large measure to the same type of factors as enumerated above for the souvenir manufacturing sector.

It remains unclear, had part of the tourism investments, if not the profits from tourism, been invested in development of a closely tourism-related sector like souvenir production or in agricultural improvements in Guilin, whether the benefits of tourism expansions to its local population would have been different in a significant manner.

## 9.4   Tourism Job Opportunities and Rural-Urban Migration

An ever-growing size of urban-ward migration, or 'floating population' as is called in most Chinese literature, is one of the most apparent responses of the Chinese peasantry to the widening income and employment opportunities between urban and rural China.[16] The influx of floating population in an economic booming city like Suzhou would occur independently of tourism. Yet, with the presence of tourism and, especially, due to the nature of some tourism jobs, rural-urban migration seems to have received added impetus in the study areas.

Obviously, differentiating the segment of migration induced by tourism from the overall rural-urban labor movements is hardly possible. Therefore, following discussions center primarily on the nature of tourism-induced job-searching activities and the identities of these low-level participants rather than their exact numbers.

### 9.4.1   Tourism Jobs as a 'Pull-Factor'

The employment effects generated by tourism go far beyond destinations themselves. In the course of development, a considerable part of tourism jobs can not been covered merely by urban labor force, though pressures of employment demand on urban labor markets in such a place as Guilin are not non-existent.

Besides seasonal fluctuations of tourism occupations, the root cause of such a structural disparity lies in the dualistic structure of tourism employment. The 'inferior' nature of some tourism jobs as well as considerations on social prestige have impeded urban labor force to take low-status jobs in the tourism employment hierarchy. Whilst indigenous urban youths hold more prestigious positions as barmen, receptionists or technicians, they often rather hesitate to take jobs to serve tourists.

Yet, for many job-searchers from rural areas, tourism represents another set of opportunities, however limited. In general, wages in tourism compare favorably with income in agriculture, and more so with earnings in subsistence agriculture which is characteristic of those major sending areas of rural migrants in China. Because jobs in the subsistence agriculture or other economic sectors in their

---

[16]Li et al. 1991, pp. 3–47; Taubmann 1991, pp. 161–78, 1993a, pp. 163–85; Yusuf 1994, pp. 88–89.

source areas are not available, let alone at higher rates of pay, job opportunities in tourism are of course very appealing to many rural migrants. Therefore, job and income opportunities in tourism and tourism-related businesses have become a strong 'pull-factor' in rural-urban migration in the study areas.

The entry of rural labor force into tourism-related service sectors has been made possible by the liberalization of China's labor markets. Besides individual and self-employment in the private sector, state and collective enterprises in Chinese cities have enjoyed increasing autonomy in labor hiring. Since the mid–1980s, contract and temporary workers as well as extra-planning labor hiring have become the prevailing form of new employment in the formal urban sector, leading to a large number of rural temporary workers flooding into many Chinese cities.[17] As tourism employment in the private sector and small collective sector is self-employment in nature, tourism-induced rural migrants are inclined to flow principally into the state-owned sector.

Over the past decade, Beidaihe's coastal zone has attracted a good deal of temporary migration as tourism employment opportunities grew. From 1985 to 1991, the number of contract and temporary workers in the urban state sector of Beidaihe rose from 2,330 to about 5,500, and their share in the state sector employment from 26% to 40% (Tab. 9–10). This means that, since the mid–1980s, about 70% of all new jobs created in the urban sector had been filled by contract and temporary jobholders.

### Table 9–10: Temporal and Contract Employment in the Urban State Sector of Beidaihe, 1985–1991[1]

| Year | Total | Temporal | | Contract | |
|------|-------|----------|------|----------|------|
| | | Absolute | $\%^2$ | Absolute | $\%^2$ |
| 1985 | 8,970 | 2,216 | 24.7 | 116 | 1.3 |
| 1987 | 11,780 | 3,490 | 29.6 | 432 | 3.7 |
| 1989 | 12,090 | 3,722 | 30.8 | 713 | 5.9 |
| 1991 | 13,540 | 4,512 | 33.3 | 977 | 7.2 |

[1] In the urban sector of Beidaihe, state-owned enterprises made up 77.6% of all employment in 1991; [2] % of all employment in the urban state sector.
Sources: Statistical Bureau Beidaihe.

---

[17]Li, et al. 1991, pp. 3–47; Feng 1991, pp. 22–43; Fu 1992, pp. 16–47.

In the case of Beidaihe, while part of the contract jobs were occupied by urban laborers, temporary jobs, which accounted for the lion's share of non-fixed employment (82%) in 1991, were filled exclusively by job-searchers from rural areas. In this tourism-dominated place, contract and temporary workers have been employed principally in the tourism sector, or 78% in 1991 (Tab. 9–11). In recent years, Beidaihe's tourism sector provided about 7,000 temporary jobs, accounting for about one-half of all direct tourism employment.

**Table 9–11: Sectoral Distribution of Temporal and Contract Employment in the State-owned Sector of Beidaihe, 1990**

| | Industry | Construction[1] | Tourism-related | | Others | Total |
| | | | Total | Accommodation[2] | | |
|---|---|---|---|---|---|---|
| Total Temporal & Contract | 526 | 229 | 9,075 | 7,446 | 3,981 | 13,811 |
| absolute | 170 | 167 | 4,088 | 3,355 | 1,037 | 5,462 |
| %[3] | 3.0 | 3.6 | 78.4 | 64.7 | 15.0 | 100.0 |
| %[4] | 32.3 | 72.9 | 45.0 | 45.1 | 26.0 | 39.5 |

[1] Local construction sector; [2] including *danwei* holiday quarters and all types of guest houses; [3] % of all temporal and contract employment; [4] % of temporal and contract employment within each sector.
Source: Statistical Bureau Beidaihe.

In the larger destinations Guilin and Suzhou, employment of contract and temporary workers in tourism takes a different form. According to local estimates, the tourism sector employed around 12,000 contract and temporary workers in Guilin, and 9,800 in Suzhou. In these two places, the share of contract and temporary jobholders in tourism lies in the range of 30–60%, depending on the type of employment and the ownership of tourism enterprises.

In general, larger state-owned tourism enterprises tend to employ more contract and temporary workers. In Guilin and Suzhou, the share of contract workers, especially in international tourism, is higher than that of temporary jobholders. According to author's survey of 245 tourism enterprises in Guilin, in 1992 about 48% of their employees were workers on a contract or temporary basis (Tab. 9–12).

## Table 9–12: Temporal and Contract Employment in the Tourism Sector in Guilin, 1992[1]

| | Establishments | Employment | | |
| | Surveyed | Total | Temporal & Contract | |
| | | | Absolute | %[2] |
|---|---|---|---|---|
| Accommodation[3] | 120 | 12,650 | 6,840 | 54.1 |
| Catering | 50 | 1,120 | 450 | 40.1 |
| Tourist Transpor- tation[4] | 28 | 2,300 | 700 | 30.4 |
| Tourist Shops | 40 | 650 | 150 | 23.1 |
| Parks & Gardens | 10 | 800 | 200 | 25.0 |
| Total | 245 | 17,520 | 8,340 | 47.6 |

[1] Excluding privately-run firms; [2] % of the total within each branch;
[3] including 30 international hotels; [4] tourist vehicles & boats.
Source: Author's field surveys, Statistical Bureau Guilin.

However, the sources of contract and temporary workers in Guilin and Suzhou are different. According to local estimates, while some 60–70% of non-fixed tourism jobs in Guilin are taken by urban laborers or laborers from its suburban areas, over 80% of contract and temporary tourism jobs in Suzhou are filled by rural migrants from other regions.

### 9.4.2 The Forms of Tourism-Induced Rural-Urban Migration

As in other urban sectors, most rural migrant laborers are employed in low-status menial and, thus, low-paid jobs, making up the lowest layer of workers in tourism. As a rule, most rural migrants enter into domestic tourist service sectors. And the share of rural migrants tends to rise with increasing seasonal fluctuations of jobs in transportation, catering, hotels to tourism-linked construction sector, and with more marginal jobs within each sector.

(1) Direct employment of temporary rural migrants
With respect to direct tourism employment, typical jobs filled by rural migrants are low-status laboring jobs in restaurants, and domestic hotels and guest houses. In Guilin, about 40–50% of waiters, room maids, and kitchen helpers are rural migrants. In Suzhou and Beidaihe, this share goes up to 60–80%.

Employment of rural migrants in tourism is seasonal in nature. According to the information from the Labor Service Company of Beidaihe, over 90% of the jobholders in the accommodation sector work 3–5 months in Beidaihe. Though seasonal fluctuations of tourism jobs in the larger destinations Guilin and Suzhou seem less apparent than in Beidaihe, most interviewed rural migrants reported that they worked 8 to 10 months each year in the city.

For the largest part of rural migrants, inter-seasonal job shifts in the same working place are hardly possible, since competitions for jobs among rural temporary workers have become increasingly intensified as their rivals from rural areas are on the rapid increase. Therefore, most rural migrants have to return to their home areas when tourism businesses become sluggish.

Personal income of rural laborers in tourism consists of two parts: (1) fixed bade wages and, (2) a certain amount of bonus, which is proportional to the business sales. In general, average income of rural migrants is much lower than that of average urban workers. Month wages for rural migrants tend to lie in the range of 150–250 yuan.

(2) Indirect job opportunities
Besides direct employment, there are other job opportunities for rural migrants. Tourism-linked infrastructure investment, especially the hotel building boom, has generated a considerable number of jobs. Local tourism planners reported that a large part of the vast hotel projects in Guilin and Suzhou, and numerous *danwei* holiday facilities and private guest houses in Beidaihe, were constructed by migrant laborers. In 1991, rural construction workers made up about 60% of all construction sector employment in Beidaihe, and 86% in Suzhou.[18] Rural construction workers usually live in temporary camps, and move on once a hotel or tourist facility is completed.

The life chances of such rural migrants are most unsecured. Once the boom of hotel construction has run its course, or when a wind of tightening policies at the national level begins to blow, they are among the first to loss jobs, causing rural-ward labor movements and deteriorating their temporarily improved life chances, if any.[19]

---

[18]BDHTN 1992, pp. 14–17; SZTN 1992, pp. 250–251.

[19]In 1992 rural construction workers comprised 40% of all employment in China's construction sector. During 1989–1990 a tightening policy in capital investment led to a decrease of 1.8 million construction workers, of which over 83% rural construction workers. ZTN 1993, p. 561. Cf. Li and Hu 1991, pp. 15–17.

Another source of indirect employment for rural migrants is the jobs left by the indigenous, in both farm and non-farm sectors. In the urban sector, as some workers have shifted from non-tourism to tourism jobs or, within tourism sector, from low-paid jobs in state- or collective-owned enterprises to individual or self-employment in the private sector, such new empty jobs are most often filled by rural migrants.

In suburban areas, as the local population responded to the new chances for better jobs and higher income, a considerable number of former farmers have been drawn into tourism, at least seasonally. In all of the study areas, part-time family engagement in farming, especially during tourism off-seasons, remains prevailing. Nevertheless, more menial jobs, which no longer interested the local population as living standard rose, have been replaced by migrants from poor rural areas. According to author's fieldwork, in two rural communities in Beidaihe and in the suburb of Suzhou where job shifts of the indigenous have occurred on a massive scale, such job opportunities are also plentiful.

## (3) Informal sector employment

In the study areas, some 'classic' informal sector occupations, such as shoe-shine boys, unregistered guides, beach boys, prostitution and the like, seem not so apparent as has been widely described in the existing tourism literature. Nevertheless, the presence of tourism has given rise to certain informal sector employment in the study areas, though little is known of its quantitative significance.[20]

Besides widespread part-time engagement of family labor, informal sector activities take place in several areas:

- in domestic hotel businesses, jobs in the sales activities at major transportation stations are informal in character;[21]

- in small private restaurants, the employment of young rural migrants is in many cases also informal in nature;

- in souvenir trading, mobile street vendors are characteristic of informal sector occupations; and

- in small private firms, informal sector employment in souvenir production appears to be a commonplace.

---

[20] For a discussion of the individual and informal sectors in China, see Heberer 1989, pp. 39–46.

[21] Compare section 7.4.4.

Informal sector occupations may loom large to tourists' perceptions, which tends to result from the over-zealous sales activities of such people at sight-seeing spots and in downtown areas. According to observed facts, explicit informal sector employment in tourism remains small in size. And, temporary rural migrants tend to have played a large part in various informal sector activities.

On the other hand, however, implicit informal sector activities appear to be widespread in the study areas. This is especially true of the employment of temporary rural labor force. The informal nature of employment of rural migrants results from three main factors:

- first, the weak bargaining strength of most migrant labor suppliers because of the increasing competitions among themselves;

- second, in general, the self-consciousness of labor rights of rural migrants remains minimal; and

- last but not least, at present, labor legislation governing the labor markets is anything but sound, binding neither for job-providers nor job-takers.

It should be pointed out that there are also informal sector activities which are occupied mainly by urban inhabitants. Illegal currency dealings, for instance, emerged as a concomitant of the expanding tourism, and were once a widespread activity in many tourist cities. In Suzhou and Guilin, such activities took place mainly at private shops. However, illegal currency transactions have lost attractions as China's foreign exchange market becomes more liberal in recent years and, especially, as FEC was expired in 1994.

Another example is the illegal activities of some guides. Such illegal activities range from 'black' currency dealings to raising extra fees from private souvenir shops and international tourists. The increasingly apparent orientation toward commercialism of a large number of guides has been sharply criticized by international tourists and, recently, by the Chinese government.

### 9.4.3 Access of Rural Migrants to Tourism Job Opportunities

There are three major channels for rural labor force to get access to tourism-induced jobs in the urban labor markets:

1. formal intermediate functions of the so-called Labor Service Companies,

2. informal introduction via family ties or friends, and
3. oral diffusions of employment opportunities among rural migrants themselves.

Labor service companies usually have not only labor demand information from local enterprises, but certain official links to lower-level organizations in rural areas. According to the information from the Labor Service Company of Beidaihe, each year 2,000–2,500 rural laborers are introduced to Beidaihe's tourism sector via this company. In some cases, labor service companies also provide or organize short-term occupational training.

A still bigger role in spreading labor demand information tends to be played by informal channels. Besides introduction of family members and friends, the oral information among rural migrants seems vital. Once some mobile members of a sleepy village have discovered job and income opportunities in a tourist place, first family members, then relatives, and finally fellow villagers are introduced to more or less similar jobs as long as there still exist possibilities, leading to a sort of observable chain migration.

According to author's interviews with temporary workers at 30 *danwei* holiday quarters 20 big guest houses in Beidaihe, in many cases room maids employed by a holiday facility or guest house originate from the same or closely neighboring villages in the counties Qianlong and Qinglong. In Suzhou, 60–70% of the 230 migrant laborers, who were employed in the private and collective-owned restaurants along the *Shiqian* Street and at other three tourist spots, originate from Northern Jiangsu province. In Guilin, 70–80% of the vender-helpers at the 'souvenir night-market', and about one-half of all employees in souvenir manufacturing in Yangshuo were rural youths from four counties of the neighboring province Hunan.

The migration of rural laborers to the study areas is selective in nature. Two categories of rural labor force appear to benefit particularly from the temporary employment opportunities in tourism: young and female people. Especially in hotel and restaurant businesses, there is an apparent tendency for young labor force at age of 18–25 to account the lion's share of all temporary workers.

As temporary rural migrants have few employment options in their home areas, the opportunity costs of their entry into the tourism sector, as is perceived by themselves, seem extremely low. This argument is affirmed by author's interviews with a large number of young rural migrants in the hotel sector in Beidaihe. Most interviewed temporary workers reported that getting a job is much more important than finding a well-paid job with good work conditions. To them considerations on job conditions and rates of pay are secondary in importance, especially at initial stages of their entry into the urban labor markets.

Nevertheless, the youths from rural areas have also experienced considerable social mobility. As soon as young rural migrants have gathered sufficient experience and information about job and income opportunities in the city, they begin to consider job changing, either on an inter-occupational or inter-regional basis.

It was reported by the Labor Service Company of Beidaihe that 60–70% of those migrant laborers who find jobs via this company, are likely to leave their first low-status jobs, usually after 2–3 years. Interestingly, there is a tendency for the empty jobs left by those 'learned' migrants to be reoccupied by their peers from the same or neighboring villages. Such newcomers are introduced to or informed about the new job opportunities most often by the 'learned', either before or after their leaves!

## 9.5  Tourism Employment and Income Effects in Rural Areas

### 9.5.1  A Small Area Case: The Rural Communities Around Beidaihe

In Beidaihe, the employment and income effects of tourism on its surrounding areas are particularly apparent. Due to the status of 'capital in summer', the three rural communities around Beidaihe were once a sleepy area in terms of economic development. By the late 1970s, this area was still dominated by an agrarian and fishery economy, with the primary sector employing nearly 90% of its labor force.

In the course of tourism expansions, the recent changes in employment structure in this area turned out to be fundamental. By the early 1990s, about 48% of the former primary sector labor force had shifted to non-farm sectors (Fig. 9–3). The principal catalyst for such a change is the tourism-centered tertiary sector, while the employment share of the secondary sector has even decreased since the mid–1980s.

Because tertiary sector activities in this area serve almost exclusively domestic tourism, it can be concluded that the principal agent of the recent structural changes in this area is tourism, or more spe-

## Figure 9–3: Changes in Employment Structure in the Rural Areas Surrounding Beidaihe, 1978–1991

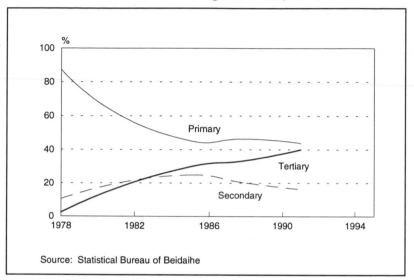

Source: Statistical Bureau of Beidaihe

## Figure 9–4: Changes in Employment Structure in Haibin *Xiang*, Beidaihe, 1978–1991

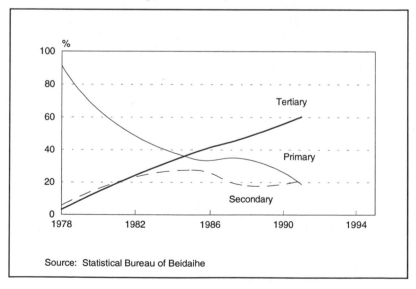

Source: Statistical Bureau of Beidaihe

cifically, the domestic tourism sector. The effects of tourism on local development are even more apparent in Haibin *xiang* (township),
which directly neighbors to the resort place of Beidaihe (Fig. 9–4).

Tourism employment effects in this rural area take several forms.

- First, a large number of former farmers have shifted fully from
  agricultural or fishery activities to tourism businesses, taking
  the form of job shifts.

- Second, besides a small number of jobs generated directly in the
  souvenir sector, a large part of employment in the secondary
  sector is also tourism-serving. Especially, the food-processing
  industry, which exclusively supplies local tourism businesses,
  takes a leading part in the local manufacturing sector.

- Third, the labor force which still remains in the primary sector
  has also profited from the expanding tourism. A considerable
  number of farmers are in fact multiple jobholders. Besides farming, they are engaged in tourism during peak seasons, either in
  formal or informal sectors. A still larger part of agricultural
  population appears to have benefited from the production of
  various agricultural goods, especially foodstuffs, whose demand
  has been expanded by tourism in a significant manner.

The income effects of such occupational changes are significant.
According to local household-survey data, per capita income of the
rural households in the three rural communities surrounding Beidaihe
had risen from 230 yuan in 1980 to 1,330 yuan in 1991. During
this period, the income growth rate of rural households had outpaced that of urban households, leading to a significant convergence
in rural-urban disparity (Fig. 9–5).[22]

Such significant employment and income effects as have been documented in Beidaihe area are also found in rural areas surrounding
the tourism-dominated town of Yangshuo in Guilin. In the cities
of Guilin and Suzhou, besides the urban population affected in the
private sector, the effects of tourism development on the employment and income situations of individual households have taken place
mainly in their suburban areas. On the whole, however, the geographical scope of tourism-affected areas in terms of employment
and income seems limited.

---

[22]In 1991 the average net income per capita of Chinese rural households was
RMB yuan 708. ZTN 1992, p. 306.

**Figure 9–5: Changing Ratio in Per Capita Income of
Urban and Rural Households in Beidaihe, 1980–1991**

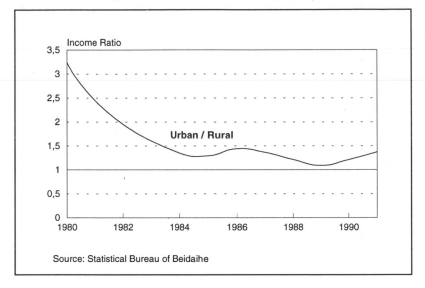

Source: Statistical Bureau of Beidaihe

## 9.5.2 A Village Case: The Chunyan Village (Guilin)

The impacts of tourism on some formerly sleepy rural villages in Guilin and Beidaihe are especially impressive. Take Chunyan village of Yangshuo county (Guilin) for example.

The Chunyan village is about 7 km from the county town Yangshuo *zhen*. Its rural landscape is typical of the whole region of Guilin. Till the late 1970s, Chunyan village was a beautiful but poor village. The whole village lived barely on a subsistence agriculture.

Since the early 1980s, Chunyan village has gradually become a sight-seeing place. It is especially famous for two scenic spots, namely, the Moon Hill and the 'Big Banyan Tree'. In the latter case, a Chinese film has made this place famous in the whole country. Today, besides individual tourists, visits to these two spots are part of the one-day river cruise program for many domestic and international tourists. In recent years, around one million tourists visited this small village per annum.

The responses of the village inhabitants to the new life chances are prompt. In 1992, this village had 90 households, 420 inhabitants and a labor force of 180 people. During tourism seasons, employment in tourism activities not only keeps all the village labor force busy, but attracts about 30 laborers from neighboring villages (Tab. 9–13). Because nearly all village laborers leave their field and hustle, a large part of farm jobs in Chunyan village have been occupied by farmers from neighboring villages. Thus, subject to the lucrative tourism businesses, agricultural activities in this village tend to get marginalized.

### Table 9–13: Tourism Employment Effects in Chunyan Village (Guilin), 1992[1]

| Tourist Service Activities | Employment |
|---|---|
| Souvenir businesses | 98 |
| Renting activities[2] | 50 |
| Photography | 26 |
| Catering | 24 |
| Others[3] | 12 |
| Total | 210 |

[1] In 1992, this village had a labor force of 180 people; [2] renting horses, ancient cloths for photography, etc.; [3] maintenance of tourist spots, etc.
Source: Author's field surveys.

The immediate payoff to the village members' participation in tourism development is sizable. Today, for most households in Chunyan village, various small-scale private businesses in tourism have become the principal source of family income. According to author's field surveys, in this village the annual income of a peasantry household earned directly from tourism lay in the range of 2,500–4,500 yuan in 1992, depending on the types and levels of engagement. In some cases, family income from tourism went up to 6,000–7,000 yuan. The mushrooming newly-built spacious peasant houses rising above the rural landscape reveal part of the story of substantial prosperity brought about by tourism at this rural place.

The impact of tourism on the local community goes far beyond mere material benefits. A new work ethic and rising entrepreneurship has shed a new release of life on this once decade-long sleepy

village. Tourism businesses have opened up possibiliti~~e~~
mobility, however moderate, for the village members a~~nu~~
for the youths. Local officials reported that, in an effort to do b~~ıgg~~
businesses in the future, 12 young people from this village have at
their own expenses participated in foreign language training courses.
For some of them, speaking English was said to have become part of
doing business.

## 9.6 Summary: A Model of Tourism Employment and Labor Mobility

The rapid rise of tourism has provided a range of jobs extending from
the unskilled to the highly specialized in forms of direct and induced
employment, generating an employment hierarchy. Under China's
new policy of economic liberalization, both urban and rural Chinese
households have exhibited a tendency to maximize their income by
allocating family resources (labor and, to a lesser degree, capital)
among occupational opportunities, for instance, between agriculture
and urban wage employment, between state and non-state sector,
etc. Obviously, tourism jobs represent different opportunities for the
different segments of the urban and rural labor markets in those areas
affected by tourism.

In Guilin, Suzhou and Beidaihe, job-taking and job-shift activities induced by tourism between and among individual labor market
segments have opened up certain chances of upward mobility for part
of their local inhabitants. The ongoing fragmentation of the urban
labor markets has also opened more chances for rural-urban migration, which tends to at least temporarily improve the life chances of
some rural migrants who otherwise live on the margin.

Fig. 9–6 attempts to illustrate the labor mobility induced by
tourism development in the study areas. With much oversimplifica-
tion, tourism-induced labor mobility can be examined at three levels:

(1) From non-tourism to tourism sector in the urban labor markets
Besides administration positions, top management posts and senior
positions at the intermediate supervisory levels which are most often held by the local privileged, the targeted jobs for urban laborers,
both as job opening and job changes, are either high-paying or more
prestigious in nature. The urban youths are inclined to take jobs in
international hotels. Job-shifts usually take place from the low-paid
in the state and collective sectors to the private sector, especially

running small souvenir shops and restaurants. As many new urban laborers are rather reluctant to take contract jobs in the state and collective sectors, they are in fact pushed to enter into private tourism businesses.

### Figure 9–6: Tourism Employment and Labor Mobility

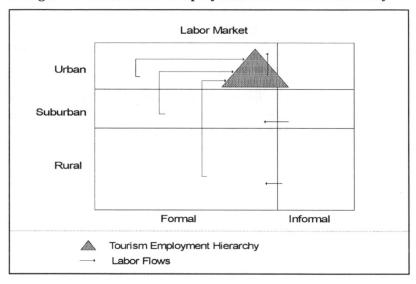

(2) From farm and to non-farm occupations in suburban areas
It seems arguable that, when mass tourism develops, tourist service activities can not only generate jobs for the indigenous in the tourist cities, but bring a considerable number of jobs to those people in areas surrounding them, especially to young laborers who would otherwise leave for the towns, thus slowing down potential rural-urban drifts. Among the study areas, nowhere is this tendency more evident than in Beidaihe and Yangshuo.

The responses of the rural population surrounding tourist cities to the new chances of work and income are prompt. A considerable number of original farmers have been drawn fully into various tourism businesses supplying services and goods directly to tourists. Others take middle-status jobs in the state or collective-owned tourism enterprises. Still others, though remaining in the agriculture sector, are engaged in part-time and seasonal work related to tourism such as mobile traders, or begin to shift to tourism-oriented cultivation or cashing crops such as vegetables, fruits, etc.

(3) From decade-long sleepy rural areas to tourist areas.

Compared to the indigenous, the employment areas of unskilled rural migrants are much broader. First, all direct tourism jobs which interest neither the urban indigenous nor the rural indigenous, are taken by temporary rural migrants. Second, the empty jobs left by former workers in urban sectors are most often filled by rural migrants. Third, temporal migrants also replace most of the more menial jobs which no longer interested the local population as living standard rose. Fourth, rural migrants are also engaged in certain informal sector activities.

Both pushed by lack of work in rural areas and pulled by the presumed employment and income opportunities in tourist cities, rural migrants are flooding into the labor markets of tourist areas, and begin to constitute an increasing proportion of their labor force. Though jobs taken by rural migrants cover a wide range, they are similar in one respect: more marginal, temporary, menial and low-paid. Rural migrants make up the lowest layer of workers in the tourism employment hierarchy. Nevertheless, for most rural migrants, employment in tourism and tourism-related sectors yields earnings higher than those available in rural sectors, especially subsistence agriculture.

# Part V

# Summary, Prospects and Policy Issues

# 10

# Summary

In responding to the decentralization policy, regional and local tourism initiatives in the post-reform era are enormous. Tourism industry is over-optimistically viewed as a promising avenue to local development. Foreign exchange receipts, vaguely-envisaged revenue effects and 'externalities' are among the first-ranked motives. While the goals of tourism development are poorly-defined on the part of local governments, the objectives of individual participation are explicit: jobs and better income opportunities.

Tourism development has pursued a quantitative maximization of tourist arrivals and gross receipts. Pursuit of sales maximization has led to a focal interest on quantitative expansions of tourism infrastructure which rely on heavy capital investment. Planning is often used as a 'trick' in alluring state investment. People-centered, community-responsive and socially responsible approaches in tourism planning and policy formulations are absent.

Local responses to the rising tourism business opportunities are prompt. Over the past decade, tourism investment has maintained at a very high level. Recent improvement in local tourism infrastructure is respectable. Tourism supply systems have followed a pluralistic development approach.

Deregulation and decentralization has stimulated enormous private initiatives. The non-state sector tends to have an increasing role to play in local tourist supplies. Especially, due to low entry barriers and plentiful lucrative market chances, domestic tourism has opened up an array of 'window of opportunity' for many small private investors. However, Broad-based participation in decision-making of the local population upon whom tourism developments affect remains non-existent. Local participation is thus partial and inconsistent.

Recent hotel investment is huge. In an economically weak area like Guilin, the growth of the international hotel sector is foreign investmentled. Hotel supply shortage has been eliminated unexpectedly within only a short span of time. However, the poor performance of the hotel industry suggests that international hotels, especially high-standard hotels, are over-developed. Hotel supply has thus changed from a seller's market to a typical buyer's market. In this process, early short-run monopolist profits, sales maximization thinking, lack of overall balance as well as difficulties in checking 'investment hunger' have all played their part.

The consequences of over-investment are multifold. Drastic decline in occupancy rates, widespread price-cutting, unfavorable terms of payment, existence problems of SOEs, heavy foreign debts and extensive leakage of foreign exchange receipts are characteristic of today's international hotel sector in Guilin. In this regard, local efforts in tourism development seem self-defeating.

In Suzhou, the penetration of international investment groups has been kept moderate. Comparatively stronger regional economy and more sophisticated commercial and industrial traditions seem crucial in explaining such a regional variation.

Commercialization and substantial growth have also taken place in domestic tourist supplies. In this development, the role of the state and non-state sector is different from one area to another. In Beidaihe, the rapid rise of small private guest houses is impressive. In big tourist cities where the growth of the private sector is impeded by lack of business space, explicit or implicit 'leasing' of collective- and state-owned facilities has gained ground. In many supply areas, the private sector has fulfilled significant supplementary functions.

The ways of functioning of the domestic tourist supply system have both under-developed and transitional features. Many Chinese danwei still play a big part in accommodation supply which is hardly observable in the supply market. Danwei guest houses have developed a hierarchy of service standards, reflecting its underpinning social and political structure.

Parallel development of international and domestic tourism is one of the most salient features of the tourism boom in China. While international tourism has followed an 'institutionalized' development, the growth of domestic tourism is spontaneous in nature. Between these two segments exist sharp discontinuities in both demand and supply, and therefore substitutability is marginal. Dualistic structure is apparent and pervasive in the entire tourism industry. Despite that international hotels and air transportation are increasingly used by domestic meeting and business travelers, direct contacts between international and domestic tourists are limited, taking place mainly at tourist spots.

Compared to the patterns observed at the national level, international tourism in Guilin and Suzhou is characterized by a higher share of foreign visitors and a faster growth rate. Since the late 1980s, international tourist demand has been undergoing remarkable structural changes in which foreigners, compatriots and overseas Chinese have played very different roles.

As overseas marketing authorities have been decentralized, local expertise has become increasingly crucial to tourism development. Shortage of human resources and marketing know-how has become an urgent issue. Decentralization in overseas marketing has exerted increasing pressures on tourism enterprises. Intensified competitions have led to continuous 'price-combats' among Chinese tour operators themselves, often resulting in unfavorable terms of business contracts. How to encourage free enterprise on the one hand and maintain rational national interests on the other remains an unsolved issue.

Domestic tourist demand is enormous, and growing at a rapid pace. The rise of mass domestic tourism has documented many ongoing economic, social and political changes in contemporary China. Improving standard of living, certain degree of individual freedom, urban growth and changing rural-urban relations, booming business and social activities as well as changing lifestyle have stimulated increasing mobility and rising demand for leisure and tourism of a considerable part of the Chinese population. Travel begins to take a higher place in consumers' scale of preferences. On the whole, domestic tourism is low-budgetary, urban-biased, sight-seeing, and highly cost- and distance-elastic in character.

Demand group has far out-ranged its traditional dimensions. Travel is no longer a merely symbolic expression of power and position in the social and political status hierarchy. Travel demand arises from both individual households and public institutions. Danwei-financed travel meetings make up a significant part of domestic tourism, whose demand is much less cost- and distance-elastic. Wealthy provinces in the eastern coastal region build up the major tourist sending areas. Well-to-do urban workers, private businessmen and the educated

211

tend to account for the lion's share of individual travelers at the inter-regional level.

China's domestic tourism is sight-seeing in nature, making a big difference to the holiday-making dominated recreational and tourism activities in the industrialized countries. Domestic travels usually take place on an individual basis and with a combination of motives of pleasure-seeking, economic and social kinds.

Domestic tourism has developed rich forms. At present, however, it is apparently dominated by one-day sight-seeing activities. One-day trips usually take place in the areas with a radius of 150 to 200 km from an urban center. Tourist flows appear in both directions. One-day tourist activities generate huge urban-rural traffics, exert enormous pressures on local infrastructure, but have little demand on local services.

Travel motives, destinations, expenditure and the range of demand on local goods and services are widely different between individual and meeting travelers, well-to-do and average tourists, and urban and rural visitors. Underpinning such a diversity are the appalling regional and urban-rural disparities, widening gap of personal income as well as the socio-political structure of the contemporary Chinese society.

International tourism tends to serve first and foremost the national goals of 'balance-of-payments'. Though tourist revenues are affected by national price policies and shifts in market compositions, the share of economic returns directly distributed to local economies is determined primarily by the ownership structure of enterprise systems (including contractual relationships), development strategies (especially investment structure and use of FDI), and the development stage and structure of local economies.

In Guilin, over-involvement of FDI has led to astonishing erosions of foreign exchange receipts. Lack of articulations between tourism and local non-tourism sectors is the most decisive explanatory factor to the lower share of returns to the local economy. In a developed and diversified economy like Suzhou, a prospering local souvenir sector has contributed the largest part of tourist revenues.

Due to its huge size, domestic tourism has significant revenue generation effects. In contrast to international tourism, domestic tourism appears to be much more friendly to the local economies. The largest part of domestic tourist revenues constitute the source of income of locally-owned tourist enterprises.

Domestic tourism has re-distributional effects in the national economy. Cross-region travels bring with them inter-regional transfers of national income. The influx of large number tourists in a destination can expand its local consumer market to a significant extent. The net effects of income transfers depend on the balance of inter-regional travel expenditure and, especially, the capacity of a destination in supplying locally-produced goods and services.

Tourism employment effects are significant. Tourism activities have opened a new area of employment in the local labor market, extending from direct to induced, skilled to unskilled, and formal to informal job opportunities. The top-three employment-generating sectors are hotels, restaurants, and souvenir trading. Both tourism- and area-specific factors are crucial in explaining the size and structure of tourism employment. International tourism has contributed no more than one-third of all direct tourism jobs.

Tourism employment effects are reflected first and foremost in tertiary sector. Tourist areas tend to have a more developed tertiary sector. Quantitative significance of direct tourism jobs rises apparently with decreasing size of local economy or its labor market. In a small economy, tourism has become an important employment factor.

During its start-up stage, tourism does not seem to be a typical labor-intensive sector. Especially, the opportunity costs of job creation in international tourism tend to be very high. On the contrary, domestic tourism is a relatively cheaper way of job generation.

Tourism can generate secondary employment and income effects. The prospering souvenir manufacturing industry in Suzhou is but one example. However, local capacity in taping potential tourism spillovers is widely different. Lack of market experience and grassroots innovations, and absence of talent entrepreneurs, who are readily to take certain perceived start-up risks, are crucial in explaining regional variations.

As individual households enjoy increasing freedom in allocating their family resources, tourism businesses have opened certain chances for certain population groups to maximize personal income and pursue upward mobility on a cross-occupation or cross-region basis.

Private business owners have benefited particularly from tourism expansions. In tourist areas, a growing tourism industry is vital to the rise of the private sector. Individual and self-employment occurs principally in domestic tourism. Job-shifts from the low-paid in the state and collective sectors to private sector employment are a com-

213

monplace. Engagement of family labor is widespread in many private business area, but seldom does a whole family get involved in the private sector. In many business areas, the private sector is far more flexible and competitive than the state and collective sectors, placing increasing pressures on lose-making SOEs.

Average wages in tourism tend to be higher than the industry averages. Within tourism, personal income in the private sector is much higher than the wage levels in the state sector, and still higher than in the collective sector. Wage levels in tourism also vary significantly among sorts of jobs and from one area to another.

The population in suburban and rural areas surrounding destinations can also benefit from a growing tourism. The employment and income effects generated by tourism on those once decade-long sleepy rural villages in Beidaihe and Guilin are particularly impressive. Growing tourism activities can lead to a convergence in rural-urban disparities and a certain form of urbanization. Tourism and tourism-related occupations have become the principal source of family livelihood. New work ethic begins to shed a new release of life on rural communities which formerly lived barely on subsistence agriculture.

Tourism and tourism-induced job and income opportunities have become a strong 'pull-factor' in rural-urban migration. Rural migrants constitute an increasing part of the labor force in tourist areas. Tourism-induced rural-urban migration is selective and seasonal. Chain migration can be observed in many cases.

A dualistic structure exists between jobs taken by the indigenous and those left to rural migrant. Rural migrants, whose general position in society is subordinate, make up the lowest layer of workers in the tourism sector. Typical jobs filled by rural migrants are low-status laboring, less secured, informal, and low-paid in character. Protection of labor rights of migrant workers has not been a political concern. Nevertheless, jobs and income in tourism and tourism-related activities can at least temporarily improve the life chances of rural migrants who otherwise live on the margin. Long-term effects of tourism-induced migration on human capital accumulation for the rural sector should not be underestimated.

# 11

# Prospects and Policy Issues

The observed facts in the study areas tend to discredit their hitherto tourism development strategies in several respects:

The role of tourism in local economic development is both sector- and area-conditioned. Tourism can be an important development factor for the tertiary sector and for relatively small areas. But, it is unlikely for a single tourism sector to play a leading industry's role in a rapid 'take-off' of the entire economy in areas of considerable population size. Thus, in a city like Guilin, local expectation of tourism as a short-cut to economic prosperity seems unrealistic.

In development of tourism, there exist a range of trade-offs between tourism and non-tourism, between types of tourism and projects, standard and size of tourist facilities, between foreign exchange objectives and local basic needs for employment and income, and so on. Different types of tourism and investment structure have significantly different impacts on the life chances and well-being of local population. Such possibilities of policy choice have to date caught inadequate attentions. Local decision-makers are interested exclusively in international tourism and big modern projects. Seldom is asked what kinds of projects are needed to establish and operate a successful tourism industry which really serves local development objectives, yet at rational and bearable investment costs.

Over the past decade, the largest part of investment has been concentrated in international tourism, especially in the hotel sector. Hitherto development of domestic tourism is spontaneous in nature. However, international tourism tends to be much less friendly than

215

domestic tourism to local economies and local participation. Development of international tourism presents high opportunity costs to the local economies in a wider sense. It requires heavy investment and, thus, the capital/labor ratio is especially high. It necessitates highly specialized industrial and marketing expertise which most destinations do not possess. But a large part of foreign exchange receipts do not constitute local revenues.

Ownership structure of enterprise systems and contractual relationships in tourism investment are decisive in determining the distribution of tourist revenues. Unfortunately, sufficient cautions have not been taken in using outside development resources, however necessary. Over-dependency on and inappropriate use of non-local capitals and skills, especially FDI, has led to a diminishing revenue base for the local economies. Too often have local efforts in seeking FDI equated means with ends.

A tourism-friendly economic structure is essential to spreading potential growth effects of tourism. Development of local sectors which supply goods and services to tourism can generate secondary employment and income effects, while drawing in large part on domestic resources. Up to now, however, nearly all investment has flown only into the narrowly-defined tourism sector. Cultivation of cross-sectoral links and strategic inter-sectoral balancing and integration have been simply neglected. Lack of industrial links between tourism and other local sectors is one of the most explicit deficits in hitherto development.

Local public sector has played an active part in tourism development. Besides infrastructure investment and operation of public utilities, local SOEs have engaged mainly in international tourism, including participation in joint-venture hotels. However, the performance of many SOEs and joint-venture enterprises appears to be very poor, leading to losses in the public sector economy. On the other hand, small investors in the private and informal sector tend to have achieved sizable returns.

On the whole, it seems clear that a short-cut to local prosperity via the vehicle of tourism, as has been hoped, does not exist. Due to the discouraging outcomes and recently rising resentment by the local population of tourism, it can be anticipated that the destination areas may begin to approach tourism more realistically, as an economic development tool. Re-adjustment and re-structuring may become a major accent in tourism development in the foreseeable future.

The structure and problems resulted from hitherto tourism development in Guilin, Suzhou and Beidaihe are different. Each destination is unique in its geography, tourism potential, position in national development schemes, stage of development, traditions in production and commerce, and so forth. Nevertheless, certain issues seem relevant for Guilin, Suzhou and Beidaihe in pursuit of sensible tourism development in the future.

(1) Goals of Tourism Development
First of all, there is a need to redefine the goals of tourism development, especially in Guilin. It can be anticipated that community objectives, in particular employment and income of local people, will occupy a higher place in tourism policy. Two factors tend to favor such a shift.

First, the priority of international tourism as an earner of foreign exchange in the national economy may reasonably be expected to decrease, as China's balance-of-payments has been significantly improving through the development of conventional export sectors.

Second, as decentralization and economic liberalization proceeds, local authorities will meet increasing pressures from local population for improvement in local well-being. Concern for local basic needs will have to be at the center of local politics. Of course, people-centered and community-responsive tourism planning only then becomes meaningful when development in the wider socio-political systems favors popular participation in politics.

(2) The Role of Tourism in Local Economic Systems
Destination areas need to rethink and redefine the appropriate place of tourism in their local economic systems. Obviously, even at the local level, many sectors may have a claim on the limited development resources available. Their potential for bringing about increases in employment and income, and even for earning foreign exchange, may be equal to or greater than that of tourism. Therefore, the logic place of tourism in the local economy depends on how it fits into overall development plan.

In defining the likely roles of tourism, both tourism- and area-specific factors are essential. Of particular importance are the size and general level of development of a destination area. Size refers to not only physical land area but population and its density. Determining the level of development is even more important, but more complicated.

In general, it seems that, in a large area, economic development can not rely merely on a single tourism sector. In a developed area, tourism tends to have a role of catalyst to play in the tertiary sector. This is of course not to be understood as excluding possibilities of tourism as a major vehicle for deliverance from backwardness of certain small areas where tourism resources are plentiful while alternative development may be limited.

(3) Inter-sectoral planning
Whatever place the tourism sector may take, one issue is crucial. That is, inter-sectoral planning. The purpose of inter-sectoral planning is twofold:

* first, to determine what priority tourism development is to receive;
* second, and more importantly, to establish articulations between tourism and tourism-related sectors. That is to say, the concept of tourism industry system should be broadened.

Obviously, solid inter-sectoral comparative analysis is essential in strategic planning.

To what extent a destination can raise the size and share of economic returns brought about by tourism to its local economy depends on how successful it is able to incorporate tourism into its local economic systems. In the long run, there is also a question of how to use the tourism-generated resources, if any, to diversify the local economy. Of particular importance is to increase the supply of locally-produced tourist goods and services. Souvenir manufactures, food production and processing, and other light manufactures are but some examples. In choosing what sectors should be developed, several factors are relevant, including but not limited to their relations to the tourism sector, elasticity of tourist expenditure, potential market capacity, kinds and levels of skills required, local expertise and resources.

As the cases of Guilin and Beidaihe have shown, local capacity in starting new production systems is generally weak. Characteristic barriers include lack of market experience, appropriate technologies, and workable organizations. Therefore, successful small-scale projects would be helpful in enlightening feasibility and motivating local participation.

From the national perspective, establishment of certain strategic industries which supply capital goods to long-term tourism development is of particular importance. At the local level, however, development of such strategic branches often meet additional economic and technical barriers. One of the most critical issues is the threshold of production. Tourism projects in individual destinations are unlikely to generate sufficient demand to spur the growth of such manufactures. In such case, a certain degree intervention of higher level government seems inevitable. Besides start-up financial and technical assistance and incentive legislation, inter-regional co-operation and sound division of demand markets from a national perspective are crucial.

Inter-sectoral planning requires considerable organizational and resource inputs. Implementation is yet more difficult. Besides lack of necessary financial resources and sufficiently legitimated authorities, implementation of integrated development plans may encounter substantial barriers resulting from considerations of maintaining current sources of local revenues. However obsolete the industrial equipment, some existing industrial branches, such as rubber processing industry in Guilin, are exactly the most important tax contributors to local revenues.

In spite of all these difficulties, the prospective gains make it worthwhile to carry out inter-sectoral plans. Only by establishing an integral and viable tourism and tourism-supporting industry system can potential growth effects of tourism and economy of scale be achieved so that dependencies on importation and erosions to local economies, broadly understood, will be reduced significantly.

(4)  International and Domestic Tourism

Within the tourism sector, there is a need to choose between the nature and types of tourism. In general, it can be expected that, besides Beidaihe, the 'key tourist city' Guilin and Suzhou will place increasing emphasis on the domestic tourism. Due to their attractions, all of them have a good prospect in taping and expanding domestic tourism businesses. At the same time, the quality of domestic tourism will rise significantly.

Undoubtedly, with rising income and more leisure time (e.g. the 5–day working system introduced in 1995) at disposal of individual households, travel will occupy an increasingly higher place in consumers' scale of preferences. Three immediate implications are:

* first, the proportion of the population taking part in leisure and tourism activities will grow steadily. Especially, the share of travelers to inter-regional destinations will be increasing rapidly. Thus,

tourist demand on local supply systems including accommodation will rise substantially. On the other hand, insufficient provision of inter-regional transportation will become a major bottleneck constraining a rapid growth of domestic tourism;

* second, the standard of demand on local tourist supplies will rise. The need for substantial improvements in the quality of local facilities and services will become more apparent;

* third, consequently, investment requirement in the development of domestic tourism will rise significantly. Nevertheless, domestic tourism remains an economic area in which local participation is most likely to take place. Especially, compared to international tourism, development of domestic tourism is a much cheaper way of job creation and income generation.

As inter-regional re-distributional effects of domestic tourism become more significant, and the balance of inter-regional travel expenditure tends to be to the advantage of economically less developed areas, domestic tourism will gain importance as a mechanism for the redistribution of income and employment at the national level. In this regard, selective provision of inter-regional transportation infrastructure, and certain financial and technical assistance to those potential destination areas seem worthy of try in achieving regional objectives. Such issues may become part and parcel of China's regional development policy.

With respect to international tourism, the continuing liberalization and deregulation of international trade, travel boom stimulated by the dynamic Asian economic and global political re-structuring tend to favor tourism expansions in Guilin and Suzhou. Especially, the construction of the new international airport in Guilin will give a big boost to its international tourism. While the role of the planned tourism and recreational center in Suzhou remains unclear.

On the other hand, however, development of international tourism in Guilin and Suzhou will meet a range of challenges in the coming years:

* First, the priorities of the 'key tourist cities' including Guilin and Suzhou in national development schemes may reasonably be expected to decrease, as international tourism will become less concentrated in the future.

* Second, inter-regional competitions will become continuously intensified. Marketing will be increasingly crucial to tourism businesses.

Especially, in Guilin, while in the past decade local efforts have focused on infrastructure development in order to accommodate rising demand, in the future it is most likely that tourism initiatives have to be placed on seeking more visitors because of the existence of tourist facilities, especially the sizable hotel stock. In the longer term, the rising demand for business offices of foreign and joint-venture companies may stimulate new development of international hotels.

* Third, in both places there is an increasing need to develop new tourism products, and more tailor-made travel arrangements besides package tours, if they try to remain viable in the marketplace.

Last but not least, in both places, further development of international tourism will be increasingly constrained by the lack of human resources in general, and shortage of marketing know-how and trained personnel in particular. On-the-job training can reduce, but not solve this problem. In addition, learning-by-doing may be at the expense of service qualities.

(5) Investment Structure and Tourism Projects

Despite of the importance of recognizing the need for a more realistic approach, mere tinkering with issues at the planning level will not accomplish this. Rather, substantive steps have to be taken in changing investment structure.

The first immediate implication is that the notion of tourism investment should be understood in a broader sense. Certain proportion of total tourism investment should be allocated in those sectors which directly support tourism. Without developing local tourism-supporting sectors, it is unlikely that the returns directly distributed to the local economies can be raised in a significant manner. Even if investment resources are limited, as are invariable the realities, a more balanced development of tourism and tourism-related sectors at a lower pace may be more desirable than an apparently single-structured development at a faster rate, if achieving local objectives enjoys high priorities.

The second implication is to improve the quality of tourism growth. A resource-saving and efficiency-enhancing development should be the central concern of future tourism initiatives.

Criteria measuring success of tourism development should be changed fundamentally. It must be recognized that increased scale alone is a very poor index. Focal interest on such aggregate incremental parameters as tourist arrivals and gross receipts is insufficient, and often misleading. Concerns have to be placed on how to reduce the opportunity-costs of tourism development by raising the efficiency in utilizing scarce resources.

While development of domestic tourism tends to require further expansions in local facilities, in the international tourism sector, however, more emphases should be put on improving the service qualities and the performance of existing facilities, instead of quantitative extensions based on reckless resource inputs.

Even in the long run, when new constructions become really necessary, wise choices between types and size of projects should be an important policy concern. It seems that big tourism projects tend to often override local preferences, leaving little room for local participation.

(6) Balance of Economic, Social and Environmental Objectives

Two issues will gain increasing weights in future tourism development. They are, social and environmental repercussions of mass tourism, which will become more apparent, and more problematic.

Obviously, tourism affects the life chances and well-being of local residents in different ways. While it creates employment and income opportunities for those engaged in tourism, especially private businessmen, its impacts on the well-being of those not directly involved in tourism can be generally regarded as negative.

The influx of large numbers of tourists exerts significant pressures on the supply of a range of goods, pushing up prices. This is particularly apparent in the case of foodstuffs, leading to perceivable negative effects on local residents as consumers, if not as producers. The distributional effects of tourism-induced inflation will become more critical as the Chinese people become increasingly price and inflation conscious.

In addition, tourists often compete with residents for limited community facilities and services. While tourism development tends to provide a basis for the restoration and improvement of historical and cultural spots as well as the survival of certain artifacts and activities, the benefits for local residents from such improvements are negligible. On the contrary, an increasing part of environmental and public facilities, which formerly provided 'free' access or at symbolic prices to local people, tend to be closed off to local residents in favor of visitors.

Accelerated inflation, over-crowded inner-city streets, and overloaded local transportation often result in a rising hostility to further tourism expansions, as have been observed at many tourist places in the study areas. The ways in which the distribution of tourism benefits affects the well-being of local communities deserve more research.

Even more critical for the long-run development is the environmental impacts of tourism, which have virtually not yet received any attentions. Degradation of physical environments resulted from inappropriate behaviors of a largest part of domestic visitors is observable at nearly all tourist spots. Therefore, concern for the environmental issues is central to future development. Especially in Guilin and Beidaihe, the physical environment per se is the basic tourism product.

Goodwill alone is not sufficient. Measures must be taken to protect the environment, broadly understood. Sustainable tourism development requires cooperation between all players in the tourism system.

At the political level, there is a need to devise policies of economic, legislative and administrative kinds which favors an environmentally sensitive tourism development.

At the planning level, comprehensive approaches are needed to incorporate environmental concerns at all levels of tourism planning and development. In this regard, such concepts as 'tourist carrying capacity' (both physically and socially understood) and 'sustainable development' are especially relevant.

At the economic level, destination areas should take into account the possible environmental costs in designing and developing their tourism products. In this respect, the concept 'low impact tourism' is instructive. More directly, appropriate environmental infrastructure should be developed for tourism facilities, especially those gardens and parks which have been under enormous pressures resulted from increasing numbers of visitors.

Still more crucial is to raise the environmental awareness on the demand side, as is suggested by the concept 'eco-tourism'. In view of mass domestic tourism and, especially, underdeveloped environmental awareness, enlightening education of current and future tourists is indispensable. In this regard, the role of state is crucial. A deepseated non-physical environmental infrastructure can be established only by incorporating environmental concerns into basic education in the entire education system. And only when individual visitors learn to respect the environment, there is still a hope. Obviously, the task to develop such an infrastructure is immense. But in spite of this, the long-term gains make such efforts worthwhile.

## (7)  The Role of Different Actors

What part will the various actors play in future tourism development depends very much on the development in the wider social and political areas. If the acceptance of the ideology of market-driven economies and the political shift to decentralization and regional autonomy continue, then following trends can be anticipated:

Certain retrenchment of direct state involvement in tourism businesses may take place. More responsibility for development and operation of tourism facilities will be transferred to the private sector, broadly understood. Government investment will be concentrated in infrastructure development, especially at the inter-regional level.

Deregulation will continue. The role of market forces in tourist supply will be growing rapidly. As the role of the market rises, deficiencies of the state-owned sector associated with the 'principal-agent' issue will become more and more apparent. Many SOEs will be under increasing pressures. In regional perspective, only those places that can offer competitive and marketable tourism products can remain viable in the marketplace.

Continuing decentralization will place more responsibility for tourism planning and development to the regional and local authorities. More active local participation, an expanding private sector, emergence of a new entrepreneurial class as well as more social mobility will be some of the outcomes of tourism development at the local level.

On the other hand, further move toward market economies may bring with it conflicts between pursuit of economic objectives and the concerns for social and environmental responsibility in tourism development. How to encourage establishing cooperative public/private partnerships, and how to balance the needs for economic efficiency, social equity and environmental sustainability will be a lasting issue in future tourism development.

# Bibliography

Adelman, I. and Fuwa, N. (1994), 'Income Inequality and Development: The 1970s and 1980s Compared', *Economie Appliquée*, XLVI (1): 7–29

Amsden, A.H. (1994), 'Why isn't the Whole World Experimenting with the East Asian Model to Develop? Review of the East Asian Miracle', *World Development*, 22 (4): 627–633

Ashworth, G.J. and Dietvorst, A.J. (1995), *Tourism and Spatial Transformations*, Oxford: C.A.B International

Ashworth, G. and Goodall, B. (1990), *Marketing Tourism Places*, London: Routledge

Aturupane, H. (1994), 'Poverty, Human Development, and Growth: An Emerging Consensus?', *American Economic Review*, 84 (2): 244–249

Bai, Z. and Li, J. (1990), 'Lüyou tizhi gaige' (Reform of Tourism Systems), in Sun, S. (ed.), *Zhongguo lüyou jingji yanjiu*, 91–119, Beijing: People's Press

Balcerowicz, L. (1994), 'Democracy is No Substitute for Capitalism', *Eastern European Economics*, 32 (2): 39–49

Baranzini, M. and Scazzieri, P. (eds) (1990), *The Economic Theory of Structure and Change*, Cambridge: Cambridge University Press

Bardhan, P. (1993), 'Economics of Development and Development of Economics', *Journal of Economic Perspectives*, 7 (2): 129–142

BDHTN: *Beidaihe tongji nianjian* (Statistical Yearbook of Beidaihe) (various issues), Beidaihe: Statistical Bureau of Beidaihe

Bell, M.W., Heo Ee Khor and Kochhar, K. (eds) (1993), *China at the Threshold of a Market Economy*, Washington DC: IMF

Bentley, R. (1991), 'World Tourism Outlook for the 1990s', in Hawkins, D.E. and Ritchie, J.R. (eds), *World Travel and Tourism Review*, Vol. 1: 55–58, Oxford: C.A.B International

Berry, B.J.L. (1990), 'Review on J. Friedmann's Book: Life Space and Economic Space – Essays in Third World Planning', *Economic Development and Cultural Change*, 38 (4): 872–876

Bodlender, J., Jefferson, A., Jenkins, C. and Lickorish, L. (1991), *Developing Tourism Destinations*, Hong Kong: Longman

Bohnet, A., Hong, Z. and Mueller, F. (1993), 'China's Open-door Policy and its Significance for Transformation of the Economic System', *Intereconomics*, 28 (4): 191–197

BMZ (Bundesministerium für wirtschaftliche Zusammenarbeit und Entwicklung) (1994), *Länderkurzbericht – VR China*, Bonn: Referat 102

Bradford Burris CMC (1991), 'Business Travel as a Segment of World Tourism', in Hawkins, D.E. and Ritchie, J.R. (eds), *World Travel and Tourism Review*, Vol. 1: 145, Oxford: C.A.B International

Briassoulis, H. (ed.) (1992), *Tourism and the Environment*, Dordrecht: Kluwer Academic Publishers

Bryant, C. (1982), *Managing Development*, Boulder: Westview Press

Bryden, J.M. (1973), *Tourism and Development – A Case Study of the Commonwealth Caribbean*, Cambridge: Cambridge University Press

Bull, A. (1995), *The Economics of Travel and Tourism*, Sydney: Pitman

Burns, P.M. and Holden, A. (1995), *Tourism: A New Perspective*, London: Prentice Hall

Butler, R.W. (1980), 'The Concept of a Tourist Area Cycle of Evolution: Implications for Management of Resources', *Canadian Geographer*, 24: 5–12

Butler, R. and Pearce, D. (1995), *Change in Tourism: People, Places, Processes*, London: Routledge

Cable, V. and Ferdinand, P. (1994), 'China as an Economic Giant - Threat or Opportunity?', *International Affairs*, 70 (2): 243–261

Cai, X. and Chen, Q. (1992), 'Xiangzhen qiye gufenzhi wenti' (Issues of Share-holding Systems in Rural Enterprises), *Suzhou xiangzhen qiye*, 71: 14–15

Cai, Y. (1986), 'Guilin lüyouye de wenti yu qianjian' (Problems and Prospects of Tourism in Guilin), in Li, H. (ed.), *Guilin lüyou fazhan zhanlüe wenji*, 146–155, Guilin: Lijiang Press

Callaghan, P., Long, P. and Robinson, M. (eds) (1994), *Travel & Tourism*, Newcastle upon Tyne: Center for Travel & Tourism, University of Northumbria

Cannon, T. (1990), 'Regions - Spatial Inequality and Regional Policy', in Cannon, T. and Jenkins, A. (eds), *The Geography of Contemporary China*, 28–60, London: Routledge

Chang, K. (1993), 'The Peasant Family in the Transition from Maoist to Lewisian Rural Industrialization', *Journal of Development Studies*, 29 (2): 220–244
– (1994), 'Chinese Urbanization and Development before and after Economic Reform: A Comparative Reappraisal', *World Development*, 22 (4): 601–613

Chaudhuri, T.D. (1989), 'A Theoretical Analysis of the Informal Sector', *World Development*, 17 (3): 351–355

Chi, J. (1993), 'Lun zhongguo lüyou fazhan de ruogan wenti' (Some Issues of Tourism Development in China), *Lüyou diaoyan* 9: 13–21

Collier, A. (1989), *Principles of Tourism*, Hong Kong: Pitman

Coates, J.F. (1991), 'Tourism and the Environment: The Reality of the 1990s', in Hawkins, D.E. and Ritchie, J.R. (eds), *World Travel and Tourism Review*, Vol. 1: 66–71, Oxford: C.A.B International

Cooper, C., Fletcher, J., Gilbert, D. and Wanhill, S., *Tourism: Principles and Practice*, Singapore: Longman

Coltman, M.M. (1989), *Tourism Marketing*, New York: Van Nostrand Reinhold

Crick, M. (1992), 'Life in the Informal Sector – Street Guides in Kandy, Sri Lanka', in Harrison, D. (ed.), *Tourism and the Less Developed Countries*, 135–147, London: Belhaven Press

Crouch, G.I. (1994), 'The Study of International Tourism Demand: A Review of Findings', *Journal of Travel Research*, 33: 12–23

D' Amore, L.J. (1991), 'Sustainable Tourism Development in the Third World', in Hawkins, D.E. and Ritchie, J.R. (eds), *World Travel and Tourism Review*, Vol. 1: 170–172, Oxford: C.A.B International

Dannhaeuser, N. (1991), 'Formal-sector Retail Trade in the Urban Third World: Conceptual Issues and the Case of Nasik City, India', *Economic Development and Cultural Change*, 39 (2): 311–329

Davey, K. (1985), *Financing Regional Development*, Chichester: John Wiley & Sons Ltd.

De Kadt, E. (ed.) (1979), *Tourism – Passport to Development? Perspectives on the Social and Cultural Effects of Tourism in Developing Countries*, Oxford: Oxford University Press

Dollar, D. (1990), 'Economic Reform and Allocative Efficiency in China's State-Owned Industry', *Economic Development and Cultural Change*, 39 (1): 89–105

Domrös, M. and Peng, G. (1988), *The Climate of China*, Berlin, Springer-Verlage

Eber, S. (ed.) (1992), *Beyond the Green Horizon: Principles for Sustainable Tourism* (A discussion paper commissioned from Tourism Concern by WWF UK)

*Economists* (1991), 'Travel and Tourism', 23 March Issue

Edgell, D.L. (1991), 'International Tourism Policy: Perspectives for the 1990s', in Hawkins, D.E. and Ritchie, J.R. (eds), *World Travel and Tourism Review*, Vol. 1: 194–196, Oxford: C.A.B International

Ellman, M. (1994), 'Transformation, Depression, and Economics: Some Lessons', *Journal of Comparative Economics*, 19: 1–21

El Shakhes, S. (1972), 'Development, Primacy and Systems of Cities', *Journal of Developing Areas*, 7: 11–36

Estrin, S. (1993), 'Enterprises in Transition', *Eastern European Economics*, 31 (5): 3–18

Ettlinger, N. (1994), 'The Localization of Development in Comparative Perspective', *Economic Geography*, 70 (2): 144–166

Fasbender, K. (1993), 'Aspects of Regional Rural Development', *Intereconomics*, 28 (2): 87–94

Feng, L. (ed.) (1991), *Zhongguo laodong shichang* (The Chinese Labor Market), Beijing: City Press

Fields, G.S. (1975), 'Rural-urban Migration, Urban Unemployment and Underemployment, and Job-search Activity in LDCs', *Journal of Development Economics*, 2: 165–187

Finsterbusch, K. (1989), 'Beneficiary Participation in Development Projects: Empirical Tests of Popular Theories', *Economic Development and Cultural Change*, 37 (3): 573–593

Freyer, W. (1995), *Tourismus - Einführung in die Fremdenverkehrsökonomie*, München: Oldenbourg Verlag

FTB (Funing Tourism Bureau) (1992), Nandaihe jianjie (Introduction to Nandaihe) (unpublished)

Fu, G. (1992), *Zhongguo laodong shichang de jingji fenxi* (An Economic Analysis of the Chinese Labor Market), Shanghai: People's Press

Gao, C. and Wang, C. (1984), 'Beijing jianguo fandian guanli de diaoyan' (Investigation of the Management of Beijing Jianguo Hotel), *Lüyou jingji*, 3: 41

Gee, C.Y., Makens, J.C. and Dexter, D.J.L. (1997), *The Travel Industry*, New York: Van Nostrand Reinhold

Gerstlacher, A., Krieg, R. and Sternfeld, E. (1991), *Tourism in the PR China*, Bangkok: Ecumenical Coalition on Third World Tourism

Gibson, B. (1994), 'A Classical Theory of the Informal Sector', *The Manchester School*, LKII (1): 81–96

GLERC (Guilin Economic Research Center) (1989), *Guilin lüyou qianjing* (Prospects of Guilin's Tourism), Guilin: Lijiang Press

GLCPB (Guilin City Planning Bureau) (1988), *Guilin chengshi fazhan guihua 1985–2000* (City Development Planning of Guilin 1985–2000), Guilin: City Planning Bureau

GLTN: *Guilin tongji nianjian* (Statistical Yearbook of Guilin) (various issues), Beijing: China Statistical Publishing House

GLURC (Guilin Urban and Rural Construction Committee) (1990), 'Baohu Lijiang' (Protecting the Lijiang River), *Guilin jingji yanjiu*, 30 (2): 33–35

Gormsen, E. (1979), 'Cancun – Entwicklung, Funktion und Probleme neuer Tourismuszentren in Mexiko', *Frankfurter Wirtschafts- und Sozialgeographische Schriften*, 30: 299–324

– (1983a), 'Der internationale Tourismus, eine neue Pionierfront in Ländern der Dritten Welt', *Geographische Zeitschriften*, 71 (3): 149–165

– (1983b), 'Tourismus in der Dritten Welt; historische Entwicklung, Diskussionsstand, sozialgeographische Differenzierung', *Geographische Rundschau*, 35 (12): 608–617

– (1985) (ed.) 'The Impact of Tourism on Regional Development and Cultural Change', Mainz: *Mainzer Geographische Studien*, 26

– (1989), 'Tourism in China: Some Aspects of Development and Social changes', *Klagenfurter Geographische Schriften*, 9: 65–72

– (1990a), 'Tourismus in China – Entwicklung, Probleme und Perspektiven', in Institut für Tourismus, FU Berlin, *Berichte und Materialen*, 8: 143–156

– (1990b), 'The Impact of Tourism on Regional Change in China', *GeoJournal*, 21 (1): 127–135

– (1991), 'Tourism as an Agent of Incorporation: Examples from Latin America', *Nijmegen Studies in Development and Cultural Change*, 8: 175–188

– (1993), 'Tourismusentwicklung in China', *Nürnberger Wirtschafts- und Sozialgeographische Arbeiten*, 46: 137–179

– (1995a), 'International Tourism in China: Its Organization and Socio-economic Impact', in Lew, A.A. and Yu, L. (eds), *Tourism in China*, 63–88, Boulder: Westview Press

– (1995b), 'Travel Behavior and the Impacts of Domestic Tourism in China', in Lew, A.A. and Yu, L. (eds), *Tourism in China*, 131–140, Boulder: Westview Press

Gormsen, E., Hemberger, R. and Wagner, S. (1991), 'Leben von den Fremden – Strukturwandel als Folge des Tourismus', *Das neue China*, 18 (1): 31–35

Gormsen, E. and Lenz, K. (eds) (1987), 'Der Fremdenverkehr in Lateinamerika und seine Folgen für Regionalstruktur und kulturellen Wandel', in *Lateinamerika im Brennpunkt*, 183–207, Berlin

Grabowski, R. (1994), 'The Successful Developmental State: Where Does It Come From', *World Development*, 22 (3): 413–422

GTB (Guangxi Tourism Bureau) (ed.) (1988), *Guangxi lüyou* (Tourism in Guangxi), Nanning: Tourism Bureau of Guangxi Zhang Autonomous Regions

Gu, Y. (1992), 'Dui shierge chengshi de guoji fandian de jingying fenxi' (Analysis of the Operation of International Hotels in 12 Cities), *Lüyou yanjiu yu shijian*, 2: 43

*Guilin shijing* (Ten Scenes of Guilin) (1987), Beijing: People's Press

Guo, L. and Bao, J. (1989), Zhongguo lüyou dili de huigu yu zhanwang (Tourism Geography in China: Retrospect and Prospect (unpublished manuscript)

Guo, W. (1988), 'Zhonguo quyu fazhan zhanlüe de zhuanbian yu xiguangjia' (The Transformation and the New Framework of China's Regional Development Policy), *Keji cenkao*, 2: 10–14

Hall, C.M. and Jenkins, J.M. (1995), *Tourism and Public Policy*, London: Routledge

Hall, D.R. (ed.) (1991), *Tourism and Economic Development in Eastern Europe and the Soviet Union*, New York: Halsted Press

Harris, J.R. and Todaro, M. (1970), 'Migration, Unemployment and Development: A Two-sector Analysis', *American Economic Review*, 60 (1): 126–142

Harrison, D. (ed.) (1992a), *Tourism and the Less Developed Countries*, London: Belhaven Press
– (1992b), 'Tourism and the Less Developed Countries: The Background', in Harrison, D. (ed.), *Tourism and the Less Developed Countries*, 1–18, London: Belhaven Press
– (1992c), 'Tourism to Less Developed Countries: The Social Consequences', in Harrison, D. (ed.), *Tourism and the Less Developed Countries*, 19–34, London: Belhaven Press

Hawkins, D. E. and Ritchie, J.R. (eds), *World Travel and Tourism Review*, Vol. 1, Oxford: C.A.B International

He, Z. (1990), 'Progress of Geography of Tourism in the P.R. China', *GeoJournal*, 21: 115–122

Heberer, T. (1989), *Die Rolle des Individualsektors für Arbeitsmarkt und Stadtwirtschaft in der Volksrepublik China*, Bremen: Bremer Beiträge zur Geographie und Raumplanung 18 (Arbeiten zur Chinaforschung)

Hemberger, R. (1990), 'Tourismus in Dali', in Institut für Tourismus, FU Berlin, *Berichte und Materialen*, 8: 169–177
– (1991), Der Tourismus in Dali – Entwicklung, Wirkungen und Perspektiven in einer chinesischen Tourismus-Region (unpublished Masters thesis), University of Mainz

Hemmer, H.R. (1990), '40 Jahre Entwicklungstheorie und -politik', *Zeitschrift für Wirtschafts- und Sozialwissenschaften*, 110: 505–570

Hillman, A.L. (1994), 'The Transition from Socialism: An Overview from a Political Economy Perspective', *European Journal of Political Economy*, 10: 191–225

Hong, J. (1995), 'Jiashu fazhan guonei lüyouye di sikao' (Some Thoughts on Promoting Domestic Tourism Development), *Lüyou jingji*, 4: 25–26

Hornik, R. (1994), 'Bursting China's Bubble', *Foreign Affairs*, 73 (3): 28–42

Hoselitz, B.F. (1955), 'Generative and Parasitic Cities', *Economic Development and Cultural Change*, 3 (2): 278–294

Höfels, T. (1990), 'Fremdenverkehr und regionale Beschäftigungseffekte in der Türkei', *Geographische Rundschau*, 42 (1): 21–26

Hu, S. (1996), 'Fazhan guonei lüyou zhi qianjian' (Prospects of Domestic Tourism), *Xueshujie*, 4: 90–93

Huebner, M. (1997), Der Tourismus und seine Folgen für Regionale Strukturen und soziokulturellen Wandel in China am Beispiel peripherer Regionen (unpublished Ph.D. thesis), University of Mainz

Hussain, A. (1994), 'Social Security in Present-day China and its Reform', *American Economic Review*, 84 (2): 276–280

Illeris, S. (1993), 'An Inductive Theory of Regional Development', *Papers of Regional Science*, 72 (2): 113–134

Jefferson, G.H. and Rawski, T.G. (1994), 'Enterprise Reform in Chinese Industry', *Journal of Economic Perspectives*, 8 (2): 47–70

Jefferson, G.H. and Xu, W. (1991), 'The Impact of Reform on Socialist Enterprises in Transition: Structure, Conduct, and Performance in Chinese Industry', *Journal of Comparative Economics*, 15: 45–64

Jiang, P. (1996), 'Guanyu fazhan guonei lüyou di shuping' (Comments on Domestic Tourism Development), *Lüyou jingji*, 3: 15–17

Kamath, S.J. (1990), 'Foreign Direct Investment in a Centrally Planned Developing Economy: The Chinese Case', *Economic Development and Cultural Change*, 39 (1): 107–130
– (1994), 'Property Rights and the Evolution of Foreign Direct Investment in a Centrally Planned Developing Economy: Reply to Pomfret', *Economic Development and Cultural Change*, 42 (2): 419–425

Kleiner, P. and Patzak, H. (1991), 'Social Economics: A New Tool for the Governing of Tourism', in Hawkins, D.E. and Ritchie, J.R. (eds), *World Travel and Tourism Review*, Vol. 1: 173–177, Oxford: C.A.B International

Körner, H. (1994), 'The Third World in the 1990s: Problems and Challenges', *Intereconomics*, 29 (2): 92–97

Krieg, R. (1993), 'Kommerzieller Tourismus in der VR China, Entwicklung mit Hindernissen', *Das neue China*, 20 (1): 10–14

Kreth, R. (1985), 'Some Problems Arising from Tourist Boom in Acapulco and the Difficulties in Solving Them', in Gormsen, E. (ed.), *The Impact of Tourism on Regional Development and Cultural Change*, 42–54, Mainz: Mainzer Geographische Studien 26

Krueger, A.O. (1994), 'Lessons from Developing Countries about Economic Policy', *The American Economist*, 38 (1): 3–9

Kulke, E. (1986), 'Regionale wirtschaftliche Entwicklung durch industrielle Kleinbetriebe in der Dritten Welt', *Zeitschrift für Wirtschaftsgeographie*, 30 (2): 23–34

Kurent, H.P. (1991), 'Tourism in the 1990s: Threats and Opportunities', in Hawkins, D. E. and Ritchie, J.R. (eds), *World Travel and Tourism Review*, Vol. 1: 78–82, Oxford: C.A.B International

Kwon, J. (1994), 'The East Asia Challenge to Neoclassical Orthodoxy', *World Development*, 22 (4): 635–644

Lall, S. (1994), 'The East Asian Miracle: Does the Bell Toll for Industrial Strategy?', *World Development*, 22 (4): 645–654

Lan, W. and Tan, Y. (1990), 'Gaishan Guilin lüyouye de jingji xiaoyi' (Improve the Economic Efficiency of Guilin's Tourism), in Wang, J. (ed.), *Guilin gucheng de baohu yu jianshe*, 124–130, Beijing: Reform Press

Laws, E. (1991), *Tourism Marketing*, Cheltenham: Stanley Thornes Ltd.

Laws, E. (1995), *Tourist Destination Management*, London: Routledge

Lea, J. (1995), *Tourism and Development in the Third World*, London: Routledge

Lee, J.R. and Malek, A. (1991), 'Multilateral Trade Negotiations and the Tourist Industry', in Hawkins, D.E. and Ritchie, J.R. (eds), *World Travel and Tourism Review*, Vol. 1: 210–212, Oxford: C.A.B International

Lew, A.A. and Yu, L. (eds), *Tourism in China: Geographic, Political and Economic Perspectives*, Boulder: Westview Press

Lew, A.A. (1995), 'Overseas Chinese and Compatriots in China's Tourism Development', in Lew, A.A. and Yu, L. (eds), *Tourism in China*, 155–175, Boulder: Westview Press

Lewis, W.A. (1954), 'Economic Development with Unlimited Supplies of Labor', *The Manchester School*, 22: 139–192

– (1958), 'Unlimited Labor: Further Notes', *The Manchester School*, 26: 1–32

Li, J. (1990), *Beidaihe daoyou* (Beidaihe: A Guide), Tianjin: Tianjin Press

Li, M. and Hu, X. (eds) (1991), *Liudong renkou dui dachengshi fazhan de yingxiang jiqi duice* (The Impact of Floating Population on the Development of Large Cities and Policies), Beijing: Economic Daily Press

Li, S. (1990), 'Lishi wenhua mingcheng Guilin de tezheng yu fazhan' (Characters and Development of the Historical and Cultural City Guilin), in Wang, J. (ed.), *Guilin gucheng de baohu yu jianshe*, 5–20, Beijing: Reform Press

– (1991), 'Huilü yu guoji lüyou jiage jiuce' (Foreign Exchange

Rates and Price Decisions in International tourism), *Lüyou jingji*, 3: 47–51

Li, W. (1986), 'Guilin chanye fazhan zhanlüe' (Industrial Development Strategy of Guilin), in Li, H. (ed.), *Guilin jingji fazhan zhanlüe wenji*, 156–163, Guilin: Lijiang Press

*Lijiang shijing* (Ten Scenes of Lijiang) (1987), Beijing: People's Press

Lillywhite, M. (1991), 'Low Impact Tourism', in Hawkins, D.E. and Ritchie, J.R. (eds), *World Travel and Tourism Review*, Vol. 1: 162–169, Oxford: C.A.B International

Lim, C. (1997), 'Review of International Tourism Demand Models', *Annals of Tourism Research*, 24 (4): 835–849

Liu, A. and Zhang, L. (1990), Suzhou lüyou shangpin xiaoshou de tezheng (Characters of Tourist goods Trading in Suzhou), in Suzhou Tourism Bureau (ed.), Suzhou lüyou shangpin kaifa wenji (unpublished)

Liu, S. (1987), *Day Tour in Guilin*, Guilin: Lijiang Press

Liu, Y. (ed.) (1991), *Zhonguo lüyou jingdian* (Tourist Attractions of China), Shanghai: People's Art Publishing House

Long, V.H. (1991), 'Government-Industry-Community Interaction in Tourism Development in Mexico', in Sinclair, M.T. and Stabler, M. (eds), *The Tourism Industry*, 185–204, Wallingford: C.A.B International

Lundberg, D.E., Krishnamoorthy, M. and Stavenga, M.H. (1995), *Tourism Economics*, New York: John Wiley & Sons Inc.

Lütkenhorst, W. and Reinhard, J. (1993), 'The Increasing Role of the Private Sector in Asian Industrial Development', *Intereconomics*, 28 (1): 22–34

*Lüyou jingji* (Tourism Economy) (various issues), Beijing: People's University

Lyons, T. (1991), 'Interprovincial Disparities in China: Output and Consumption, 1952–1987', *Economic Development and Cultural Change*, 39 (3): 471–506

Ma, L.J.C. and Cui, G. (1987), 'Administrative Changes and Urban Population in China', *Annals of Association of American Geographers*, 77 (3): 373–395

Ma, S. (1991), 'Zhonguo guoji lüyou jiage tiaozheng de pingjia yu qianjing' (Assessment and Prospects of Price Adjustment in China's International Tourism), *Lüyou jingji*, 2: 42–44

Ma, X. (1990), 'Taihu diqu chengshihua yu xiangcun jingji fazhan' (Urbanization and Rural Economic Development in the Taihu Area), in Ma, X. and Yu, X. (eds), *Taihu diqu xiangcun dili*

(Rural Geography of the Taihu Area), 178–196, Beijing: Science Press

Mackie, V. (1992), 'Japan and Southeast Asia: The International Division of Labor and Leisure', in Harrison, D. (ed.), *Tourism and the Less Developed Countries*, 75–84, London: Halsted Press

Mathieson, A. and Wall, G. (1993), *Tourism: Economic, Physical and Social Impacts*, Essex: Longman

McIntyre, G. (1993), *Sustainable Tourism Development: Guide for Planners*, Madrid: WTO

McIntosh, R.W. and Goeldner, C.R. (1986), *Tourism: Principles, Practices, Philosophy*, New York: John Wiley & Sons, Inc.

Mei, L. (1994), 'Shilun woguo guonei lüyouye fazhan di xianzhuang, qushi ji duice' (Domestic Tourism: Current Situation, Trends, and Policies), *Xiaofei jingji*, 5: 24–28

Meng, Z. (1992), 'Zhonguo hezi fandian de waizhai wenti' (Foreign Debts of Joint-venture Hotels in China), *Lüyou yanjiu yu shijian*, 11: 7–12

Middleton, V.T.C. (1993), *Marketing in Travel & Tourism*, Oxford: Butterworth-Heinemann Ltd.

Müller, B. (1983), *Fremdenverkehr und Entwicklungspolitik zwischen Wachstum und Ausgleich. Folgen für die Stadt- und Regionalentwicklung in peripheren Räumen: Beispiele von der mexikanischen Pazifikküste*, Mainz: Mainzer Geor. Studien 25

Nash, M. (1955), 'Some Notes on Village Industrialization in South and East Asia', *Economic Development and Cultural Change*, 3 (2): 271–277

Naughton, B. (1994), 'Chinese Institutional Innovation and Privatization from Below', *American Economic Review*, 84 (2): 266–270

Nee, V. (1991), 'Peasant Entrepreneurs in China's Second Economy', *Economic Development and Cultural Change*, 39 (2): 293–310

Nozawa, H. (1991), 'Pacific-Asia Travel Market', in Hawkins, D.E. and Ritchie, J.R. (eds), *World Travel and Tourism Review*, Vol. 1: 103–105, Oxford: C.A.B International

NTA (National Tourism Administration of the People's Republic of China), *Yearbook of China Tourism Statistics* (various issues), Beijing: China's Tourism Press

NTA (National Tourism Administration of the People's Republic of China) (1991), 'Zhongguo lüyouye fazhan zhanlüe' (Development Strategies of China's Tourism Industry), in *Zhongguo lüyou tongji nianjian*, 105–116, Beijing: China Tourism Press

Oakes, T. (1995), Tourism in Guizhou: Place and the Paradox of Modernity (unpublished Ph.D. thesis), Seattle: University of Washington

Page, J.M. (1994), 'The East Asian Miracle: An Introduction', *World Development*, 22 (4): 615–625

Pang, T. and Ding, M. (1994), 'Dui guonei lüyou di jidian sikao' (Some Thoughts on Domestic Tourism), *Lüyou xuekan*, 2: 32–35

Pearce, D. (1991), 'Tourism Policy: A Multi-Scale Policy Approach', in Hawkins, D.E. and Ritchie, J.R. (eds), *World Travel and Tourism Review*, Vol. 1: 178–179, Oxford: C.A.B International

Pearce, D. (1995), *Tourism Today: A Geographical Analysis*, New York: Longman

Peng, Y. (1988), *Zhongguo gudian yuanlin fengxi* (Analysis of Classical Chinese Gardens), Beijing: China's Architectural Industry Publishing House

Perkins, D. (1994), 'Completing China's Move to the Market', *Journal of Economic Perspectives*, 8 (2): 23–46

Perkins, D.H. (1994), 'There are at Least Three Models of East Asian Development', *World Development*, 22 (4): 655–661

Pomfret, R. (1994), 'Foreign Direct Investment in a Centrally Planned Developing Economy: Lessons from China: Comment in Kamath', *Economic Development and Cultural Change*, 42 (2): 413–418

Putterman, L. (1992), 'Dualism and Reform in China', *Economic Development and Cultural Change*, 40 (3): 467–493

Pye, E.A. and Lin, T. (eds) (1983), *Tourism in Asia: The Economic Impact*, Singapore: Singapore University Press (NUS)

Qian, Z. and Zhu, X. (1989), *Discover Chinese Cities – Suzhou*, Beijing: New World Press

Qiao, L. (1993), 'Shilun zhongguo guonei lüyou' (On China's Domestic Tourism), *Caimao jingji*, 5: 54–57

Qiao, Y. (1995), 'Domestic Tourism in China: Policies and Development', in Lew, A.A. and Yu, L. (eds), *Tourism in China*, 121–130, Boulder: Westview Press

Qin, Z. (1986), 'Lun Guilin de lüyou fazhan' (On Tourism Development in Guilin), in Li, H. (ed.), *Guilin jingji fazhan zhanlüe wenji*, 182–196, Guilin: Lijiang Press

Qiu, L., Wei, B. and Shi, L. (1990), 'Zhongguo lüyou fazhan shinian' (Ten Years of Tourism Development in China), in Sun, S. (ed.), *Zhongguo lüyou jingji yanjiu*, 1–32, Beijing: People's Press

QTB (Qinhuangdao Tourism Bureau) (ed.) (1990), *Qinhuangdao daoyou* (Qinhuangdao: A Guide), Beijing: People's University Press

Quick, P.D. (1991), 'Travel and Tourism in National Economies: Present and Future', in Hawkins, D.E. and Ritchie, J.R. (eds), *World Travel and Tourism Review*, Vol. 1: 72–77, Oxford: C.A.B International

Rakowski, C.A. (1994), 'Convergence and Divergence in the Informal Sector Debate: A Focus on Latin America, 1984–92', *World Development*, 22 (4): 501–516

Ranis, G. and Fei, J.C.H. (1961), 'A Theory of Economic Development', *American Economic Review*, LI (4): 533–565

Rawski, T.G. (1994), 'Chinese Industrial Reform: Accomplishments, Prospects and Implications', *American Economic Review*, 84 (2): 271–275

Richter, L.K. (1991), 'Political Issues in Tourism Policy: A Forecast', in Hawkins, D.E. and Ritchie, J.R. (eds), *World Travel and Tourism Review*, Vol. 1: 189–193, Oxford: C.A.B International

Riskin, C. (1994), 'Chinese Rural Poverty: Marginalized or Dispersed?', *American Economic Review*, 84 (2): 281–284

Ritchie, J.R.B. (1991), 'Global Tourism Policy Issues: An Agenda for the 1990s', in Hawkins, D.E. and Ritchie, J.R. (eds), *World Travel and Tourism Review*, Vol. 1: 149–158, Oxford: C.A.B International

Roland, G. (1994), 'The Role of Political Constraints in Transition Strategies', *Economics of Transition*, 2 (1): 27–41

Romeiss-Stracke, F. (1993), 'Sanfter Tourismus – die Lösung für alle Probleme?', *Raumforschung und Raumordnung*, 6: 363–369

Rostow, W.W. (1956), 'The Take-off into Self-sustaining Growth', *Economic Journal*, 66: 25–48

Rozelle, S. (1994), 'Quantifying Chinese Villages' Multiple Objectives', *Journal of Comparative Economics*, 18: 25–45

Sachs, J. and Woo, W.T. (1994), 'Reform in China and Russia', *Economic Policy*, 18: 101–145

Santiago, C.E. (1988), 'A Multisectoral Framework for the Analysis of Labor Mobility and Development in LDCs: An Application to Postwar Puerto Roco', *Economic Development and Cultural Change*, 37 (1): 127–148

Scharping, T. (1993), 'Rural-Urban Migration in China', in Taubmann, W. (ed.), *Urban Problems and Urban Development in*

# Bibliography

*China*, 77–93, Hamburg: Mitteilungen des Instituts für Asienkunde

Seaton, A.V. (ed.) (1994), *Tourism: The State of the Art*, New York: John Wiley & Sons Inc.

Segal, G. (1994), 'China's Changing Shape', *Foreign Affairs*, 73 (3): 43–58

Shaw, G. and Williams, A.M. (1994), *Critical Issues in Tourism: A Geographical Perspective*, Oxford: Blackwell Publishers

Shen, Z. and Jiang, Y. (1988), *Suzhou de zhuyao jingdian* (Major Attractions of Suzhou), Nanjing: Jiangsu People's Press

Sinclair, M.T. (1991), 'The Tourism Industry and Foreign Exchange Leakage in a Developing Country: The Distribution of Earnings from Safari and Beach Tourism in Kenya', in Sinclair, M.T. and Stabler, M. (eds), *The Tourism Industry*, 185–204, Wallingford: C.A.B International

Sinclair, M.T. and Stabler, M. (eds) (1991a), *The Tourism Industry: An International Analysis*, Wallingford: C.A.B International
– (1991b), 'New Perspectives on the Tourism Industry', in Sinclair, M.T. and Stabler, M. (eds), *The Tourism Industry*, 1–14, Wallingford: C.A.B International

Sovani, T.V. (1964), 'The Analysis of Over-Urbanization', *Economic Development and Cultural Change*, 12 (2): 113–122

Srinivasan, T.N. (1994), 'Human Development: A New Paradigm or Reinvention of the Wheel?', *American Economic Review*, 84 (2): 238–243

Stark, O. (1982), 'On Migration and Risk in LDCs', *Economic Development and Cultural Change*, 31 (1): 191–196

Stiglitz, J.E. (1988), *Economics of the Public Sector*, New York: W.W. Norton & Company

Stöhr, W. B. and Taylor, D.R. (eds) (1981), *Development from Above or Below*, Chichester: John Wiley & Sons Ltd.

Suarez-Villa, L. (1993), 'Regional Economic Integration and the Evolution of Disparities', *Papers of Regional Science*, 72 (4): 369–387

Sulc, Z. (1994), 'Some Theoretical Issues on Transformation', *Eastern European Economics*, 32 (2): 23–38

Sun, L. (1984), 'Kuaisu fazhan de guonei lüyou' (Rapid Development of Domestic Tourism), *Lüyou jingji*, 3: 17–18

Sun, S. (ed.) (1990), *Zhongguo Lüyou Jingji Yanjiu* (A Study of China's Tourism Economy), Beijing: People's Press

Sun, Z. (1991), 'Huilü bianhua dui lüyou de yingxiang' (The Effects of Exchange Rate Variations on Tourism), *Lüyou jingji*, 1: 66

SZCPB (Suzhou City Planning Bureau) (1988), *Suzhou chengshi fazhan guihua 1985–2000* (City Development Planning of Suzhou 1985–2000), Suzhou: City Planning Bureau

SZGMB (Suzhou Garden Management Bureau) (1991), *Suzhou yuanlin* (Suzhou Gardens), Shanghai: Tongji University Press

SZTN: *Suzhou tongji nianjian* (Statistical Yearbook of Suzhou) (various issues), Beijing: China Statistical Publishing House

Tan, Y. (1991), 'Jiangu zhongyang he difang liyi, diaodong fazhan lüyou jijixing' (Take into Account of both Central and Local Interests; Promote Local Initiatives in Tourism Development), *Guilin jingji yanjiu*, 2: 44

Tang, R. (1990), 'Guonei lüyou' (Domestic Tourism), in Sun, S. (ed.), *Zhongguo lüyou jingji yanjiu*, 143–181, Beijing: People's Press

Tang, X. (1990), 'Gaishan tozi jigou, kaichuang Guilin lüyou xinqianjing' (Improve Investment Structure and Open a New Prospect for Tourism Development in Guilin), in Wang, J. (ed.), *Guilin gucheng de baohu yu jianshe*, 124–130, Beijing: Reform Press

Taubmann, W. (1986), 'Stadtentwicklung in der VR China', *Geographische Rundschau*, 38 (3):114–123

– (1987), 'Die Volksrepublik China – ein wirtschafts- und sozialgeographischer Überblick', in Landeszentrale für politische Bildung, Baden-Württemberg (ed.), *Die Volksrepublik China*, 13–42, Stuttgart: Verlag W. Kohlhammer

– (1991), 'Räumliche Mobilität und sozio-ökonomische Entwicklung in der VR China seit Beginn der 80er Jahre', *Die Erde*, 3: 161–178

– (1993a), 'Socio-economic Development and Rural-urban Migration in China since the Beginning of the 1980s', in *Urban Development in China and South East Asia*, 163–85, Bremen: Bremer Beiträge zur Geographie und Raumplanung 25

– (1993b), 'Rural Urbanization in the PR China', in Taubmann, W. (ed.), *Urban Problems and Urban Development in China*, 94–127, Hamburg: Mitteilungen des Instituts für Asienkunde

– (1993c), 'Die Chinesische Stadt', *Geographische Rundschau*, 45 (7–8): 420–428

Teltscher, S. (1994), 'Small Trade and the World Economy: Informal Vendors in Quito, Ecuador', *Economic Geography*, 70 (2): 167–187

Thomas, L.J. (1994), 'Neoclassical Development Theory and the Prebisch Doctrine: A Synthesis', *The American Economist*, 38 (1): 75–81

Tribe, J. (1997), *Corporate Strategy for Tourism*, London: International Thomson Business Press

Tsui, K. (1993), 'Decomposition of China's Regional Inequalities', *Journal of Comparative Economics*, 17: 600–627

UN Center on Transnational Corporations (1980), *Transnational Corporations in International Tourism*, New York: UN

Vincent, C. and Ferdinand, P. (1994), 'China as an Economic Giant: Threat or Opportunity', *International Affairs*, 70 (2): 243–261

Vorlaufer, K. (1990), 'Dritte-Welt-Tourismus: Vehikel der Entwicklung oder Weg in die Unterentwicklung?', *Geographische Rundschau*, 42 (1): 4–13

Vornholz, G. (1994), 'The Sustainable Development Approach', *Intereconomics*, 29 (4): 194–199

Wagner, S. (1990a), 'Fremdenverkehr in den Huangshan-Bergen', in Institut für Tourismus, FU Berlin, *Berichte und Materialen*, 8: 157–167
– (1990b), Fremdenverkehr in Huang Shan-Entwicklung und struktureller Wandel in einer Bergregion Chinas (unpublished Masters thesis), University of Mainz

Wang, D. (1991), 'Huilü bianhua dui lüyoujingji de yingxiang' (The Effects of Exchange Rate Variations on Tourism Economy), *Lüyou jingji*, 4: 51

Wang, J. (ed.) (1990), *Guilin gucheng de baohu yu jianshe* (Protection and Construction of the Ancient City of Guilin), Beijing: Reform Press

Wang, S. (1987), 'Guonei youke shichang diaocha' (Surveys of Domestic Tourist Markets), *Lüyou jingji*, 5: 74

Wang, T. and Shen, Y. (1990), 'Huilü bianhua dui lüyou de yingxiang' (The Effects of Exchange Rate Variations on Tourism), *Lüyou jingji*, 3: 73–76

Wang, W. (1986), 'Zhichi yi lüyou wei zhongxin de disan changye fazhan' (Support the Development of a Tourism-centered Tertiary Sector), in Li, H. (ed.), *Guilin jingji fazhan zhanlüe wenji*, 201–206, Guilin: Lijiang Press

Wang, W. (1991), 'Guoji fandian xiaoyidi de yuanyin jiqi duice' (The Causes of Low Efficiency in the International Hotel Sector and Instruments to Improve the Situation), *Guilin jingji yanjiu*, 1: 63

Wang, Y. (1996), 'Fazhan lüyou, baituo pinqiong' (Get Rid of Poverty by Developing Tourism), *Lüyou jingji*, 1: 12

Wei, X. (1988), 'Zhongguo de waihui liushi wenti' (Problems of Foreign Exchange Leakage in China), *Lüyou jingji*, 6: 93–94

Weitzman, M.L. (1994), 'Chinese Township-Village Enterprises as Vaguely Defined Cooperatives', *Journal of Comparative Economics*, 18: 121–145

Wiemer, C. (1994), 'State Policy and Rural Resource Allocation in China as Seen Through a Heibei Province Township, 1970–85', *World Development*, 22 (6): 935–947

Willaims, A.M. and Shaw, G. (eds) (1991), *Tourism and Economic Development*, London: Belhaven Press

Williamson, J.G. (1965), 'Regional Inequality and the Process of National development', *Economic Development and Cultural Change*, 13 (4): 3–45

Wilson, P. (1994), 'Tourism Earnings Instability in Singapore, 1972–88', *Journal of Economic Studies*, 21 (1): 41–51

World Tourist Organisation (1994), *Global Tourism to the Year 2000 and Beyond. Vol. 4: East Asia and the Pacific*, Madrid: WTO

World Tourist Organisation (1994), *National and Regional Tourism Planning: Methodologies and Case Studies*, London: Routledge

World Tourist Organisation (1994), *Sustainable Tourism Development: Guide for Local Planners*, Madrid: WTO

World Tourist Organisation (1994), *Marketing Plans & Strategies of National Tourism Administrations*, Madrid: WTO

Wu, C. (1985), Suxichang chengshi yongdi yanjiu (Study of Urban Land use in Suzhou, Wuxi and Changzhou) (unpublished research report of Nanjing Institute of Geography, the Chinese Academy of Sciences)

– (1987), 'Suxichang chengshi yongdi de dongtai bianhua' (Changing pattern of Urban land use in Suzhou, Wuxi and Changzhou), Mem. of Nanjing Institute of Geography, *Acad. Sinica*, 4: 113–132

Xi, P. (1996), 'Chongxin renshi guonei lüyouye' (Rethinking Domestic Tourism), *Lüyou xuekan*, 2: 13–16

Xia, G. (1995), 'Fazhan minzu dequ lüyou di jige wenti' (Some Issues of Tourism Development in the Minority Areas), *Sixiang zhanxian*, 4: 51–57

Xie, D. (1990), 'Guilin lüyou fazhan de wenti yu duice' (On Problems and Policies of Tourism Development in Guilin), in Wang,

J. (ed.), *Guilin gucheng de baohu yu jianshe*, 152–164, Beijing: Reform Press

Xin, D. (1990), 'Lüyou ziyuan Kaifa' (Develop Tourism Resources), in Sun, S. (ed.), *Zhongguo Lüyou Jingji Yanjiu*, 251–275, Beijing: People's Press

Xing, S. and Wang, B. (1991), 'Guanyu guonei lüyou tongji wenti' (On Domestic Tourism Statistics), in *Zhongguo lüyou tongji nianjian*, 356–360, Beijing: China Tourism Press

Xu, G. (1998), 'Domestic Tourism and Its Economic Effects in Beidaihe, the Largest Seaside Resort of China', *Pacific Tourism Review*, 2 (1) (Forthcoming)
– (1999), 'Socioeconomic Impacts of Domestic Tourism in China', *Tourism Geographies*, 1 (1) (Forthcoming)

Xu, G. and Gormsen, E. (1999), 'The Role of Tourism in Regional Development in China', *Regional Development Studies*, 5 (UN Center for Regional Development/Nagoya) (Forthcoming)

Yanagihara, T. (1994), 'Anything New in the (East Asian) Miracle Report? Yes and No', *World Development*, 22 (4): 663–670

Yang, G. (1994), 'Lun guonei lüyouye' (On Domestic Tourism Industry), *Xueshu luntan*, 4: 35–39

Yang, Y. (1996), 'Dui fazhan neilu lüyou shichang di sikao' (On Tourism Development in Inland China), *Lüyou jingji*, 1: 24–29

*Yangshuo shijing* (Ten Scenes of Yangshuo) (1987), Beijing: People's Press

Yao, S. (1992), *Zhongguo chengshiqun* (The Urban Agglomerations of China), Hefei: University of Science and Technology of China Press

Ye, P. (1986), 'Guilin jingji fazhan de zhanlüe de xuanze' (On Economic Development Strategy of Guilin), in Li, H. (ed.), *Guilin jingji fazhan zhanlüe wenji*, 207–212, Guilin: Lijiang Press

Young, A. (1994), 'Lessons from the East Asian NICs: A Contrarian View', *European Economic Review*, 38: 964–973

Yu, L. (1992a), 'Emerging Marketing for China's Tourism Industry', *Journal of Travel Research*, 31 (1): 10–13
– (1992b), 'China's Hotel Development and Structures', International Journal of Hospitality Management, 11 (2): 99–110

Yu, W. (1996), 'Guanyu minzu pinkun shanqu fazhan lüyouye di sikao' (Some Thoughts on Tourism Development in Poor Mountain Areas), *Minzu luntan*, 2: 31–32

✓Yusuf, S. (1994), 'China's Macroeconomic Performance and Management during Transition', *Journal of Economic Perspectives*, 8 (2): 71–92

ZCFS: *Zhonguo chengshi fazhan sishinian* (Forty Years of Urban Development in China), Beijing: China Statistical Information & Consulting Service Center

ZCTN: *Zhongguo chengshi tongji nianjian* (Statistical Yearbook of Chinese Cities) (various issues), Beijing: China Statistical Publishing House

Zequn, M. (1992), 'Guoji fandian de waizhai wenti' (On Foreign Debts of International Hotels), *Lüyou yanjiu yu shijian*, 1: 7

Zhang, C. (ed.) (1988), *Suzhou daoyou* (Suzhou: A Guide), Nanjing: Jiangsu People's Publishing House

Zhang, G. (1995), 'China's Tourism since 1978: Policies, Experience, and Lessons Learned', in Lew, A.A. and Yu, L. (eds), *Tourism in China*, 3–17, Boulder: Westview Press

Zhang, W. (1988a), 'Woguo keyunliang de jueding yinsu he quyu chayu' (Determinants and Regional Differentiation of Passenger Traffics in China), *Acta Geographica Sinica*, 43 (3): 192–198
– (1988b), 'Woguo de quji keyunliang' (Inter-regional Passenger Traffics in China), *Scientia Geographica Sinica*, 8 (4): 314–322

√ Zhang, Y. (1995), 'An Assessment of China's Tourism Resources', in Lew, A.A. and Yu, L. (eds), *Tourism in China*, 41–59 Boulder: Westview Press

Zhao, X. (ed.) (1985), *Tourism Atlas of China*, Beijing: Cartography Press

Zhao, X. and Wei, X. (1990), 'Lüyou touzi' (Tourism Investment), in Sun, S. (ed.), *Zhongguo lüyou jingji yanjiu*, 225–250, Beijing: People's Press

Zhen, L. (1993), 'Guonei lüyou de xianzhang yu fazhan' (Current Situation and Future Development of Domestic Tourism) *Lüyou diaoyan*, 7: 3–6

Zhen, H. and Wang, H. (1996), 'Lun lüyouye xiandao changye diwei di queli he bianjiang chengshi di fazhan' (The Role of Tourism as a Leading Industry and the Urban Development along the Border Areas), *Minzu yanjiu*, 3: 28–32

Zhen, L. (1993), 'Woguo guonei lüyou di xianzhuang yu fazhan silu' (Domestic Tourism: Current Situation and Future Development), *Lüyou diaoyan*, 7: 3–6

Zheng, J. (1990), 'Lüyouye zai guomin jingji fazhanzhong di zuoyong yu diwei' (The Role of Tourism in National Economic Development), in Sun, S. (ed.), *Zhongguo Lüyou Jingji Yanjiu*, 48–62, Beijing: People's Press

Zhong, J. (1983), *Suzhou fengjing* (Sights and Scenes of Suzhou), Beijing: Zhaohua Press

Zhong, M. (1991), 'Haiwai youke shichang fenxi' (Analysis of Overseas Tourist Markets), in *Zhongguo lüyou tongji nianjian*, 127–132, Beijing: China Tourism Press

Zhou, J. (1989), 'Overprovision in Chinese Hotels', *Tourism Management*, 10 (1): 63–66

Zhou, T. (1988), *Meili de Lijiang* (The Beautiful Lijiang River), Changsha: Education Press

√Zhu, X. (1991), 'Dui fengli karst tezheng he yanbian de xinsikao' (New Thoughts on the Characteristics and Evolution of Fenglin Karst), *Carsologica Sinica*, 10 (1): 51–62; 10 (2): 137–150; 10 (3): 171–182

Zhu, Z. (1987), *Suzhou daoyou* (Suzhou: A Guide), Shanghai: Shanlian Shidian Press

Zimmer, R.D. (1991), 'Sustainable Development: A New Paradigm for Global Tourism', in Hawkins, D.E. and Ritchie, J.R. (eds), *World Travel and Tourism Review*, Vol. 1: 159–161, Oxford: C.A.B International

ZNJFB: *Zhongguo nongcunjingji fazhan baogao* (Annual Report of Chinese Rural Economy) (1992), Beijing: Social Sciences Press

ZNZD: *Zhongguo nongcun zhuhu diaocha* (Surveys on Chinese Rural Households) (1992), Beijing: China Statistical Publishing House

ZTN: *Zhongguo tongji nianjian* (Statistical Yearbook of China) (various issues), Beijing: China Statistical Publishing House